JANUA LINGUARUM

STUDIA MEMORIAE
NICOLAI VAN WIJK DEDICATA

edenda curat

C. H. VAN SCHOONEVELD

Indiana University

Series Minor, 214

THE ANAGOGIC THEORY OF WITTGENSTEIN'S 'TRACTATUS'

by

ROY EMANUEL LEMOINE

*Sometime Professor
of Philosophy and Religion
at the Iowa State University*

1975
MOUTON
THE HAGUE · PARIS

LIBRARY OF CONGRES CATALOG CARD NUMBER: 74-80541
ISBN: 90 279 3393 6

Printed in The Netherlands by Mouton & Co., The Hague

To Ludwig Wittgenstein who consciously gave himself to the glory of the most high god while being of service to his two countries, both native and adopted, and his neighbors; and in fond appreciation of the loving concern of my daughter, Fannie John, and my wife, Jane, who encouraged me to preserve in the writing of this book. In addition, although he still lives, I wish to memorialize my friend and teacher, William H. Werkmeister, whose constant criticism and continuing approbation made this book possible.

By means of strange tongues and by the lips of strangers will I speak . . .
"Tongues" are a sign of God's power.

I Corinthians 14:20-21a
Philips

CONTENTS

Foreword 9

I. Introduction: A Literary Perspective 11

II. A Religious, Esthetic, and Linguistic Treatise . . 40

III. Russell and Wittgenstein 61

IV. The *Tractatus*: A Mirror; not a Riddle 87

V. Wittgenstein and Spinoza 96

VI. The Central European Philosophical Background . 115

VII. Wittgenstein and Schopenhauer 125

VIII. The Anagogic Theology of the *Tractatus* . . . 140

IX. The *Tractatus* and Post-Symbolist Poetry . . . 159

X. The Revelatory Event 176

Bibliography 204

Index 207

List of Citations 212

FOREWORD

The following essay is an attempt to demonstrate that there is an implicit metaphysical theology in the *Tractatus Logico-Philosophicus* of which its own author may have been unaware. It is in this sense that we must speak of an author as only his own first reader.

The essay departs radically from the traditional interpretations of the *Tractatus* which have usually associated Wittgenstein with the British empiricists or their continental cousins, the logical positivists. Ludwig Wittgenstein was of central European Jewish descent and a true member of that group of famous Jews who came to maturity in the last decades of the dying Austro-Hungarian monarchy. Although Wittgenstein spent most of his mature years in England, he seems never to have left Vienna.

The *Tractatus* is probably the most significant philosophical document since the *Critique of Pure Reason*, from which it is in some ways derivative; but it is much harder to read. Even Wittgenstein, as he stated in his own foreword, was aware that perhaps only those who had thought similar thoughts would understand him. It may be that my contribution to the study of the *Tractatus* comes from the fact that my own background is different from that of most scholars and has some similarity to Wittgenstein's. I have been both a line officer and a chaplain, and I also served in a great war.

The use of German throughout the essay was prompted by three factors: (1) some of the authors quoted have not been translated; (2) parallelisms show up much more clearly if the untranslated German selections are placed together; (3) translations, whether mine or another's, inevitably betray the author by offering a point of view which may not be his.

Some of the same considerations which led to the use of German in the text led also to the choice of a number of different authors against whose writings the text of the *Tractatus* might be illuminated. If one looks at the text of the *Tractatus* directly, it is likely that the meaning which the author intended will not appear. As one compares and contrasts the text with other writings which Wittgenstein himself may well have read, one is offered many different perspectives. It is probably only in such a comparison and contrast that one can make sense of the penultimate proposition; can see the coherence within the incoherence which inevitably results if one takes the propositions as parts of a non-dialectical argument.

Finally, although my essay is a "saying", the *Tractatus* itself must be regarded both as a great mirror and a "showing" which helps us to see language, logic, and the world aright. The images of the *Tractatus* are designed to lead us into an ever deeper understanding of all things, particularly ourselves. I myself have found working with the *Tractatus* over a period of many months the most exciting and frustrating experience of my life. I believe that most who have worked seriously with the *Tractatus* have felt a similar excitement and a similar frustration.

Tallahassee, Florida 1972

I

INTRODUCTION: A LITERARY PERSPECTIVE

1

Although it has taken several decades for Americans to understand, World War I marked the end of an era which had begun two centuries earlier in western and central Europe. The confidence of eighteenth century man in human rationality and his belief in the inevitability of human progress after the shackles of superstition had been broken came to a visible end in the mindless slaughter on the western front. The Enlightenment continues in our technological progress, our increased control over nature; but the confidence is gone. As Yeats said in a poem written between the two world wars, the center will no longer hold; and we are afraid that the future will give us not the Superman, but a mindless beast in a broken and meaningless wilderness.

In many ways World War I broke in on an unsuspecting world; but those who had not anticipated the horror had not really looked at the social scene and had not seen the intellectual and moral inconsistencies which lay at the base of the prevailing optimism. More perceptive minds had already noted that the center was giving way. The deep sense of loss was probably best expressed by Matthew Arnold in the middle of the century (1867). The last stanza of "Dover Beach" anticipates the mindless slaughter of the next century, but the pain of the loss is most distinctly expressed in the third stanza.

> The Sea of Faith
> Was once, too, at the full and round earth's shore

> Lay like the folds of a bright girdle furl'd
> But now I only hear
> Its melancholy, long withdrawing roar,
> Retreating, to the breath
> Of the night-wind, down the vast edges drear
> And naked shingles of the world.

John Henry Newman equally recognized the loss of faith; but he was of sufficient genius to recognize that a return to an earlier faith could not be achieved with the intellectual tools of an earlier period or an apparently arbitrary condemnation of modern errors. His great work, the *Grammar of Assent*, was written in the eighteen-sixties, but it anticipates at least two contemporary modes of thought: phenomenology and ordinary language analysis. Newman stands firmly within the British empirical tradition, but he is equally at home with the languages of antiquity and with Aristotelian thought. Notions are abstractions created by the mind for use in inference and the systematic exposition of schemes of thought, including theological systems. The assent given to notions and to abstract propositions is not psychologically binding on the individual in the same way that the individual is bound by his assent to the existence of things and singular propositions. The assent to singular propositions is real assent; assent to abstractions is notional assent.

For Newman, the intellectual problem for his time was the question of what is real. What we believe to be real is dependent on our use of language and the cultivation of our imaginations. The religious man, the Aristotelian practically wise man, and the poetic man share a similar quality. They each are able to picture the unique and to speak and reason about congeries of uniques. These men are the realists of any age; and those who live by abstractions and project their abstractions on the world are not realists. Arnold, because he had accepted the contemporary scientific worldview, saw the external world as empty, void of all meaning; Newman found the world filled with meaning and beauty.[1]

---

[1] John Henry Newman, *An Essay in Aid of a Grammar of Assent* (Garden City, N.Y.: Doubleday, 1955), 52, 90, and Chap. 9.

Newman believed that the dependence on abstract reasoning was the death of all real life in men and nations and that this dependence was a factor in the decay of the nineteenth century.[2] In fact, Newman was persuaded that philosophers of the school of Hume, among whom he must have included J. S. Mill, had allowed their imaginations to usurp the function of reason and had imposed on nature something which is not in actual fact to be found there: necessary, inviolable laws.[3]

This universal living scene of things is after all as little a logical world as it is poetical; and, as it cannot without violence be exalted into poetical perfection, neither can it be attenuated into logical formula. Abstract can only conduct to abstract; but we have need to attain by our reasonings to what is concrete.[4]

The mode in which we ordinarily reason is with a personal grasping of things as they stand toward each other and with respect to ourselves, and our language about the things we grasp is stated in concrete rather than abstract terms. Newman did not deny the value of abstract reasoning; he was concerned to demonstrate that men in their usual lives possess a different and more concrete way of dealing with their world. "In reasoning on any subject whatever, which is concrete, we proceed, as far indeed as we can, by the logic of language." The Illative Sense, which Newman equates with the Aristotelian *phronesis*, is that which judges the truth or falsity of all concrete premises and the appropriateness of all forms, including those of poetry.[5]

Newman's purpose in writing the *Grammar of Assent* was to change the character of the arguments for and against the Christian religion, but his analyses of the way that men actually live, think, and talk have a perennial validity. It is significant that Wittgenstein while preparing the materials for the work which was posthumously entitled *On Certainty* should have read Newman. He

[2] Newman, *An Essay*, 88.
[3] Newman, *An Essay*, 81.
[4] Newman, *An Essay*, 215.
[5] Newman, *An Essay*, 281.

made a reference to Newman at the very beginning of the work,[6] and it is obvious that his understanding of certainty owes much to Newman's discussion of certitude. It is most unlikely that the young Wittgenstein had read Newman before writing the *Tractatus*; but there seems to have been a similar attitude toward captious scepticism throughout their lives. In the *Tractatus* Wittgenstein says:

Scepticism is *not* irrefutable, but palpably senseless, if it would doubt where nothing can be asked. For doubt can only exist where a question exists; a question only where an answer exists, and this only where something *can* be *said* (6.51).[7]

For both Newman and Wittgenstein the world was filled with things which one could grasp or apprehend and about which one could speak. They agreed about the nature of propositions; Newman assumed that we could transcend language to the ultimately "real". Wittgenstein did not. The *Tractatus Logico-Philosophicus,* to which most of this essay is given, analyzes the possibilities of our transcending language and comes up with negative conclusions. We can stretch language; but if we transcend language we cannot talk about the experience. At best we can reveal it by a showing.

In Germany a contemporary of Newman equally saw that the place to begin a viable philosophy was with logic and language. A great portion of the first book of Arthur Schopenhauer's *The World as Will and Idea* is concerned with demonstrating the difference between reasoning about perceptions and reasoning about and with concepts. For Schopenhauer, who considered himself to be the true follower of Kant, reasoning about perceptions is reasoning about objects which appear to us under the categories of space, time, and causality. Our assent to their existence and interrelations is an assent to that which is real. We share this understanding with the lower animals in so far as they share our senses; and there is

[6] Ludwig Wittgenstein, *On Certainty,* ed. by G. E. M. Anscombe and G. H. von Wright, trans. by Denis Paul and G. E. M. Anscombe (New York: J. & J. Harper, 1969), 2.

[7] Ludwig Wittgenstein, *Tractatus Logico-Philosophicus,* trans. by C. K. Ogden (London: Routledge and Kegan Paul, 1960). Future citations to the *Tractatus* will be to this edition and will appear in the text, in German, in accordance with the decimal notation.

nothing to distinguish our understanding from that of the other animals; it is evident that this understanding is not the product of language or dependent on language for its existence. Animals, including man, in so far as they operate within the framework provided by the understanding (*Verstand*) function effectively in their several worlds, but they are not able to rise above the limited spatial and temporal aspects of those worlds.[8] Man, however, through the use of abstract reasoning and judgment is able not only to see the limits of the understanding, but is equally able to project himself into the past and the future of his world. Abstract reasoning is, as it was for Newman, very frequently fallacious; but it is through and with reasoning about concepts that man is able to free himself from the limits of the understanding. Speech comes into existence as "the necessary organ of . . . reason".[9]

Speech, as an object of outer experience, is obviously nothing more than a very complete telegraph, which communicates arbitrary signs with the greatest rapidity and the finest distinctions of difference.[10]

Sometimes we use the more concrete of the words of our languages to describe objects of our perception; but the relation is never more than a loose one.[11]

Schopenhauer is concerned throughout the first book to make clear both the limits and advantages of abstract reasoning. In a famous chart between pages sixty-four and sixty-five he demonstrates how easy it is to move by use of abstractions from a particular event or experience to contrary assessments of the event by accepting some rather than other characteristics of the various abstractions used in the reasoning process. The dangers in the reasoning process are inescapable because we must reason if we are to free ourselves from the solipsism of the present moment; but we must recognize that only the experience of the present moment is

---

[8] Arthur Schopenhauer, *The world as Will and Idea*, trans. by R. B. Haldane and J. Kemp (3 vols.; London: Kegan Paul, Trench, Trübner and Co., 1907), I, 18.
[9] Schopenhauer, *The World as Will and Idea*, 47.
[10] Schopenhauer, *The World as Will and Idea*, 51.
[11] Schopenhauer, *The World as Will and Idea*, 53.

real and that there are, in fact, no words which are adequate to describe the present moment. It is for this reason that Schopenhauer makes so much of the faculty of judgment. Judgment is the faculty which mediates between the understanding and the reason. Correct judgments provide a basis for a developed science; poor judgments lead to *silliness*.[12] Newman was right in believing that we should strive for the concrete and that poetry best expresses the concrete; but Schopenhauer, with his Kantian background, was more precise in stating the problem: our language, despite our care, can be said to depart from abstractions only in the loosest way. As we shall have occasion to see, Wittgenstein was deeply concerned with this problem in the *Tractatus*; and he remained concerned, as the posthumous *On Certainty* shows, until the end of his life.

Both Newman and Schopenhauer came to believe that the men of their time had become lost in abstractions which purported to give men the truth; they believed that abstractions take men away from the actuality of real experience. Newman's answer was within language, and he divided propositions into two kinds: those which ask only a notional assent and those which ask a real assent. In each case, both men were seeking a way to talk about the real and to uncover for their readers what constitutes real experience. Significantly, Kierkegaard, who lived at the same time, saw the problem in the same way. By his use of the pseudonymous method he sought to *show* men that the real is something other than the notions with which men put together their science and their philosophy. It is likely that all three men would have seen the experience of World War I as the experience of real men dying real deaths. Probably all of them would have said that the center did not hold because the center had been described in otiose abstractions rather than shown through the activities of individual human lives or through poetry.

---

[12] Schopenhauer, *The World as Will and Idea*, 85.

2

The choice of the figures of Newman, Schopenhauer, and Kierkegaard to begin an essay on Wittgenstein and the theology of the
Tractatus was not by chance. These men, each so exceptional,
shared a common attitude toward the unique; and all, to varying
degrees, were poetical and philosophical. Newman had made the
distinction between real and notional assent and identified the proposition about the singular as being about the real; Schopenhauer
claimed that the idea is singular and applies truly only to the species,
the individual's existence (except for those men who had made
themselves exceptional) having only numerical significance; Kierkegaard's concern was for those individual men who through
their encounter with ultimacy had become unique. In each case
there was a definite rejection of the dominant thrust of eighteenth
and nineteenth century thought which had identified the rational,
the real, and the universal. It was Newman who had seen that
philosophers of the school of Hume had in fact reified their notions and given their allegiance to abstract ideas which on their
philosophical premises had no grounding in reality. Without rejecting reason or the sciences, each of these men had come to see that
the intellectual pressure to universalize all thoughts about reality
was in fact destroying most men's understanding of themselves as
singular beings. Kant had made a place for the unique in the *Critique of Judgment*, but most thinking men of the nineteenth century saw the world ultimately as matter in motion in accordance
with inexorable laws.

Of course there were other exceptions than the men whom I have
named. There were the men of lyrical talents, the romantics, the
reactionaries, the practical men of political affairs and business.
There were men who interpreted the various evolutionary schemes
postulated through the earlier years of the century in an optimistic
light; but for an increasingly large number of men the only escape
from the dismal intellectual landscape was by a retreat to a private world of fantasy or romantic love. The last stanza of "Dover
Beach" displays both this kind of retreat and the mindlessness of

the external world, including increasingly the world of men.

Schopenhauer, Newman, and Kierkegaard in varying degrees moved the discussion away from the clash between "scientific" and "religious" metaphysics to language. Even though each in a way offered a metaphysic, they individually recognized that the problems were in fact linguistic and phenomenological. Each could have said with Wittgenstein, "if all possible scientific questions are answered, our questions about life are not yet touched" (6.52). It is significant that the later Wittgenstein could be quoted as saying that poetry is a higher and more difficult discipline than philosophy.[13] There is no reason to believe that this was not the position of the author of the *Tractatus* if we can trust the testimony of Rudolph Carnap, a member of the Vienna Circle.[14] Paul Engelmann, who maintained a friendship and a correspondence with Wittgenstein from 1916 until the late nineteen thirties, spoke frequently of Wittgenstein's interest in several poets during the war years when he was writing the *Tractatus*.[15] Obviously, when Wittgenstein said that we must be silent when we cannot speak clearly (7.) he did not intend to imply that the poet should not speak or that what the poet says is nonsense. Certain problems in the *Tractatus* can be clarified only through an understanding of what the poet is trying to do.

Newman had seen the poet as one who seeks an immediate and full contact with things as they are; he had seen the logician and the scientist as persons who in their work prescind from the unique because the unique is unimportant, irrelevant, or fortuitous. But is poetry in actual contact with the unique? The answer must be no; but the same must equally be said of logic and science. Both dis-

---

[13] D. A. T. Gasking and A. C. Jackson, "Wittgenstein as a Teacher", *Ludwig Wittgenstein: The Man and His Philosophy*, ed. by K. T. Fann (New York: Dell Publishing Co., 1967), 55. Hereafter referred to as Fann (ed.), *Ludwig Wittgenstein*.

[14] Rudolf Carnap, "Autobiography", in Fann (ed.), *Ludwig Wittgenstein*, 33-39.

[15] Paul Engelmann, *Letters from Ludwig Wittgenstein with a Memoir*, trans. by L. Furtmuller, ed. by B. F. McGuiness (New York: Horizon Press, 1968), nos. 5, 6, 8, 43, 49. Engelmann in a note on page 47 speaks of Wittgenstein reading Tagore and other poets to members of the Circle.

ciplines stand within the world of speech and not the world of things; but they stand in it in a different way, and when they speak they speak in different ways. At first approximation we can say that the logician is interested in extension or denotation; the poet, in intension or connotation. The logicians' objects are located in logical space; the poets' objects are in poetical space. Yet these spaces are not entirely distinct since an object can never be purely an intensional or extensional thing. There will be occasion to return to this problem again and again throughout the essay since the question of intension and extension does come up in the *Tractatus* itself (4.1211-4.2) with the discussion of proper and formal relations, external and internal relations. Failure to realize that Wittgenstein is trying to relate intensional and extensional objects within a language world has been a source of much confusion. Wittgenstein was fond of good poetry and good music; both are languages as exact as logic, but they are exact in a different way. It would surely be quite wrong to suggest, as many have done, that poetry and music are purely emotive and are, as compared to logic or scientific statements, nonsense. We must, however, recognize that the spaces in which logic and poetry exist are spaces within language itself. Men are, at least in their communication with each other, confined to a language world. That which is outside the language world is what it is. We may in fact have a relation with that which is outside; but about that relation itself we must be silent, because the relation necessarily transcends the reality of language (5.6, 5.61).

3

Wittgenstein has left us several clues for the understanding of the *Tractatus*. Among these clues are his later works where he indicates, as he does in *Philosophical Investigations*, differences between his earlier and later views. It does not appear that he so much rejected the earlier viewpoints as that he came to realize that the problem was much more complicated and that his approach had been much too elliptical. Dennis O'Brien makes a very good case for a fundamental unity in Wittgenstein's thought from the *Tractatus* to the posthumous works.[16] The major thesis of this essay is that we must take the penultimate statement of the *Tractatus* seriously and that, if we do, we can see the *Tractatus* more as the record of a search than a collection, no matter how systematic, of philosophical truths. The next to the last proposition reads:

Meine Sätze erläutern dadurch, dass sie der, welcher mich versteht, am Ende als unsinnig erkennt, wenn er durch sie — auf ihnen — über sie hinausgestiegen ist. (Er muss sozusagen die Leiter wegwerfen, nachdem er auf ihr hinaufgestiegen ist.) Er muss diese Sätze überwinden, dann sieht er die Welt richtig (6.54).

We can speak of the *Tractatus* in its entirety as being true, for it is a true record of a most significant investigation. Careless use of language inevitably leads to incoherence (4.003). Philosophy like philology is a critique of language (4.0031). The *Tractatus* is both a philological and a philosophical treatise.

At 4.0031 Wittgenstein sharply distinguished what he was doing from what Fritz Mauthner had done in the latter's *Beiträge zu einer Kritik der Sprache* which was published toward the end of the nineteenth century. Mauthner's position was that of an extreme relativism which saw an infinite array of individual languages forming themselves, according to similarities of words and structures, into families of greater or less extent and richness. No man speaks an identical language with any other man or even with himself from one moment to the next. The world as it is in itself is an ultimately strange thing; the worlds in which individual men and groups of men live are brought into being by transient states of intentionality (*Aufmerksamkeit*). If it were possible to place Mauthner in any philosophical school, it would be that of Mach and Avenarius; but Mauthner, himself, denied the possibility of any philosophy or logic. There could be only philosophies and logics reflecting the varying grammars of the individual languages. The following quotations illustrate not only the points mentioned

---

[16]   Dennis O'Brien, "The Unity of Wittgenstein's Thought", in Fann (ed.), *Ludwig Wittgenstein*, 380-404.

above, but Mauthner's own attractive style:

Die Sprache eines Einzelmenschen ist nicht ein falsches Bild seines Denkens, sondern ein falsches Bild seiner Aussenwelt; er spricht alles aus, was er individuell denkt, nur sein Denken über die Wirklichkeit ist individuell und darum falsch.[17]

Nicht zwischen der Sprache und dem Denken ist eine Brücke zu schlagen, sondern zwischen dem Denken und der Wirklichkeit.[18]

Es gibt nur individuelles Denken und nur individuelle Sprachen. Alles andere ist Abstraktion.[19]

Wir müssen aber hier den Begriff der Individualsprache noch näher betrachten und uns erinnern, dass auch dieser Begriff nur eine ungenaue Abstraktion ist, dass der einzelne Mensch nicht sein Leben lang das zunftgemässe Werkzeug Sprache in gleicher Weise besitzt, dass es in Wirklichkeit auch für den Einzelmenschen in jedem Augenblicke nur eine ererbte und erworbene Sprachbereitschaft und ihre gegenwärtige konkrete Anwendung gibt.[20]

As one studies the *Tractatus*, one is struck by the continuing effort which Wittgenstein is making to come to terms with Mauthner's relativism and to find an answer to it. In the very same proposition (4.0031) where he mentions Mauthner, he suggests that "Russell's merit is to have shown that the apparent logical form of the proposition need not be its real form". Mauthner had said that logic was only "a house of cards",[21] and had denied that language was an organism:

Man hat viel Missbrauch getrieben mit dem Bilde, die Sprache sei ein Organismus. Sie kann gar nicht ein Organismus sein, denn wenn dieses Wort überhaupt einen Sinn haben soll, so müsste doch, was ein Organismus sein will, eine Einheit sein, die durch sich selbst, die allein leben kann. Die Sprache existiert aber niemals für sich allein, sondern immer nur zwischen den Menschen.[22]

---

[17] Fritz Mauthner, *Beiträge zu einer Kritik der Sprache* (3 vols., 3rd ed.; Leipzig: Felix Meiner, 1923; photocopy: Georg Olms, Hildesheim, 1969), I, 193.
[18] Mauthner, *Beiträge*, I, 193.
[19] Mauthner, *Beiträge*, I, 195.
[20] Mauthner, *Beiträge*, I, 196.
[21] Mauthner, *Beiträge*, I, 34.
[22] Mauthner, *Beiträge*, I, 28.

Wittgenstein's answer is not only the logical analysis which Russell had provided, but the following statement:

Die Umgangssprache ist ein *Teil des menschlichen Organismus* und nicht weniger kompliziert als dieser. Es ist menschenunmöglich, die Sprachlogik aus ihr unmittelbar zu entnehmen (4.002 italics added).

One might even say further that not only in the *Tractatus* but even in his later works Wittgenstein was continually searching for answers to deeply sceptical statements such as the following:

Die menschliche Sprache an sich ist — wie gesagt — ein Abstraktum, ein unfassbarer Schatten wie die alten Seelenvermögen; die menschliche Sprache an sich besitzt überhaupt keine Grammatik, geschweige denn eine *philosophische Grammatik*.[23] [Italics added.][24]

Die objektive Wahrheit müsste, um uns etwas zu sein, ein Verhältnis aussprechen, das Verhältnis einer Idee, eines Satzes, einer Vorstellung zu der Wirklichkeit. Man wollte denn anders diese Wirklichkeit selbst die Wahrheit nennen, was sehr hübsch klänge, nur dass dann die Wahrheit aus unserem Denken, wo allein sie einen Schein von Dasein hat, hinausgeworfen wäre in das Gebiet, von dessen Bezirk kein Wanderer wiederkehrt, von welchem Gebiet wir nichts wissen. Ja der Satz, "die Wirklichkeit allein ist wahr", wäre für uns unfreiwillig komisch.

Die bescheidenere subjektive Wahrheit ist aber wieder an das Individuum gebunden; sie ist nicht mehr und nicht weniger als das Wissen oder Zu-wissen-glauben eines Menschen. Die subjektive Wahrheit, die Überzeugung von der Richtigkeit eines Urteils ist nur ein Unterstreichen des Selbstverständlichen, dass wir nichts Falsches vorstellen oder glauben. Wobei man vergisst, dass unsere Sprache oder unser Gedächtnis, wie wir gesehen haben, wesentlich falsch sein muss. Die subjektive Wahrheit ist der Akt des Aufmerkens auf das, was wir gerade wahrzunehmen oder zu wissen glauben.[25]

---

[23] Mauthner, *Beiträge*, I, 193.
[24] Fann reports that Rush Rhees has edited a typescript of Wittgenstein's "divided into titled chapters and sections as in conventional learned works", entitled *Philosophische Grammatik (1932)*. K. T. Fann, *Wittgenstein's Conception of Philosophy* (Berkeley: University of California Press, 1969), 115. *Philosophische Grammatik* finally appeared in 1970 with Rush Rhees as the editor. No English translation is shown. The publisher is Barnes and Noble, New York.
[25] Mauthner, *Beiträge*, I, 694-95.

Es gibt Philosophen und es gibt ihre Philosophien; aber es gibt keine Philosophie.[26]

Unbestimmt und unklar legt sich Logik und Syntax um den Kern unseres Denkens, um die Eindrücke der Wirklichkeit. Die Wirklichkeit ist weder logisch noch syntaktisch.[27]

Es gibt keine Logik, es gibt nur Logiken.[28]

Wo keine Logik der Sprache ist, da hat die Algebra der Logik ihr Recht verloren.[29]

Mauthner carried his scepticism, his radical Humeanism, so far that he was unable to affirm more than a similar *Weltanschauung* among those who had spent much of their time in similar situations.[30] Nor was it impossible for subject and object to change their places within the language world.[31] The atomicity of the impressions and conjectures out of which individual worlds may be built is complete.[32] Wittgenstein considers atomicity, both in its ontological and phenomenal aspects, in the earlier portions of the *Tractatus* and finds atomicity incoherent except as determined by intention (1, 1.11, 2.011, 2.0121, 2.0231, 2.024, 2.025, 2.027). Within language, atomicity is not incoherent; but its meaning or use at any one moment is dependent on whether the use is intensional or extensional. It could be said, however, that the philosophical position of *Philosophical Investigations* is closer than that of the *Tractatus* to Mauthner's *Beiträge*.[33] Nevertheless, as *On Certainty* shows, Wittgenstein never became the very deep sceptic that Mauthner was. Scepticism is palpable nonsense because one

---

[26] Mauthner, *Beiträge*, I, 708.
[27] Mauthner, *Beiträge*, III, 214.
[28] Mauthner, *Beiträge*, III, 445-46.
[29] Mauthner, *Beiträge*, III, 237-47.
[30] Mauthner, *Beiträge*, III, 258.
[31] Mauthner, *Beiträge*, III, 234-36.
[32] Mauthner, *Beiträge*, III, 397-402.
[33] The relation between Wittgenstein and Mauthner is carefully explored in Gershon Weiler, *Mauthner's Critique of Language* (Cambridge: Cambridge University Press, 1970). Although more concerned with the later Wittgenstein, Weiler believes that no portion of Wittgenstein's writings can be understood without reference to Mauthner (pp. 325, 327).

must be able to affirm before one can doubt (6.51). Nevertheless, it is quite questionable that, either in the *Tractatus* or later, Wittgenstein was able to affirm a definitely formed reality lying beyond language itself. Proposition 2.0211 is in the subjunctive.

4

Although it is important to recognize that the *Tractatus* owes part of its content to Wittgenstein's determination to find a way out of Mauthner's relativism, it is equally important to recognize that the *Tractatus* and Wittgenstein's later works are unique responses to some of the important questions of our time. We can discern Mauthner's influence as we can discern that of others; but Wittgenstein's responses are his own. Wittgenstein's importance lies not only in the nature of his responses, but in that he grasped the problems of our time far earlier than most.

Wittgenstein's mind was unusually gifted in its ability to analyze while drawing the boundaries within which the analysis was legitimate. In this sense his mind was not unlike Spinoza's and Kant's. But Wittgenstein lived at the end of a period; and he was perceptive enough to know that most of what passed for knowledge in his time was but a congeries of empty phrases.[34] As Engelmann saw at a very early period in Wittgenstein's life, the latter had come to realize that only by developing a new understanding of language and what actually could be said with assurance was it possible for men to find a way to live deeply and religiously.[35]

Further corroboration for this understanding of the purpose of the young Wittgenstein may be seen in his relations to and correspondence with Ludwig Ficker, the long-time editor and publisher of the Christian intellectual weekly *Der Brenner*. The editor of the Engelmann volume was able to talk with Herr Ficker before the latter's death and to look over some correspondence between Wittgenstein and Ficker. It was to Ficker that Wittgenstein turned

[34] Engelmann, *Letters*, 133.
[35] Engelmann, *Letters*, 135.

in 1914 when he decided to give away a portion of his estate.
Ficker was the administrator of one hundred thousand crowns to
be spent for the promotion of literature.[36] Ficker has disclosed
that one of the earliest beneficiaries was Rainer Maria Rilke who
had been living in Paris when the war broke out and who was
stranded without means in Vienna.[37] Wittgenstein wrote to Ficker
when the latter was seeking a publisher for the *Tractatus* that the
Tractatus was both a literary and a "strictly philosophical work".[38]
In another letter Wittgenstein said:

... der Sinn des Buchs ist ein ethischer. Ich wollte einmal in das [sic]
Vorwort einen Satz geben, der nun tatsächlich nicht darin steht, den
ich Ihnen aber jetzt schreibe weil er Ihnen vielleicht ein Schlüssel sein
wird: Ich wollte nämlich schreiben, mein Werk bestehe aus zwei Teilen:
aus dem, der hier vorliegt, und aus alledem, was ich *nicht* geschrieben
habe. Und gerade dieser zweite Teil ist der Wichtige [sic]. Ich würde
Ihnen nun empfehlen das *Vorwort* und den *Schluss* zu lesen, da diese
den Sinn am Unmittelbarsten zum Ausdruck bringen.[39]

Ficker himself could not afford to publish the *Tractatus*, but did
enlist the services of Rilke who sought to introduce it to several
other publishers.[40] It is important for the purposes of this essay
to recognize that there was a relation, although not a close one,
between Wittgenstein and Rilke. A few common concerns will be
explored in the latter part of this introductory chapter. At this point
it need only be said that Rilke, also, was seeking a way to ground
his writing firmly in "reality".

The thoroughgoing relativism of Mauthner's work led him to a
deep sadness which can be seen in the conclusion of the *Beiträge*.
The relativism is so complete that it in some ways vitiates the whole
work. With all things relative, there is no place to stand to judge
anything which has been written; and the work itself becomes a
congeries of *aperçus*. The *Tractatus* is an attempt to answer the
relativism of the *Beiträge* and the other forms of relativism which

---

36   Engelmann, *Letters*, 137, 139.
37   Engelmann, *Letters*, 143.
38   Engelmann, *Letters*, 143.
39   Engelmann, *Letters*, 144n.
40   Engelmann, *Letters*, 143.

were beginning to surface at the end of the nineteenth century. If there were to be a fixed point, that point had to be either a form of transcendentalism or some form of a meta-language; but, as Lord Russell himself was to point out in his "Introduction" to the *Tractatus*, to invent meta-languages was to involve oneself in an infinite regress.[41] Wittgenstein chose to investigate language itself. In the *Tractatus* he claims to have discovered that, despite Mauthner, there is in fact a transcendental logic within language. It may be that Wittgenstein was led to this way of looking at language by his studies in Frege and his knowledge of Kant. He explicitly acknowledges his indebtedness to Frege and Russell in his Preface; and there are several references to Frege's *Grundgesetze der Arithmetik* in the *Letters to Engelmann* (numbers 19 and 37). In a significant way Wittgenstein's *Tractatus* also has an analogy in Heraclitus' *Logos* doctrine which developed in a similar period in the Aegean world when men had come to realize that language itself was that which had to be explored. Cassirer reports the situation thus:

Not the material but the human world is the clue to a correct interpretation of the cosmic order. In this human world the *faculty of speech* occupies a central place. We must, therefore, understand what speech means in order to understand the "meaning" of the universe. If we fail to find this approach — the approach through the medium of language rather than through physical phenomena — we miss the gateway to philosophy. Even in Heraclitus' thought the word, the Logos, is not merely anthropological phenomenon. It is not confined within the narrow limits of our human world, for it possesses universal cosmic truth. But instead of being a magic power the word is understood in its semantic and symbolic function. "Don't listen to me", writes Heraclitus, "but to the Word and confess that all things are one".[42]

The confusion in so many interpretations of the *Tractatus* begins with the conflation of logical space with an ontological space. Wittgenstein is not doing ontology; he is doing an analysis of that por-

---

[41]   *Tractatus*, p. 23.
[42]   Ernst Cassirer, *An Essay on Man: An Introduction to a Philosophy of Human Culture* (Garden City, New York: Doubleday Anchor Books, 1954), 145. [Italics added.]

tion of language over which logic has in the past asserted some control; and he is carefully defining the limits of language in order to avoid the metaphysical nonsense which has come about in the past through a misuse of language. As an example of the latter, one needs only to cite a part of 4.003:

Die meisten Sätze und Fragen, welche über philosophische Dinge geschrieben worden sind, sind nicht falsch, sondern unsinnig. Wir können daher Fragen dieser Art überhaupt nicht beantworten, sondern nur ihre Unsinnigkeit feststellen. Die meisten Fragen und Sätze der Philosophen beruhen darauf, das wir unsere *Sprachlogik* nicht verstehen. [Italics added.]

It is at 1.13 that he says: "Die Tatsachen im logischen Raum sind die Welt". Wittgenstein is not attempting to tell us what "space" is. He is talking about something other than an ontological space. Were he talking about an ontological space, then the two following passages would raise all sorts of additional problems. They contradict each other.

Etwas Logisches kann nicht nur-möglich sein. Die Logik handelt von jeder Möglichkeit und alle Möglichkeiten sind ihre Tatsachen (2.0121).

Unter den möglichen Gruppen Wahrheitsbedingungen gibt es zwei extreme Fälle. In dem einen Fall ist der Satz für sämtliche Wahrheitsmöglichkeiten der Elementarsätze wahr. Wir sagen, die Warheitsbedingungen sind *tautologisch*. Im zweiten Fall ist der Satz für sämtliche Wahrheitsmöglichkeiten falsch: Die Wahrheitsbedingungen sind *kontradiktorisch* (4.46).

In actual fact "Tautologie und Kontradiktion sind sinnlos", (4.461) but they are not *unsinnig* (4.4611). They do not refer to objects in space, or even in logical space, but refer only to the structure of languag eitself. Mauthner states that contradiction is a construct only of the logicians.[43] "Ein Widerspruch ist in der Wirklichkeitswelt undenkbar. Denkbar und wirklich ist er nur im Denken oder im Sprechen der Menschen".[44] In language itself we can at most find contrarieties,[45] and in a perfect natural language

---

43 Mauthner, *Beiträge*, III, 367.
44 Mauthner, *Beitrage*, II, 48.
45 Mauthner, *Beiträge*, III, 367.

there could be no negations of any sort.[46] Although he is not explicit, Mauthner apparently agrees with Spinoza that "all determination is negation". Perhaps, Mauthner's criticism of the whole problem of negation stands in back of Wittgenstein's remark at 3.03: "Wir können nichts Unlogisches denken, weil wir sonst unlogisch denken müssten". At 3.031 he says: "Wir könnten nämlich von einer 'unlogischen' Welt nicht sagen, wie sie aussähe."

As will be apparent in the sequel, Wittgenstein approved of poetry which was coherent although it might stretch the boundaries of logical discourse. The *Tractatus* in this sense is a poetical document: it presses against the boundaries of language in its efforts to clarify the limits of language (5.6). Rilke and the French symbolists were concerned with the same problem. In so far as the symbolists used private languages or self-contradictory images, the message of the *Tractatus* is unequivocal. Their poetry is incoherent (*unsinnig*). It is quite doubtful, considering his high respect for poetry, that Wittgenstein would equate *unsinnig* with *sinnlos*.

On page 19 above, there was a preliminary discussion of the problem of intension and extension. One must understand this distinction in order to understand the *Tractatus*, but the distinction in the *Tractatus* is a much subtler one than in the school logic which assumes that there is an objective correlate and that intension and extension are dependent variables with respect to each other. Mauthner, in discussing the difference at the beginning of his discussion of logic in the third volume, attempts to make the distinction clear by coining two German words: *Begriffsumfang* and *Begriffsinhalt*. Neither word appears in the *Tractatus*, but roughly the first word corresponds to extension and the second to intension. One must say "roughly" because Mauthner does not believe that the distinction is a really valid one, but rather that it was imposed on German by the long dominance of Latin in technical discussions.[47] It is likely that he would expand his statement to all of the western tongues because Latin was the technical language everywhere in western Europe for many centuries.

46 Mauthner, *Beiträge*, III, 367.
47 Mauthner, *Beiträge*, III, 282, 283.

With Mauthner there is a further complication, for he is continually using psychology in his analysis. As far as he is concerned, both animals and men are capable of making concepts. The difference between men and animals lies in men's ability to speak easily and in the fact that they index their concepts with their words. The relation between concepts and words is purely arbitrary,[48] and the difference between *Begriffsinhalt* and *Begriffsumfang* is in fact made possible only by words:

Der Begriff oder das Wort ist nämlich psychologisch aus dem Begriffsumfang entstanden; das Wort ist für jeden Volksgenossen ein Assoziationszentrum nur für den Umfang, den er kennt. Dabei kann es recht gut zugegeben werden, dass grosse Gruppen eines Volkes, . . . über den Begriffsinhalt einig zu sein glauben oder es auch wirklich sind, so weit die Worte die gleichen sind, die den Begriffsinhalt bilden. Aber jedes dieser Worte geht psychologisch wieder auf seinen Umfang zurück, der für jedes Individuum ein anderer ist. So ist zuletzt auch die Übereinstimmung über den Begriffsinhalt nur ein Schein; über den Begriffsumfang sind aber sicherlich nicht zwei Menschen einig, mag der Begriff nun so konkret sein wie ein Kalb oder so abstrakt wie gut und böse.[49]

Formal logic is dependent on the careful definition of a sign so that all who use the sign use it in a univocal way. But:

Die formale Logik ist nur dann wertvoll, wenn die Begriffsinhalte ihren Begriffsumfängen absolut genau entsprechen, das heisst, wenn es allen Menschen gemeinsame abstrakte Begriffe gibt. In die formale Logik kann ein Begriff eigentlich erst eingehen, wenn er vorher abstrakt geworden ist. Abstrakt ist aber immer nur der künstlich gebildete Begriffsinhalt; der Begriffsumfang oder der Assoziationsbereich des Begriffs ist immer konkret. Und mit diesem einzig Wirklichen am Begriff kann die Logik als mit etwas Konkretem nichts anfangen.[50]

It is Mauthner's conviction that formal logic began to lose its position in the world with the rise of the new science and the vernacular languages in the beginning of the modern period.[51] Mauthner dates a critical awareness of the new way of thinking not to Des-

[48] Mauthner, *Beiträge*, III, 265.
[49] Mauthner, *Beiträge*, III, 280-81.
[50] Mauthner, *Beiträge*, III, 281-82.
[51] Mauthner, *Beiträge*, III, 282.

cartes, but to Locke and the latter's recognition that reality appears to us in terms of similarities and not in terms of identities.[52] It is speech which transforms a similarity into a comparison and a contrast of things which are held to possess rigid and objective qualities.[53] Wittgenstein owes much to Mauthner's analysis, but Mauthner's analysis, as noted above, is vitiated by its extreme relativism, and Wittgenstein is attempting to get away from the psychologizing which permeates much of Mauthner's work. The relevant passages in the *Tractatus* are: 4.112 and 4.1121. The first part of the latter reads as follows: "Die Psychologie ist der Philosophie nicht verwandter als irgend eine andere Naturwissenschaft. Erkenntnistheorie ist die Philosophie der Psychologie." For Mauthner, there is ultimately no common world.

Jedes Individuum, jede kleine und grosse Menschengruppe, jedes Volk hat ein bestimmtes Weltbild, das sich von dem Weltbild anderer Individuen, anderer Gruppen, anderer Völker unterscheidet.[54]

Speech provides a common repository of memory signs which can be converted into images, but the images are uniquely the individual's. Nevertheless, this treasury of memory signs and the possibility of their use by the individual makes it possible for the individual human being to transcend his present spatial and temporal moment.[55] Yet the danger of *Wortaberglaube*, word superstition or fetishism, is always present. *Begriffsinhalt* and *Begriffsumfang* represent boundaries within which language can operate without certain self-deception.

Die Unklarheit, welche jedem Wortzeichen anhaftet im Verhältnis zur Anschauung, steigert sich mit der Zahl der Anschauungen und der Stufenreihe der Anschauungsgruppen, die das Wort bezeichnen soll. An dem einen Ende ruht die Einzelvorstellung, die *vor* der Sprache ist, an dem anderen Ende gähnt der Abgrund der Allgemeinsten Begriffe oder Kategorien, die *jenseits* der Sprache liegen und nur

---

[52]   Mauthner, *Beiträge*, III, 283
[53]   Mauthner, *Beiträge*, III, 284.
[54]   Mauthner, *Beiträge*, III, 230.
[55]   Mauthner, *Beiträge*, I, 456, 457.

missbräuchlich von künstlichen Worten mythologisch vorwerden; zwischen diesen beiden Enden schwebt die menschliche Sprache über der Wirklichkeitswelt wie ein Nebelduft, verschönernd und die Grenzen auflösend.[56] The possibilities of self-deception are never absent, and the wise man is either silent or laughing.[57] Mauthner has a great deal of sympathy with the late medieval mystic, Meister Eckart, and his understanding of the necessity of silence before the inexpressible.[58] The last two propositions of the *Tractatus* may be construed as saying the same thing: that which is incoherent is necessarily ridiculous and a cause for laughter; about all else we must be silent.

At this point we may draw another insight from Mauthner which will help us to understand the *Tractatus* and the possible meaning of "unsinnig" in the penultimate proposition. Proposition 6.41 reads as follows:

Der Sinn der Welt muss ausserhalb ihrer liegen. In der Welt ist alles wie es ist und geschieht alles wie es geschieht; es gibt *in* ihr keinen Wert — und wenn es ihn gäbe, so hätte er keinen Wert. Wenn es einen Wert gibt, der Wert hat, so muss er ausserhalb alles Geschehens und So-Seins liegen. Denn alles Geschehen und So-Sein ist zufällig. Was es nicht-zufällig macht, kann nicht in der Welt liegen, denn sonst wäre dies wieder zufällig.

Although, as we shall see below, there are relations between this statement and certain statements of Kant's and Aristotle's, there is a direct correlation between the statement and a number of Mauthner's statements about the accidental. Mauthner's understanding of the problem of the accidental came out of his historical and empirical research on the various meanings of the word *Zufall* over the centuries. The word *Zufall* is essentially a negation of some other unclear concept,[59] and its meaning has varied with the concept it was negating.

Es wäre denn, dass man jedesmal Zufall benennt, was die betreffende

---

56 Mauthner, *Beiträge*, III, 288.
57 Mauthner, *Beiträge*, III, 632-34.
58 Mauthner, *Beiträge*, III, 617, 618.
59 Mauthner, *Beiträge*, III, 572.

Wissenschaft nicht mehr weiss. In diesem Sinne verliert sich jede Wissenschaft in Zufälligem, und es ist kein Spiel mit Worten, wenn ich nun behaupte: Alles Wirkliche ist zufällig. Nur muss man sich davor hüten, beim Versinken in diesen Abgrund mythologisch zu werden und den Zufall für irgend etwas positiv Wirkendes zu halten. Was wir nicht wissen, was wir uns vorstellen, unsere Bilder von der Welt, nur das ist unser. Was wir nicht wissen, das ist unsere Wissenschaft, das ist notwendig. Was wir wissen möchten, die Wirksamkeit, das Wirkliche, das ist zufällig.[60]

The world as it appears to us, about which we can make significant propositions in Wittgenstein's sense, is actually incoherent, *unsinnig*; and the only thing we can really do about it is laugh. In later life Wittgenstein said that a good philosophy book could consist only of jokes.[61] If there is a meaning to the world it must lie outside of the world. Surely, there is also some relation to the above passage from Mauthner and the following two propositions from the *Tractatus*.

Einen Zwang, nach dem Eines geschehen müsste, weil etwas anders geschehen ist, gibt es nicht. Es gibt nur eine logische Notwendigkeit (6.37).

Der ganzen modernen Weltanschauung liegt die Täuschung zugrunde, dass die sogenannten Naturgesetze die Erklärungen der Naturerscheinungen seien (6.371).

Logical necessity is transcendental; for the author of the *Tractatus* scientific laws are at best shorthand or heuristic devices. Something is being said about the world; but what has been said can, in fact, only be shown (6.36).

With reference to *Begriffsinhalt* and *Begriffsumfang* it is fairly obvious that in the *Tractatus* Wittgenstein is exploring the possibilities of their ultimately being identical (4.1211-4.128) distinguished only by the intentionality (*Aufmerksamkeit*) of the speaker. It will be necessary to return again and again to the problem of extension and intension as it exists in language and not in reality; but for the

---

[60]   Mauthner, *Beiträge*, III, 576, 577.
[61]   Norman Malcolm, *Ludwig Wittgenstein: A Memoir* (New York: Oxford University Press, 1962), 29.

moment let us leave the question with a quotation from the *Tractatus*:

Ausdrücke wie "1 ist eine Zahl", "es gibt nur Eine Null" und alle ähnlichen sind unsinnig. (Es ist ebenso unsinnig zu sagen "es gibt nur eine 1", als es unsinnig wäre, zu sagen: "2+2 ist um 3 Uhr gleich 4".) (4.1272).

These sentences are incoherent; unless we are talking about marks on a sheet of paper.

5

Some who were fortunate in their possessions and not too thoughtful about the presuppositions of their society have called the two decades before World War I *La Belle Époque*. In fact, however, the eighteenth century synthesis which sustained nineteenth century progress was beginning to break apart in two radically different directions.

On the one hand, the determinism which had provided the basis for the vast increase in scientific knowledge began, increasingly, to be applied to men themselves. Darwin's theses suggested that men are no different from any other objects in the physical world and that men's societies and cultures change in determinable ways. Although Mauthner proclaims an ultimate arbitrariness in the ways in which languages change, it is obvious from the various headings in the *Beiträge* that Darwinism presented a considerable threat to Mauthner; for, in the form of naturalism, Darwinism strongly affected the literature of the period as we can see in the novels of Hardy and Zola. But Wittgenstein was able to dismiss Darwinism as one more scientific hypothesis (4.1122), on the whole irrelevant for the philosopher who was seeking to ground his thought on something other than a passing fashion. If this thesis is correct, Wittgenstein saw the challenge of his time not so much in determinism as in the extreme relativism which began to emerge in the same period.

It would be difficult to prove that the literary movement we call Symbolism was a retreat from Darwinism and the harsh consequences which were necessarily drawn from the Darwinian theses; but when one considers Rimbaud's call for the "disordering of all the senses" and the solipsistic exploration of the inner world by the French Symbolists, one is tempted to suggest that these men sought within the creations of their minds other worlds than those offered by the "benevolent bourgeois" and their faith in a triumphant social Darwinism. The Symbolists learned to use language connotatively as it had never been used before. They came to realize that words were in fact symbols and were rarely signs and that the things (Rilke's *Dinge*) of the poetic world were at best the reified concepts to which the words in their various contexts refer.

This does not mean that all of the Symbolists refused to write about things outside their own minds. It means that all of them, from Baudelaire to Valéry, were concerned not so much with what was denoted by a word, or even a word's normal connotations, but rather with *what a word could be made to connote* through special handling of that word in poetry. They were concerned with exploiting possibilities of connotation, experimenting with the resources of connotation. And naturally enough they concentrated in their experimentation on the inner world of the creative spirit: a world which might be characterized loosely as the world of imagination or of memory; a world where every type of conceptual, sensuous, sensible emotional image moved and intermingled: a world that could be called "le Rêve", whether the dream was hysteric, absinthe-inspired, or the vision of a god-like "moi projeté absolu".[62]

The Symbolists created their own worlds and their only controls were the ways in which they placed their words within their verses. They sometimes spoke about things, but they spoke about them connotatively rather than denotatively. As our discussion about *Begriffsinhalt* and *Begriffsumfang* demonstrated there is really no other way in which one can speak about things since we are, as soon as we try to communicate, trapped in the symbolic world of language. Words are symbols and are very rarely signs. They al-

---

[62] Genesius Jones, *Approach to the Purpose: A Study of the Poetry of T. S. Eliot* (New York: Barnes and Noble, 1966), 33.

ways carry a load of connotative meanings which vary with the individual. The poet experiments with words and their usage and if successful in his experiments, with his enlarged metaphors, the language is enriched. But the poet is quite likely to fail and to lapse into incoherence. He must recognize the boundary situations: silence and chaos.

It is obvious if we look at his life that Wittgenstein neither in the *Tractatus* nor later was denying the legitimacy of a connotative use of language. Again, he suggests that pure solipsism coincides with pure realism (5.64), a position which the French Symbolists sometimes assumed to be the case. "Dass die Welt meine Welt ist, das zeigt sich darin, dass die Grenzen der Sprache (der Sprache, die allein ich verstehe) die Grenzen meiner Welt bedeuten" (5.62). Poetry needs at least as many guards as philosophy; and there is no justification for making noises and calling the result poetry. The French Symbolists in their exploration of the limits of language sometimes fell into incoherence. The German poet, Rilke, learned from the French experiments and tried to ground his poetry into the very stuff of the world. Yet he also recognized that in the early twentieth century the stuff of the world had become very elusive.

Rilke's new discoveries and inventions in the world of words amount to an unparalleled extension alike of sensibility and of the capacity for expression. To a degree inconceivable before him, the German language seems to have been softened, made more intimate, inward and spiritual, more limpid — and yet at the same time more precise, intellectual and factual. . . . The extraordinary intensity of Rilke's sensory and emotional perception . . . reminds one in many ways of the contemporary philosopher's "phenomenological" view of the world.[63]

La Belle Époque was an era of increasing social madness which finally culminated in World War I. Apparently, it became Wittgenstein's view that only by purifying language would it be possible to reconstruct a world. In another time of troubles, Confucius had spoken of the necessity of rectifying names; Socrates, himself, can

---

[63] Hans Egon Holthusen, *Rainer Maria Rilke: A study of His Later Poetry*, trans. by J. P. Stern (New Haven, Connecticut: Yale University Press, 1952), p. 11.

be seen more clearly as a purifier of language than as a metaphysician. As Mauthner had shown, language has a tendency toward constructions and concepts which mislead men when they attempt to deal with the world. Nevertheless, as human beings, men have no choice but to purify language by the use of language itself. This is the task that the young Wittgenstein gave himself while at the front in the midst of World War I: to create and defend a logic which, while relying on language, could provide a criterion by which nonsense could be judged. The tragedy of the *Tractatus* was that it was mis-understood by so many, including many who were personally close to Wittgenstein, and interpreted as requiring men to speak only in the forms of a mathematical logic. The Vienna Circle seems on the whole to have read the *Tractatus* in this philistine manner; and the consequences can be seen in the reductionist absurdities of Ayer's *Language, Truth and Logic*. Wittgenstein, in writing the *Tractatus*, stayed entirely within the boundaries of language; his followers very frequently overstepped those boundaries and converted the *Tractatus* into an essay in antimetaphysical phenomenalism. Wittgenstein's statement as to the nature of the boundary is precise:

Die Grenzen meiner Sprache bedeuten die Grenzen meiner Welt. Die Logik erfüllt die Welt; die Grenzen der Welt sind auch ihre Grenzen. Wir können also in der Logik nicht sagen: Das und das gibt es in der Welt, jenes nicht. Das würde nämlich scheinbar voraussetzen, dass wir gewisse Möglichkeiten ausschliessen und dies kann nicht der Fall sein, da sonst die Logik über die Grenzen der Welt hinaus müsste; wenn sie nämlich diese Grenzen auch von der anderen Seite betrachten könnte (5.6, 5.61).

The *Tractatus* is not poetry; but neither is it a straightforward exposition in logic. Wittgenstein points this out both in the Preface and in his letter to Ficker about the *Tractatus*. It could be said that the *Tractatus* as a literary essay lies between and covers the boundaries of logic and poetry. A good poem and a good philosophical essay show in their forms what they point to in their contents: form and content cannot be divided. Considered as a whole, the *Tractatus* is neither *sinnlos* nor *unsinnig* because it is talking about what language must be if it is not to mislead; but individual statements can be both *sinnlos* and *unsinnig* because, taken by themselves and out of context, they make no sense. The same kind of judgments must be made about good poetry; but good poetry explores a larger field than does the *Tractatus*: on the one hand, poetry presses toward the stuff of the world (*Gegenstände, Sachen, Dinge*) which nevertheless always eludes the poet; on the other hand, poetry presses toward *das Mystische* which, however, the poet can never apprehend. Significantly, the stuff of the world is pointed to in the earliest portions of the *Tractatus*; the boundaries at the end. Of neither can one speak, although one may point.

Good poetry is other than noise, pleasing sounds or an expression of the emotions of the poet. Good poetry is coherent and extremely exact. The discussion of internal and external properties within the *Tractatus* may very well be considered as a discussion of the nature of the significant proposition in poetry. The relations in a verse are internal.

Wir können in gewissem Sinne von formalen Eigenschaften der Gegenstände und Sachverhalte bezw. von Eigenschaften der Struktur der Tatsachen reden und in demselben Sinn von formalen Relationen und Relationen von Strukturen. (Statt Eigenschaft der Struktur sage ich auch "interne Eigenschaft"; statt Relation der Struktur "interne Relation". Ich führe diese Ausdrücke ein, um den Grund der, bei den Philosophen sehr verbreiteten Verwechslung zwischen den internen Relationen und eigentlichen (externen) Relationen zu eigen.) Das Bestehen solcher interner Eigenschaften und Relationen kann aber nicht durch Sätze behauptet werden, sondern es zeigt sich in den Sätzen, welche jene Sachverhalte darstellen und von jenen Gegenständen handeln (4.122).

Das Bestehen einer internen Eigenschaft einer möglichen Sachlage wird nicht durch einen Satz ausgedrückt, sondern es drückt sich in dem sie darstellenden Satz, durch eine interne Eigenschaft dieses Satzes aus. Es wäre ebenso unsinnig, dem Satze eine formale Eigenschaft zuzusprechen, als sie ihm abzusprechen (4.124).

Das Bestehen einer internen Relation zwischen möglichen Sachlagen drückt sich sprachlich durch eine interne Relation zwischen den sie darstellenden Sätzen aus (4.125).

Hier erledigt sich nun die Streitfrage "ob alle Relationen intern oder extern" seien (4.1251).

Reihen, welche durch *interne* Relationen geordnet sind, nenne ich Formenreihen. Die Zahlenreihe ist nicht nach einer externen, sondern nach einer internen Relation geordnet (4.1252).

Dass etwas unter einen formalen Begriff als dessen Gegenstand fällt, kann nicht durch einen Satz ausgedrückt werden. Sondern es zeigt sich an dem Zeichen dieses Gegenstandes selbst. (Der Name zeigt, dass er einen Gegenstand bezeichnet, das Zahlenzeichen, dass es eine Zahl bezeichnet etc.) (4.126).

If these propositions are considered against the background of Mauthner's work and the problems of poetic expression which Rilke and the French Symbolists explored, one can make several observations which will serve to clarify them. In the first place, Wittgenstein is speaking about language, not things. Secondly, whether words or sentences (*Sätze*) are used connotatively or denotatively depends on the intention of the person constructing the sentence and of the person hearing it. Thirdly, to assume a meaning for "object", "thing", "event (*Sache*)" in the external world apart from our speech and our imaginations is to go beyond the evidence. Mauthner, in this connection, quotes R. Wahle, *Das Ganze der Philosophie* (S.356) approvingly:

Es gibt einen Unterschied zwischen einer Vorstellung und dem Wissen davon, dass wir diese Vorstellung haben. Eine *Vorstellung oder ein Gegenstand* wird nämlich dann als *gewusster* bezeichnet, wenn eine Vorstellung in ihrer Existenz als von einer Ich-Tätigkeit abhängig gegeben ist.[64]

Although Mauthner shares with Schopenhauer the conviction that both men and other animals operate *vis-à-vis* the outer world with a kind of "animal faith" which does not use words and which they both call "Verstand", he is equally convinced that as soon as men become men in the sense that they use language they are trapped by the language they use. "Kein Mensch kann mit seiner Sprache aus seiner Vorstellungswelt herausspringen, denn Sprachschatz und

[64]   Mauthner, *Beiträge*, I, 695. [Italics added.]

Weltanschauung ist eins und dasselbe."[65] The *Tractatus Logico-Philosophicus* is not written from some kind of a realist position as most commentators presuppose. The *Tractatus* explores the possibility of getting outside of the world of language; but the author of the *Tractatus* finds that when the propositions are alleged to refer to an external world which exists apart from all human knowing, the propositions begin to contradict themselves. The propositions control and the facts are those things to which the propositions refer. The similarities to Bradley's explorations in the world of appearances are close. The difference is, however, very significant. Wittgenstein does not find it meaningful to try to talk about anything other than language itself. About "Reality", "das Mystische", we must be silent. Bradley wrote a fairly large book about "Reality", but in the Preface to *Appearance and Reality* he confesses that his reasoning was necessarily faulty.[66] Wittgenstein is attempting to avoid Bradley's error by treating not of "reality", but of the *Logos*.

---

[65]   Mauthner, *Beiträge*, III, 600.
[66]   Francis H. Bradley, *Appearance and Reality* (2nd ed.; London: George Allen and Unwin, 1897), xiv. In the appendix Bradley says "the actual starting-point and basis of his work is an assumption about truth and reality. I have assumed that the object of metaphysics is to find a general view which will satisfy the intellect, and I have assumed that whatever succeeds in doing this is real and true" (553-54). Mauthner's position was, of course, the almost complete antithesis of Bradley's position. Whether Wittgenstein read Bradley while he was in England before World War I does not appear to be known; but it seems inconceivable that he would not have at least glanced at Bradley's major works and found them unsatisfactory. Bradley's *Principles of Logic* (1883) is deeply concerned with the problem of internal relations.

II

A RELIGIOUS, ESTHETIC, AND
LINGUISTIC TREATISE

1

The *Tractatus Logico-Philosophicus* has an attraction for anyone who does more than glance at it and for whom the subjects with which it wrestles have more than a passing interest. It is, apparently, a treatise about modern logic; and there is much logic in it. Yet Wittgenstein in the Preface denies that the work can in anyway be construed as a textbook. Again, the *Tractatus* seems to be saying something about the ultimate constituents of the world. Yet again, in the Preface, the author denies the possibility of going beyond the reach of language itself. In other words, we cannot talk about the ultimate constituents of the world unless these constituents can at least be named. As *Philosophical Investigations* tells us, this was Wittgenstein's intention when he wrote the *Tractatus*.[1] Yet the author does talk about the ultimate constituents of "reality". They appear, at least at first reading, to be atoms in logical space, possibly analogous to the point-events of some space-time continuum. But we do not actually know any logical atoms and can only presume their existence as constituents of elementary facts. Yet, although we can define elementary facts and can define how they are related to elementary propositions, we cannot, in fact, point to any, although we can make negative judgments about the incompatibility of certain, presumably elementary, facts (4.123,

[1] Ludwig Wittgenstein, *Philosophical Investigations*, ed. by G. E. M. Anscombe and Rush Rhees (2nd ed.; New York: Macmillan, 1958), Part I, sec. 46, 50, 57.

6.5751). We can, at best, know only combinations of elementary facts, and of elementary propositions. We can know only symbols: sentences and facts presumably built up from more fundamental constituents.

Perhaps the discussion of atoms, facts, propositions is only a prelude to statements which affirm that all of these are only appearances, and that we cannot affirm of any of them that they are the constituents of existence itself. Rather, reality is beyond these appearances, both in terms of the "I" which holds individual worlds together, and of the "reality" which gives meaning to the whole: *das Höhere* or *das Mystische*. Before *das Höhere* and the "I" we, as empirical beings, can only sit in awareness; we can say nothing. We can, at most, point, and allow those who are able to see to look and share the experience with us.

The *Tractatus* promises to answer many philosophical questions. In fact, its author claims in the Preface that he has, in essentials, solved the philosophical problems with which others have been wrestling. There is really nothing else to do except a little tidying up; the structure of the building heretofore known as philosophy is now in place, and the apprentices can finish up. At first, one is tempted to agree. As one reads the beautiful German for the first time, one has the sense of being on the threshold of great discoveries; but as one continues to read and to try to think with the author, as he suggests is the only proper method, one becomes less sure. The questions become ever more obscure and so do the answers. One begins to wonder whether the author was mad, whether the reader (oneself) is mad, or whether the world has been confronted with some magnificent hoax. If one could be sure of the sanity or madness, one could walk away despite the original promise; but the book alternately repels and attracts. After the first enticements, one is hooked as by some exotic drug; becoming involved with the *Tractatus* is most analogous to a serious illness. One must see it through to some kind of resolution, even if one has to impose a resolution on it; this is what has happened heretofore. While the present essay is but another attempt to impose a resolution, different from the resolutions which have been imposed in the past, its virtue may lie in the fact that the difference is so extreme that someone else may find a common ground which may include the best out of all.

The bright people of the Vienna Circle thought the *Tractatus* a great work. Bertrand Russell, who was at least a clever philosopher, wrote an introduction for the *Tractatus*, which is still printed with it. The logical positivists, who pride themselves on the clarity of their thought, claim the *Tractatus* as a major source of their understanding of the world and of what philosophy is all about. On the whole, one may well say that many comments and commentaries on the *Tractatus* approach the work from a logical positivist or logical empiricist point of view. It may be that these Humeans are, in the main, right; but it is the thesis of this essay that they are, in fact, wrong. Their fault is not that they are not intelligent; their fault is not that their comments do not illuminate. Their fault is that they take a portion of the work, sometimes *seriatim*, and treat that portion as a whole, even though that portion is frequently in contradiction to other portions. The next chapter will examine, although not in detail, a tragic example of this kind of writing: G. E. M. Anscombe's *An Introduction to Wittgenstein's Tractatus*.[2] Anscombe's book is not even about the *Tractatus*; it is about Frege, Russell, and Ramsey. Yet Anscombe was among Wittgenstein's closest friends.

Although Wittgenstein may have been mad, he was obviously not a fool; it is most questionable that he would unconsciously write at one place what he would deny at another, or, if he did so, that he did so without a purpose. Too little attention has been paid to the mood of some of the statements made in the *Tractatus*. They are not always in the indicative, but are frequently in the subjunctive; and practically no attention has been paid to the penultimate statement which claims that all which has appeared earlier in the *Tractatus* is *unsinnig*. The least that this statement could mean is that those earlier statements which are in the indicative should be construed as in some fashion in the conditional. The author of the

---

[2]   (2nd ed., rev.; New York: Harper & Row, 1965).

Tractatus, as the Preface shows, felt quite strongly that he had given us the truth; but perhaps the truth is not so much in the individual statements as in the whole. In fact, the individual statements taken in isolation might very well be false while the statements as parts of a larger whole may contribute to the truth of the whole. It may very well be that the truth of the *Tractatus* is similar to that of a great poem. The truth is connotative, not denotative; and the truth to which the *Tractatus* refers is the *Logos* which is hidden in our language, but which can be revealed if we can find the proper mirrors (*Spiegel*, 5.511). Other uses of the mirror figure are to be found at 4.121, 5.512, 5.514, and 6.13. The mirror figure is very common in the ancient Gnostic literature and in early Zen; but it is most unlikely that Wittgenstein was familiar with either. It is, however, a natural figure for those who are wrestling with the esoteric or the hidden. Saint Paul speaks of seeing through a glass darkly (I Cor. 13 : 12).

If the truths of the *Tractatus* are connotative rather than denotative, they must be treated as parts of a whole — as Wittgenstein obviously intended. This means that any attempt to treat the parts of the *Tractatus* denotatively or in isolation will not only miss the point of the work, but will falsify it. If we are to find a way to understand the *Tractatus*, we must find a way to treat it synoptically. The poetic essay, which is what the *Tractatus* is, is itself a showing rather than a saying.

The use of German throughout this essay is owing to the author's conviction that all translations in one fashion or another falsify what Wittgenstein was trying to show. The essay, itself, is an attempt to say what he was trying to show; and it must be a failure insofar as it takes Wittgenstein's sentences out of context. But insofar as the essay, by proceeding obliquely, is a showing rather than a saying, it may be successful.

2

A subordinate, but necessary purpose of this essay is to place the

Tractatus Logico-Philosophicus within another literary genre than that to which the heading "technical philosophy" is usually applied. A work in technical philosophy is either an argument or an exposition. The *Tractatus* is neither. Rather, the *Tractatus* belongs with that group of literary works which is bounded on one side by technical philosophy, and on the other by poetry. There are no fixed boundaries, and the placing of a particular piece within the genre is surely at least in part determined by the tastes of the classifier. Wordsworth's *Preludes* are at one boundary; the *Ethica Ordine Geometrico Demonstrata* is at the other. Within the genre are *De Rerum Natura, Also Sprach Zarathustra* and the *Tractatus*. They appear to be arguments or expositions and they seem to proceed methodologically through a series of propositions; but when one examines the alleged argument or exposition one finds that the work does not quite hold up either as an argument or as an exposition.

Nevertheless, something important is being said, and it would be an error to say that an argument is not going on. If one were to use the figure of a net rather than a line, one could call these semi-poetical works arguments because the totality of the propositions is closely bound together and every part illuminates all of the others. It is well to hold to the figure of the net for works like the *Tractatus* and the *Ethics* because they pretend to be linear arguments. There is, in fact, no beginning nor end. Rather there is a constant movement of the many parts illuminating one whole: *Natura naturata.*

The *Tractatus* is obviously the fruit of many logical, psychological, and linguistic investigations by the author. It reflects those investigations, and, as the author says in the Preface, it can only really be understood by someone who has made similar investigations. Each of the statements, sentences, propositions (*Sätze*) is as dependent on all of the others and on the whole as are the sentences of a well written poem. The *Tractatus* has a being even as Cleanth Brooks describes being in *The Well Wrought Urn* (1947). There is nothing accidental in the *Tractatus*; and the author tells us in his next to the last statement that each of the propositions taken singly is *unsinnig*. Whatever meaning the propositions may have, that meaning is not going to be immediately apparent nor is it going to be denotatively unequivocal.

A book in philosophy should seek at least to be denotatively unequivocal; and there should be little doubt when one has studied a good piece of philosophical writing that one has understood it. If it is a difficult piece of writing, such as we see in the case of Saint Thomas, Aristotle or Hume, we assume that further study will give us deeper insights of the same general character that we already have obtained. This cannot be said of the *Tractatus*. It cannot be said of Spinoza's *Ethics* or of most of Plato's *Dialogues*. They appear to be expository, and they are not; they appear to be arguments, and they are not. Rather, like good pieces of poetry, they lead the reader further and further into the thought of the author and of the reader's own self; sometimes, as with the *Tractatus*, the thought is labyrinthine indeed. The *Tractatus* is not so much a philosophic as a religious treatise, and the purpose is to entice the reader into an understanding of himself and his relation to the *Logos*. Dr. K. T. Fann, whose native speech is Chinese, compares the *Tractatus* with the ancient far eastern classic: The *Tao Teh Ching*.

Both are composed of short oracular remarks which cover the whole range of philosophy in a short span. Both philosophers use paradoxes to convey their most important insights. One starts with a metaphysical statement about the nature of the world and ends with practical advice: Whereof one cannot speak one must be silent; while the other starts with a metaphysical statement about the Way of Nature and concludes with a practical message: Do nothing and nothing will be left undone.[3]

The comparison is apt; but it is surely only another beginning in our search for the key to the *Tractatus*. In the *Tao Teh Ching* we are reminded that the world has its own way and that, if we are to be effective, we must allow things to work out their own destinies. In the *Tao* sharp distinctions are avoided; but in the *Tractatus* careful distinctions are made. It appears that certain things can be

---

[3]   Fann, *Wittgenstein's Conception of Philosophy*, 3n.

talked about with complete clarity. These are the facts to which the elementary propositions of the natural sciences refer. These facts are depictable; and the matrices of the truth tables have been devised to depict them, or at least depict the propositions which describe them by standing in a one to one relation with them. Most of the *Tractatus* is concerned to talk about the boundaries of the realm of the depictable, showing clearly where the scientific writ runs and where it does not. Clearly, most so-called scientific laws are at best short-hand or heuristic devices which cannot be depicted, although they may be quite useful (6.34-6.361). In addition, the *Tractatus* shows us the logical form of the world by showing us the logical form which pervades our language and understanding. In a way not dissimilar from that of the *Tao Teh Ching* the *Tractatus* shows us the structure of the human world by indirection, obliquely. He who would learn what the *Logos* is like must not so much look with the third eye, but out of the corner of his natural eyes as he contemplates human speech as it is actually in use. Only then will the *Logos* begin to appear. And "die Logik ist keine Lehre, sondern ein Spiegelbild der Welt" (6.13). Heraclitus would not have said it better.

3

In his radical examination of speech in the *Tractatus*, Wittgenstein shows us, among others, two things which have the quality of necessity as soon as we really observe them. Both have had a significant influence on linguistic studies since the publication of the *Tractatus*. The first is a redefinition of the meaning of Occam's razor in terms of symbolism and necessity rather than convenience or practicality. At 3.328 Wittgenstein says:

Wird ein Zeichen *nicht gebraucht*, so ist es bedeutungslos. Das ist der Sinn der Devise Occams. (Wenn sich alles so verhält als hätte ein Zeichen Bedeutung, dann hat es auch Bedeutung.)

Significantly, the Ogden translation of the italicized words is "not necessary". What Wittgenstein says is more subtle; it is almost reminiscent of the later *Philosophical Investigations*. A sign which is not used is surely not necessary; but there may be a mental "spinning of the wheels" as the result of the sign being in the proposition (*Satz*). Wittgenstein refers to Occam's razor again at 5.4731, and points out that the rule is not to be respected because of its practical efficacy. In the passages which surround the two references to Occam's razor, Wittgenstein points out that neither Frege nor Russell had really come to understand that purpose and the use of a sign were intrinsically rather than extrinsically joined. At 5.4731 Wittgenstein writes:

Das Einleuchten, von dem Russell so viel sprach, kann nur dadurch in der Logik entbehrlich werden, dass die Sprache selbst jeden logischen Fehler verhindert. — Dass die Logik a priori ist, besteht darin, dass nicht unlogisch gedacht werden kann.

Similarly, he says:

In der logischen Syntax darf nie die Bedeutung eines Zeichens eine Rolle spielen; sie muss sich aufstellen lassen, ohne dass dabei von der *Bedeutung* eines Zeichens die Rede wäre, sie darf *nur* die Beschreibung der Ausdrücke voraussetzen (3.33).

Von dieser Bemerkung sehen wir in Russell's "Theory of Types" hinüber: Der Irrtum Russell's zeigt sich darin, dass er bei der Aufstellung der Zeichenregeln von den Zeichen reden musste (3.331).

Speaking of Frege, he says:

Frege sagt: Jeder rechtmässig gebildete Satz muss einen Sinn haben; und ich sage: Jeder mögliche Satz ist rechtmässig gebildet, und wenn er keinen Sinn hat, so kann das nur daran liegen, dass wir einigen seiner Bestandteile keine *Bedeutung* gegeben haben (5.4733).

The differences which Wittgenstein is here drawing between himself and two thinkers whom he called his mentors may seem overly subtle; but the issues are, in fact, fundamental and vital. Apparently, Wittgenstein saw that both Frege and Russell in some fashion related their logical operations to a world which lay beyond language. In effect, both Russell and Frege could stand outside of language or logic and judge the congruence of their propositions by common sense or self-evidence. Wittgenstein did not believe that it is possible to get outside of the language world (5.6). Therefore, any discussion about logic and language must take place within the medium being discussed. If distinctions are to be made, and they must be made, they must be made within the medium. It is this kind of thought which lies in back of the following passages:

Kein Satz kann etwas über sich selbst aussagen, weil das Satzzeichen nicht in sich selbst enthalten sein kann, (das ist die ganze "Theory of types") (3.332).

An unseren Notationen ist zwar etwas willkürlich, aber *das* ist nicht willkürlich: Dass, *wenn* wir etwas bestimmt haben, dann etwas anderes der Fall sein muss. (Dies hängt von dem Wesen der Notation ab.) (3.342).

Die Logik muss für sich selber sorgen. Ein mögliches Zeichen muss auch bezeichnen können. Alles was in der Logik möglich ist, ist auch erlaubt (5.473).

Although not immediately relevant, it is very important to distinguish the thought of 3.342 from that of Mauthner. Mauthner knew no necessity; all was arbitrary.

At the beginning of this section we spoke of two lasting influences resulting from the publication of the *Tractatus*. The first, with which we have been concerned at some length, pertains to a redefinition of Occam's razor. Occam was concerned with an unnecessary multiplication of entities; but as he offered his rule, he spoke heuristically. As Wittgenstein was to point out later in his discussion of natural laws, we have no objective criterion for choosing a shorter rather than a longer explanation (6.363, 6.3631). But Occam's razor is more than a heuristic device; an unnecessary sign is a meaningless sign within language; and the sense of a sign is dependent on the intentionality of the users. Within language Occam's razor is a device to prevent incoherent sentences. As a corollary, once we have chosen a sign and given it a meaning, other signs follow by necessity (3.342). That this is the case shows that there is at least a minimal order in the world (3.3421). Mauthner was most doubtful of this: order exists only where we impose it, and we impose order out of ignorance rather than knowledge.[4]

The second lasting influence of the *Tractatus* is related to the first: it concerns the ubiquity of logic and the necessary synonymity which must lie at the base of all language if Wittgenstein's analysis of the meaning of Occam's razor for language is in fact the true one. There seems little doubt that the author of the *Tractatus* was, on the whole, committed to synonymity.

Wir können einem Zeichen nicht den unrechten Sinn geben (5.4732).

Definitionen sind Regeln der Übersetzung von einer Sprache in eine andere. Jede richtige Zeichensprache muss sich in jede andere nach solchen Regeln übersetzen lassen: *Dies* ist, was sie alle gemeinsam haben (3.343).

Das, was am Symbol bezeichnet, ist das Gemeinsame aller jener Symbole, durch die das erste den Regeln der logischen Syntax zufolge ersetzt werden kann (3.344).

Der Mensch besitzt die Fähigkeit Sprachen zu bauen, womit sich jeder Sinn ausdrücken lässt, ohne eine Ahnung davon zu haben, wie und was jedes Wort bedeutet (4.002).

Alle Sätze unserer Umgangssprache sind tatsächlich, so wie sie sind, logisch volkommen geordnet (5.5563).

Yet at 5.62 the heritage of Mauthner is demonstrated by the parenthetical phrase "der Sprache, die allein ich verstehe". Every language is, after all, an individual thing. This parenthetical phrase is not, however, the major thrust of the *Tractatus*. The major thrust is that languages can be translated into each other without remainder and that languages control how we see and build reality (4.01-4.023, 3.04-3.26). We are prisoners of our language worlds; propositions are the means by which we articulate these several worlds; but the projected worlds, with accidental exceptions (3.34-3.3421), are identical. It is not reality which judges the language, but language which judges reality.

Der Satz *zeigt* seinen Sinn. Der Satz *zeigt,* wie es sich verhält *wenn* er wahr ist. Und er *sagt,* dass es sich so verhält (4.022).

[4] Mauthner, *Beiträge*, III, 576, 577.

"Die Wirklichkeit muss durch den Satz auf ja oder nein fixiert sein" (4.023). The importance of language study, including the study of logic and mathematics, is that only through the certainty that we are not incoherent in our use of language can we be certain that we are living in a common world with our fellows. Mauthner concludes his monumental three volume work with a quotation from Dante (*Paradiso* II) to the effect that we are, in fact, on a boundless sea without any guide whatsoever. The thrust of Wittgenstein's argument is to assert that this simply is not the case. Within language there are some certainties; and they show themselves to him who really looks. These certainties do not show themselves in the world, which for Wittgenstein is as strange as it is for Mauthner, but in our common speech patterns. But again these speech patterns, insofar as we can uncover them with a kind of mirror (*Spiegel*) (5.511, 6.13), reveal something about the nature of the world (3.342-3.343). At no point in the *Tractatus* does Wittgenstein say that we can discover the logic of either our language or the world by looking at language directly. That was Mauthner's way; and it had obviously failed: it had given us as many logics as there were languages which could be empirically explored. In the *Tractatus* Wittgenstein is not making an empirical investigation, nor is he seeking to find that which is common to all languages. He is, in fact, seeking to find that which makes language itself possible; and his tool is the *Principia Mathematica*.

It appears that the later Wittgenstein retreated from the rigorous views about logic and its ubiquity which he had held in his youth. In *Philosophical Investigations* he seems to be saying that logic rests on essentially empirical grounds. The crucial quotation is to be found at section xii, Part II:

Wenn die Begriffsbildung sich aus Naturtatsachen erklären lässt, sollte uns dann nicht, statt der Grammatik, dasjenige interessieren, was ihr in der Natur zugrunde liegt? — Uns interessiert wohl auch die Entsprechung von Begriffen mit sehr allgemeinen Naturtatsachen. (Solchen, die uns ihrer Allgemeinheit wegen meist nicht aufallen.) Aber unser Interesse fällt nun nicht auf diese möglichen Ursachen der Begriffsbildung zurück; . . . Wer glaubt, gewisse Begriffe seien schlechtweg die richtigen, wer andere hätte, sähe eben etwas nicht ein, was wir einsehen, — der möge sich gewisse sehr allgemeine Naturtatsachen anders vorstellen, als wir sie gewohnt sind, und andere Begriffsbildungen als die gewohnten werden ihm verständlich werden.[5] It is very questionable that Mauthner could have said this. For Mauthner, language was a purely accidental congeries of sounds and gestures. The author of the quoted material is saying neither that language has no relation to the external world nor that the relation is accidental. In fact, it is more likely that the world is accidental than that language is. Speech patterns are the inevitable result of certain developments within the human organism, and the logic proceeds as a consequence of those developments. We may not assume that all is arbitrary. At most, we can assume that the range of possibilities is considerably greater than we had originally thought possible. The author of the *Tractatus* has not been repudiated; his vision has been extended. The quotation given above concludes in this fashion:

Vergleiche einen Begriff mit einer Malweise: Ist denn auch nur unsere Malweise willkürlich? Können wir nach Belieben eine wählen? (z.B. die der Ägypter). Oder handelt sich's da nur um hübsch und hässlich?

At 6.37 the author of the *Tractatus* had said that there is only logical necessity and that everything else, including the several worlds, is accidental. He had found that logical necessity exists transcendentally within the world of language; and that logic is the logic of the *Principia Mathematica* perfected. The author of *Philosophical Investigations* still has the same doubts about the existence of an external world; but the logic of the *Tractatus* has become a congeries of logics, none of them arbitrary, all of them dependent on the intentionality of the user. Equally, all lie within language and its various games. The logic of the *Tractatus* is one of the games within language; but there are others for which notations still need to be worked out. *Philosophical Investigations* is an expansion of the thought of the *Tractatus*; not a repudiation. At no place does the later Wittgenstein affirm the possibility of an illogical world; and, significantly, he says of beings other than men, such

[5] *Philosophical Investigations*, 230.

as lions and gods, that if they wish to talk to men they must do so in the language of men.[6]

4

Although this essay explores Wittgenstein's philosophical and personal development down to and including the writing of the *Tractatus* as clearly as published materials permit, it must be recognized that some conjecture is necessary if we are to make a plausible account. Chapter X is concerned to present a picture of the mature Wittgenstein, the man who came back from World War I, and his theology. At this place in our discussion we are concerned only with Wittgenstein's probable position at the time he went to England for the first time, a young man of nineteen, and his apparent development under the influence of Russell, Whitehead, Frege, and Moore.

Until very recently, it has been assumed that Wittgenstein was influenced only by the four men mentioned at the end of the preceding paragraph and Schopenhauer, whom he had read as a boy.[7] Miss Anscombe, who is one of Wittgenstein's literary executors[8] and was supported by the Rockefeller Foundation for a number of years while she worked on Wittgenstein's manuscripts,[9] reports that "Wittgenstein's philosophical influences are pretty well confined to Frege and to Russell".[10] Whitehead must be added because he did share the authorship of the *Principia Mathematica* with Russell. Although Moore may be discounted, it is true that Wittgenstein attended his classes[11] and that a friendship was established which lasted until Moore's death.[12] Yet is not this whole way of speaking

---

6   *Philosophical Investigations*, 217, 223.
7   Anscombe, *An Introduction*, 12.
8   Engelmann, *Letters from Ludwig Wittgenstein*, xiv.
9   Anscombe, *An Introduction*, Acknowledgments.
10   Anscombe, *An Introduction*, 12.
11   G. E. Moore, "Autobiography", in Fann (ed.), *Ludwig Wittgenstein*, 39.
12   G. H. von Wright, "A Biographical Sketch", in Fann (ed.), 23.

fundamentally fallacious? It assumes that a life, even though it may only be the life of a mind, can be constructed out of bits and pieces of other lives and other minds. Wittgenstein's friendship with Keynes[13] demonstrates that there were other and significant influences at work in England. Can we doubt that there were others in central Europe? The young Wittgenstein was as much a genius as the older. Surely, we are wrong if we attempt to make Wittgenstein an epigone of either Frege or Russell, or both, and at the same time imply that we have explained Wittgenstein if we have explained his mentors.

If Wittgenstein had mentors, which was obviously the case, they were far more numerous than Frege and Russell. His relations with Kant, Spinoza, and Schopenhauer will be explored at some depth in this essay; but this exploration does not attempt to say that these, any more than Frege and Russell, explain Wittgenstein. He was *sui generis*. It would be difficult to explain his influence if he had not been. It is most likely that the attempt to explain Wittgenstein by referring back to Russell and Frege is owing both to his obviously very sincere acknowledgment of his indebtedness to the latter two and to Russell's "Introduction"; but we know that he did not approve of Russell's "Introduction".[14] Then, again, there is the common assumption that he could not have known any philosophy since he came to England to study engineering. The same line of reasoning denies the possibility of his knowing any music since he was an engineer; but no one has any doubt of his great musical genius.[15] Wittgenstein came from a remarkably gifted and very wealthy family which had access to every reach of the Viennese society of the late nineteenth and early twentieth centuries.[16] Although decadent, that society was also very fertile, as we soon realize when we consider the names of the men who grew up within it. It seems incredible that Wittgenstein is assumed to have

13 Engelmann, *Letters*, 54f.
14 Engelmann, *Letters*, 31.
15 Von Wright, *Biographical Sketch*, 17.
16 Von Wright, *Sketch*, 14.

grown up in a philosophical vacuum and to have read only the works of Schopenhauer, Frege, and Russell.

5

It was perfectly natural for Wittgenstein to have studied engineering since his family controlled a large portion of the steel industry of the Danube Basin;[17] but there was nothing in the environment in which Wittgenstein grew up which would have prevented him from thinking or discouraged him from pursuing philosophical questions. One of the questions about which he apparently thought a great deal was solipsism and how to escape from it. Miss Anscombe was conscious that this problem still occupied Wittgenstein at the end of his life,[18] and it is certainly a major thread running through the *Tractatus*. Mauthner offered no way out of the solipsism; and Schopenhauer encouraged it; but Schopenhauer did offer a radical gambit, sainthood, which could make the human predicament worthwhile. From a close reading of the *Tractatus*, it appears that the young Wittgenstein finally accepted his solipsism and the new logic, the latter as an aspect of the way in which people communicate between their isolated worlds (4.463, 5.6-5.641). If his life after his return from the war is any indication, it seems most likely that Wittgenstein had also accepted the Schopenhauerian gambit during the war.

It is a thesis of this essay that the *Tractatus* is both an exploration of the ontological implications of the new logic and a rejection of any application of that logic beyond language itself. Mauthner entitled the first part of his *Beiträge: Wesen der Sprache,* and here explored the difficulties of the subject, coming out with quite negative conclusions which are reflected in the *Tractatus*. There is no essence of speech. Momentarily, we may call speech a tool which distinguishes men from other animals, but speech can become a tyrant and betray us. Our job, as speech critics, is to try to under-

---

17   Von Wright, *Sketch*, 14.
18   Anscombe, *An Introduction*, 12.

stand where we can and where we cannot trust speech; but we cannot stand apart from speech to do the job of criticizing because the very signs which speech uses are the counters with which we must perform the critic's task. Compare "Gedächtnis ohne Gedachtniszeichen ist nicht möglich; und Zeichen sind im weitesten Sinn sprachliche Akte",[19] with Wittgenstein's statement that we cannot get outside of the limits of our language (5.6-5.62). In the widest sense, however, it is wrong to call language a tool. Language is what it is; and yet it has no being. Consider the following quotation, so reminiscent of the later Wittgenstein. In the *Tractatus,* language is a part of the human organism (4.002), in the *Beiträge,* it is not.

Die Sprache ist aber kein Gegenstand des Gebrauchs, auch kein Werkzeug, sie ist überhaupt kein Gegenstand, sie ist gar nichts anderes als ihr Gebrauch. Sprache ist Sprachgebrauch. Da ist es doch kein Wunder mehr, wenn der Gebrauch mit dem Gebrauche sich steigert.[20]

Mauthner, like Wittgenstein, finds it necessary to define his terms by indirection as they apply to language. He does so by the exploration of alternative meanings until the true meaning at last appears. Surely, this process is what is meant by the last sentence of the quotation; and, as the penultimate proposition of the *Tractatus* states, it is the process which may be seen in action throughout the *Tractatus.* Language controls our understanding of the world; and there is no way in which we can get outside of our language worlds for a correction. The very nature of language requires that a discussion of language must proceed dialectically. The whole of the *Tractatus* falls into place if we come to realize that Wittgenstein is testing the limits of language and that *Wirklichkeit, Wahrheit,* and *Welt* have their meanings as words within language rather than as *Dinge-an-sich* or *Vorstellungen* apart from language.

Nevertheless, Wittgenstein, unlike Mauthner, does attempt to show that there is some correlation between the pictures in our minds evoked by our propositions, and the world out there. In the sense that the elements "out there" provide the raw stuff of our

---

[19] Mauthner, *Beiträge,* I, 227.
[20] Mauthner, *Beiträge,* I, 24.

individual worlds there is a correlation. This is surely the purpose of the whole discussion about *Gegenstände*; but we do not know *Gegenstände*. We know only facts (1.-2.01) and the pictures of those facts (2.1-2.1512); *and* it is not an illogical world since we cannot think illogically (3.031). The truth of our picture of the world is dependent not on its congruence with a *Wirklichkeit* independent of our knowledge; although at times Wittgenstein seems to be saying this (2.203-2.225). Rather, the truth of our picture of the world is dependent on its coherence (3.032-3.1432), but not only on its coherence. Wittgenstein is not an idealist. Perhaps what he was trying to say is most clearly shown by the interesting proposition and figure in 5.5432. What I see is dependent on me, but the raw material is something other than me. In either of the two possible choices, coherence still guides the development of the picture which appears; and the two pictures are mutually exclusive facts although made of the same elements. Mauthner concludes his discussion of the *Wesen der Sprache* with this interesting sentence: "Denn die objektive Welt stammt von unsrer Begriffswelt ab, die eroberte Gedankenwelt von der ererbten Sprache."[21]

For Mauthner, the ultimate control of our understanding of the world is dependent on our inherited language in all of its arbitrariness; for Wittgenstein, language still controls, but our colloquial languages are logically in order as they are (5.5563), and the worlds which they give us are coherent worlds. The worlds themselves may be different, even at some points mutually exclusive (5.5423), but they share the quality of logical coherence. Our worlds are controlled by the elementary propositions, the significant propositions, describing any particular world. Tautology and contradiction are the external boundaries for any possible description and therefore for any possible world; but tautology and contradiction have only a linguistic existence and have no correlate in any possible world.

Die Tautologie lässt der Wirklichkeit den ganzen — unendlichen — logischen Raum; die Kontradiktion erfüllt den ganzen logischen Raum und lässt der Wirklichkeit keinen Punkt. Keine von beiden kann daher die Wirklichkeit irgendwie bestimmen (4.463).

[21]   Mauthner, *Beiträge*, 232.

Es ist klar, dass das logische Produkt zweier Elementarsätze weder eine Tautologie noch eine Kontradiktion sein kann. Die Aussage, dass ein Punkt des Gesichtsfeldes zu gleicher Zeit zwei verschiedene Farben hat ist eine Kontradiktion (6.3751).

Although the major purpose of this chapter is to place the *Tractatus* within a certain literary genre, it would not be amiss to point out the relation of this whole discussion of tautology, contradiction and logical form to the discussion of the metaphysical "I" in the *Tractatus* and *The World as Will and Idea*. In both books there is an objective world correlate to a knowing subject, itself not a part of that world. There may be many worlds and many subjects, but it is legitimate to talk about the world and the "I" correlated with it as the paradigm case. In *The World as Will and Idea* Schopenhauer does not find it possible to place any boundaries to the kinds of possible worlds.[22] Wittgenstein, on the other hand, found such boundaries, at least as far as human knowledge is concerned, in the linguistic concepts of contradiction and tautology. Schopenhauer was aware of the human origin of tautology and contradiction; and he suggested toward the end of the first volume of *The World as Will and Idea* that there may be, either in the Will or beyond it, a reality which is open to those who deny the world both as will and idea.[23] Although there will be many more references to Schopenhauer, it is important for our purposes in this chapter to make it clear that Wittgenstein's understanding of the nature of solipsism was much influenced by Schopenhauer's analysis. The series of propositions running from 5.6 to 5.641 presuppose the kind of knowing subject which Schopenhauer describes; and the mystical of 6.522 again presupposes that reality which Schopenhauer suggested as possibly existing, which becomes a Presence when the world as both will and idea is successfully denied.[24]

In the next chapter we shall be concerned with the relations between Bertrand Russell and Wittgenstein and the great influence of Russell's "Introduction" on the early interpretations of the *Trac-*

---

[22] Schopenhauer, *The World as Will and Idea*, III, 298.
[23] Schopenhauer, *The World as Will and Idea*, III, 528-32.
[24] Schopenhauer, *The World as Will and Idea*, I, 528-32.

tatus, but there should be at least a note about the possible relation between Wittgenstein and Alfred North Whitehead, the co-author of *Principia Mathematica* (1911). By the time that Wittgenstein came up to Cambridge, Whitehead was already in London; but there is no reason to believe that he did not make frequent trips back to the University. We must assume some meetings between Whitehead and Wittgenstein because it is unlikely that Russell would have hidden his most promising pupil. What is strange is the apparent lack of communication between Whitehead and Wittgenstein. Wittgenstein mentions Whitehead only as the co-author of the *Principia*; and Whitehead does not mention Wittgenstein in any of his later books when he would have had an opportunity to read the *Tractatus*. The apparent lack of communication seems to rest finally on the fact that Whitehead and Wittgenstein came to see the world quite differently. Each of them was devoted to the new logic of the *Principia*; but Whitehead chose to use the new logic as a means of erecting a comprehensive metaphysics. Wittgenstein saw the new logic as ruling out the possibility of any metaphysics.

In *Science and the Modern World* and *Process and Reality,* Whitehead erected a metaphysics which presupposes the Humean analysis, the achievements of modern science and the existence of eternal objects, Platonic-like forms, which provide the substance of the world. At first sight, the *Gegenstände* of the earlier portions of the *Tractatus* seem to be the equivalent of the eternal objects; but they fall under Wittgenstein's destructive analysis. Wittgenstein's analysis, in the end, rules out everything except language and mystical experience. From the viewpoint of the *Tractatus* the elaborate metaphysics of *Process and Reality* would have seemed absurd. It may have been his awareness of this differing point of view which caused Whitehead to write some cautionary notes in the Preface to *Process and Reality*. In these notes he claimed to reject several contemporary positions in modern philosophy:

(i)   The distrust of speculative philosophy.
(ii)   The trust in language as an adequate expression of propositions.
(vii)   The Kantian doctrine of the objective world as a theoretical

construct from purely subjective experience.
(viii) Arbitrary deductions in *ex absurdo* arguments.
(ix)   Belief that logical inconsistencies can indicate anything else
       than some antecedent error.[25]

Each of these statements pertains to an aspect of the *Tractatus*.
In most respects the author of this essay is in deep sympathy
with Whitehead's conclusions which are not very different from
Bradley's;[26] but the course of investigation over the past four decades seems to indicate that we must begin with language rather than
with metaphysics. Wittgenstein's procedure in the *Tractatus* is to
explore language by throwing it against itself until the meaning appears. The failure to understand the *Tractatus* is the failure to understand its author's method; even more frequently to impose a
radical empiricism upon him. The only possible way out of Wittgenstein's world of language is a radical leap of faith to a wholly
other. Whitehead's own sense of failure even after the completion
of such a magnificent book as *Process and Reality* can be found in
the Preface in a phrase very similar to Bradley's expressed sense
of failure in the Preface to *Appearance and Reality*. Whitehead's
statement reads:

There remains the final reflection, how shallow, puny, and imperfect
are efforts to sound the depths in the nature of things. In philosophical
discussion, the merest hint of dogmatic certainty as to the finality of
statement is an exhibition of folly.[27]

Whitehead's importance is that, in attempting to create a metaphysics with one of the best mathematical brains of this century,
he failed; Wittgenstein's importance is in his showing that we are
forever imprisoned within the sounds and symbols of our languages.
Insofar as *Process and Reality* is a showing rather than a saying,
it is highly useful; insofar as it attempts to say what cannot be said
it is a striking failure. The author of the *Tractatus* is surely a radical sceptic about the possibility of any metaphysics; but he is a

[25] Alfred North Whitehead, *Process and Reality: An Essay in Cosmology*
(New York: The Humanities Press, 1955), viii.
[26] Whitehead, *Process and Reality*, vii.
[27] Whitehead, *Process and Reality*, x.

sceptic who is convinced that it is possible to talk meaningfully and with certainty with his fellows. Nevertheless, with his distinction between "showing" and "saying", Wittgenstein also made a good case for taking a leap of faith.

III

RUSSELL AND WITTGENSTEIN

1

It is difficult, perhaps impossible, to reconstruct the relation between Russell and Wittgenstein in that period just before World War I when they were studying together. It was obviously very exciting for both of them; and one is tempted to draw a parallel with the earlier association between Whitehead and Russell which resulted in the *Principia Mathematica*. In the tenth chapter of this essay, the chapter which attempts to demonstrate certain aspects of Wittgenstein's personal life after the war years as an explication or showing of the meaning of the *Tractatus* as a work in theology, we shall look at the available evidence as it points toward a decision on the part of the mature Wittgenstein to become, if possible, a Schopenhauerian saint. At the present stage of our discussion, however, our interests are purely intellectual: to try to determine how and in what way the young Wittgenstein was influenced by his older teacher. Both Wittgenstein and Russell give evidence that the relation before the war was extraordinarily close. Wittgenstein mentions Russell's name several times in the *Tractatus;* and Russell made frequent references to the friendship in "The Philosophy of Logical Atomism", a series of lectures delivered in early 1918. Of the lectures, Russell said that they were

largely concerned with explaining certain ideas which I learnt from my friend and former pupil Ludwig Wittgenstein. I have had no opportunity of knowing his views since August, 1914, and I do not even know whether he is alive or dead.[1]

To what degree the lectures represent truthfully the kind of thinking that went on between the two friends in the period before the war we cannot tell. Surely Russell believed that they did, and it is apparent that he believed the *Tractatus* to be primarily a development of the thoughts which the two had shared. His "Introduction" confirms this understanding; but we know that Wittgenstein did not believe the "Introduction" truly represented the thought of the *Tractatus*.[2] There is a discrepancy in the two understandings of what Wittgenstein was trying to say. What makes it so difficult to understand the nature of the discrepancy is that the two friends had thought they were in agreement in the period before the War. Either they were not, in fact, in agreement or one or the other or both had changed. Russell, apparently, never did really understand what the difficulty was; and most commentators seem, on the whole, to understand the *Tractatus* in the same manner that Russell did.

The issue is not a simple one. In fact, it lies at the heart of this essay. Russell was not untruthful in his 1918 lectures, although one feels at times that the exposition is not as clear as it might have been had the lecturer really made the material his own. One might say that Wittgenstein had changed, and this seems to have been Russell's decision. But there is another alternative which includes the possibility that Wittgenstein and Russell were not actually as close as they both had thought themselves to be; and that during the four year separation certain central European speech and thought patterns, which had always been in the mind of the young Wittgenstein, emerged as dominating patterns. While in England, Wittgenstein presumably thought and spoke in English and carried on his logical research in English. But between that time and the publication of the *Tractatus*, while Wittgenstein had been in the Austrian Army, he had spoken nothing but German. Logic became the tool which the German-speaking Austrian used to serve his philosophic purposes. These purposes, at first meta-

---

[1]   Bertrand Russell, *Logic and Knowledge: Essays 1901-1950*, ed. by Robert Charles Marsh (New York: Macmillan, 1968), 177.
[2]   Engelmann, *Letters*, 29-31.

physical, seem to have become more and more religious and linguistic as the war was prolonged. It is significant that Wittgenstein was unable to read Russell's English with ease and that he had to wait for a German translation before he was able to state emphatically that the "Introduction" would not do.[3] There was a difference between the two men. In this section we shall try to display what it was.

The difference concerns ultimately their respective metaphysical visions of the world. The issue may be essentially revealed if we consider the relation between a fact and a proposition which is held to be descriptive of that fact. Which is prior: the fact or the proposition? Max Black summarizes Russell's position as follows:

Russell . . . tended to assimilate logical and mathematical truths to scientific truths in a way which Wittgenstein could not stomach. Logical truths are distinguished from empirical generalizations only by their superior generality (cf. *Principia,* Vol. I, p. 93); logical words stand for subsistent "universals", our apprehension of which is "as ultimate as sensation" ("Mathematical Logic", p. 492); and logic is an abstract natural science which "must no more admit a unicorn than zoology can; for logic is concerned with the real world just as truly as zoology, though with its more abstract and general features" *(Mathematical Philosophy,* p. 169). So Russell consistently took the primitive propositions of *Principia* to be hypotheses and held the chief reason for adopting his reduction of mathematics to logic to "be inductive . . . [and to] lie in the fact that the theory in question enables us to deduce ordinary mathematics" *(Principia,* preface, para. 2)[4]

Obviously, for Russell, the fact is prior to the description, and it exists somewhere out there in the external world. Furthermore, there is only one world. Our propositions, whether complex or simple, are attempts to describe the complex and simple facts of the world. But, for Russell, even in the 1918 lectures, the ultimate facts are themselves logical simples: individuals which can be no further analyzed. Black states it in this way:

Russell's philosophical grammar is dominated by the category of

---

[3]   Engelmann, *Letters,* 31.
[4]   Max Black, *A Companion to Wittgenstein's "Tractatus"* (Ithaca, New York: Cornell University Press, 1964), 4.

name: broadly speaking, words or symbols are ultimately acceptable for him only when they *stand for* real entities, are names of things.[5]

When we consider the attention paid to *Gegenstände* in the earlier portions of the *Tractatus*, we are tempted to say the same thing of Wittgenstein, but, in fact, this is not the case. Again quoting Black, we can say:

In his conception of elementary propositions Wittgenstein introduced two important novelties which distinguish his view from the semantical theories of Russell and Frege: he insisted that propositions must be regarded as *facts*, not complex objects; and he extended a famous doctrine of Frege's by holding *all* names to have reference only in context.[6]

This distinction, if acceptable, is more than enough to explain why Wittgenstein had so much difficulty with Russell's "Introduction" and why there is a frequent blurring as Russell attempts, in his 1918 lectures, to be true to the thought of his student. Yet one is forced to wonder as one reads Black's *Companion* whether Black himself really understood the radical nature of Wittgenstein's break with Russell.

In actual fact it was not a break since Wittgenstein's solipsistic position had probably not altered during all the time he was studying with Russell. Wittgenstein's position, as he tells us in *Philosophical Investigations*, was to give to the *Gegenstände* the ontological status of meontic non-being.[7] The *Gegenstände* do not have being until they are united by us with other *Gegenstände*, thereby creating our several worlds. What is out there in the world of all possible worlds and to which contradiction and tautology give the boundaries is a world of possibilities: *Sachlage*, possible *Sachverhalte*. Russell insisted that there were definite somethings open to our inspection out there in the one world; it was this that Wittgenstein denied, but his denial is also a partial affirmation: my world is created out of something, not nothing; but the something does not have being until it is linked with other similar somethings into a chain. Only in a complex does a *Gegenstand* have being; only

---

[5]   Black, *A Companion*, 12.
[6]   Black, *A Companion*, 12.
[7]   *Philosophical Investigations*, Part I, sec. 46.

when there is a complex is there a world. Propositions are *facts*, as Black says, and the totality of propositions or facts with which I am acquainted is my world (1.11).

It would seem appropriate at this point to attempt to prove the concluding sentence of the preceding paragraph, but, in fact, the whole essay is directed to that end. For Wittgenstein there are a very large number of private worlds; but their possibilities range within definite boundaries, and communication is possible. What Lenin saw as a threat of total relativism in the philosophies of Mach and Avenarius and against which he wrote *Materialism and Empirio-Criticism*, Wittgenstein saw as a problem of language and logic. Lenin's book was a rather complete failure; Wittgenstein's a rather distinguished success.

In an earlier paragraph it was stated that, in attempting to publish Wittgenstein's earlier thoughts, Russell had not thoroughly appropriated them and ended by blurring some distinctions which should have been made. It is not possible to discover whether Russell read Mauthner or, if he did, that he read the *Beiträge* in the same way that Wittgenstein apparently did. Nevertheless, one may distinguish certain passages in the 1918 lectures as having their ultimate roots in Mauthner's discussion of language. As an example, the following passage may be offered as a paraphrase of similar passages from Mauthner:

The whole question of the meaning of words is very full of complexities and ambiguities in ordinary language. When one person uses a word, he does not mean by it the same thing as another person means by it. I have often heard it said that that is a misfortune. That is a mistake. It would be absolutely fatal if people meant the same things by their words. It would make all intercourse impossible, and language the most useless thing imaginable, because the meaning you attach to your words must depend on the nature of the objects you are acquainted with, and since different people are acquainted with different objects, they would not be able to talk to each other unless they attached quite different meanings to their words. . . . It would be altogether incredibly inconvenient to have an unambiguous language, and therefore mercifully we have not got one.[8]

8 Russell, *Logic and Knowledge*, 195-96.

This should remind us of the discussion about *Begriffsumfang* and *Begriffsinhalt* in Mauthner; but Mauthner would not have written a statement which is actually as incoherent as this one is, for what Russell is saying here is that we can only understand each other because, in fact, we do not understand each other. The end result is, of course, that if we are to make sense to each other we must reject the temptation to get outside of our language world. Russell attempts to rescue himself in the following statement:

In a logically perfect language, there will be one word and no more for every simple object and everything that is not simple will be expressed by a combination derived, of course, from the words for the simple things that enter in, one word for each simple component. A language of that sort will be completely analytic and will show at a glance the logical structure of the facts asserted or denied. The language which is set forth in *Principia Mathematica* is intended to be a language of that sort. . . . Barring the omission of a vocabulary I maintain that it is quite a nice language. It aims at being that sort of a language that, if you add a vocabulary, would be a logically perfect language . . . [but] a logically perfect language, if it could be constructed, would not only be intolerably prolix, but, as regards its vocabulary, would be very largely private to one speaker.[9]

Russell has given us an intolerable dilemma: if we speak with others we cannot speak with understanding; if we speak with understanding, we can speak only to ourselves. Nonsense! Russell's trap, at least with respect to symbolism, was his belief that occasionally we could get outside of our symbolic worlds into the "real world",[10] where "real facts" subsist. Wittgenstein says we can, of course, get outside of our symbolic worlds as actors or as showers; but we cannot get outside as sayers. This is surely a major portion of the message of the *Tractatus*. In the *Tractatus* we, as sayers, cannot get outside of that particular portion of the world of symbolic forms which we call language. With that understood, the differences between Wittgenstein and Russell become much clearer. The following quotations are important:

9 Russell, *Logic and Knowledge*, 197-98.
10 Russell, *Logic and Knowledge*, 185.

Wir machen uns Bilder der Tatsachen (2.1).

Die Tatsache muss, um Bild zu sein, etwas mit dem Abgebildeten gemeinsam haben (2.16).

Das Bild bildet die Wirklichkeit ab, indem es eine Möglichkeit des Bestehens und Nichtbestehens von Sachverhalten darstellt (2.201).

Das Bild stellt eine mögliche Sachlage im logischen Raume dar (2.202).

Im Satz drückt sich der Gedanke sinnlich wahrnembar aus (3.1).

Wir benützen das sinnlich wahrnehmbare Zeichen (Laut- oder Schriftzeichen etc.) des Satzes als Projektion der möglichen Sachlage. Die Projektionsmethode ist das Denken des Satz-Sinnes (3.11).

Das Satzzeichen ist eine Tatsache (3.14). (Italics added.)

Der Satz ist ein Bild der Wirklichkeit (4.01).

Der Satz ist ein Modell der Wirklichkeit, so wie wir sie uns denken (4.01).

Der Satz *zeigt* seinen Sinn. Der Satz zeigt, wie es sich verhält, *wenn* er wahr ist. Und er *sagt,* dass es sich so verhält (4.022).

Die Wirklichkeit muss durch den Satz auf ja oder nein fixiert sein. . . . Der Satz konstruiert eine Welt mit Hilfe eines logischen Gerüstes und darum kann man am Satz auch sehen, wie sich alles Logische verhält, *wenn* er wahr ist. Man kann aus einem falschen Satz *Schlüsse ziehen* (4.023).

Im Satz wird gleichsam eine Sachlage probeweise zusammengestellt. Man kann geradezu sagen: statt, dieser Satz hat diesen und diesen Sinn; dieser stellt diese und diese Sachlage dar (4.031).

Beachtet man nicht, dass der Satz einen von den Tatsachen unabhängigen Sinn hat, so kann man leicht glauben, dass wahr und falsch gleichberechtigte Beziehungen von Zeichen und Bezeichnetem sind (4.061).

Der Satz stellt das Bestehen und Nichtbestehen der Sachverhalte dar (4.1).

Der Sinn des Satzes ist seine Übereinstimmung, und Nichtübereinstimmung mit den Möglichkeiten des Bestehens und Nichtbestehens der Sachverhalte (4.2).

At first, one is tempted to read all of these statements as referring to an external world which controls the truth or falsity of any significant sentence; but there is the possibility in all of them that the control lies in the sentence and not in the external world. Wittgenstein's position is actually more subtle and more discriminating than either of these alternatives. If there are, in fact, objects out there in the world — individuals as Russell calls them — it should be possible to arrange these individuals into classes or sets, and it should be possible also, at least in theory, to name each of the individuals (2.011-2.027, 4.1211). Under these conditions, Russell's "Axiom of Infinity" is at best an heuristic device (5.535), if we are not to get into serious difficulties and even into self-contradictory assertions.[11] Wittgenstein obviously considered all of the possibilities in connection with individuals out there and rejected all except his own theories: that we can talk about entities only within language. The quotations which follow show, however, that the objects are possibilities rather than actualities and become actualities only as parts of complexes, correlates of "I"s. It is the intentionality of the "I"s which determines which possibilities become actual in any particular world; and language is the actualization according to rules of the common world which we share. Classes or sets do not exist in the external world and are "wholly superfluous in mathematics" (6.031). Presumably, however, a theory of sets or classes could be worked out which concerned itself with arbitrary marks within certain arbitrary groupings. The quotations dealing in this way with Wittgenstein's answer to Russell's theory of individuals (or objects) and his theory of numbers are as follows:

Der Satz ist kein Wörtergemisch. — (Wie das musikalische Thema kein Gemisch von Tönen). Der Satz ist artikuliert (3.141).

Nur Tatsachen können einen Sinn ausdrücken, eine Klasse von Namen kann es nicht (3.142).

So zeigt ein Satz "fa", dass in seinem Sinn der Gegenstand a vorkommt,

---

11 Black, *A Companion*, 5, 314-17.

zwei Sätze "fa" and "ga", dass in ihnen beiden von demselben Gegenstand die Rede ist (4.1211).

Reihen, welche durch *interne* Relationen geordnet sind, nenne ich Formenreihen. Die Zahlenreihe ist nicht nach einer externen, sondern nach einer internen Relation geordnet (4.1252).

Die logischen Formen sind *zahllos*. Darum gibt es in der Logik keine ausgezeichneten Zahlen und darum gibt es keinen philosophischen Monismus oder Dualismus, etc. (4.128).

Der Elementarsatz besteht aus Namen. Er ist ein Zusammenhang, eine Verkettung, von Namen (4.22).

The last quotation seems to be an exact correlate of 2.03: "Im Sachverhalt hängen die Gegenstände ineinander, wie die Glieder einer Kette." If this is all there is, then the external world rather than the locution controls the meaning. In this light 4.2211 seems but an afterthought, added because of Russell's difficulties with the "axiom of infinity":

Auch wenn die Welt unendlich komplex ist, so dass jede Tatsache aus unendlich vielen Sachverhalten besteht und jeder Sachverhalt aus unendlich vielen Gegenständen zusammengesetzt ist, auch dann müsste es Gegenstände und Sachverhalte geben.

But "müssen" is in the subjunctive. The question of whether there are independent *Gegenstände* and *Sachverhalte* is left open. At 1.1 Wittgenstein states that "Die Welt ist die Gesamtheit der Tatsachen, nicht der Dinge", and at 2.01 he makes an identity between *Gegenstände, Sache,* and *Dinge.*

Das, was das axiom of infinity sagen soll, würde sich in der Sprache dadurch ausdrücken, dass es unendlich viele Namen mit verschiedener Bedeutung gäbe (5.535).

Wittgenstein's position is that there is something out there in the world outside of my "I", but whether it takes this form or that is dependent on me. Nevertheless, the form is not a purely arbitrary thing, as it is with Mauthner. Rather, the appearance of the form follows quite definite rules which may be discerned in the way we use our languages. The propositions in which Wittgenstein considers the nature of form run from 5.55 through 6, although the

consideration of the nature of form in itself stands in back of much
of the argument in the *Tractatus*. As one contrasts Wittgenstein
with Russell one finds that the former did not believe that Russell
made a sufficient distinction between accidental and necessary
generality. For instance, Wittgenstein is able to say: "Es lässt sich
eine Welt denken, in der das Axiom of Reducibility nicht gilt"
(6.1233). With Russell the distinction between accidental and
necessary generality is not very important because he believed that
there is only one world; but Wittgenstein was interested in dis-
covering a logic which is valid for all possible worlds. Necessarily,
such a logic would then apply to the world of our common experience and to our private worlds as well. The general proposition
which meets this demand is given at 6. Its characteristics are to be
seen in the following statement:

Man kann die Welt vollständig durch vollkommen verallgemeinerte
Sätze beschreiben, das heisst also, ohne irgend einen Namen von vorn-
herein einem bestimmten Gegenstand zu zuordnen (5.526).

2

In some respects, it may appear that in this essay Lord Russell is
under attack; and, in a sense, this is true. However, the intent is
somewhat different. Bertrand Russell was a clever philosopher
who exercized a great influence over many minds in American and
England during the first half of this century. Throughout his life
he attempted to relate human knowledge to our relation with the
external world; but, in fact, he never quite brought human knowledge and the external world together. On the whole he seems never
to have been very far from that peculiar kind of British solipsism
which stands on a Humean rather than a Kantian, perhaps Leib-
nizian, base. Yet, Russell wrote a book on Leibniz which has
been justly praised. He was aware of the problem, but he seems
never to have found himself with those Europeans who approached
solipsism from continental rather than British premises. Any attacks on Earl Russell come not from a view that his solipsism was

jejune, because it was not, but because he had not considered, at least not in an existential fashion, the effect of a solipsism which was not his own. In capsule form we might very well distinguish the two forms of solipsism as "the problem of other minds" and the "problem of why I am not God". The second has as its corollary "the problem of why there is a world" (5.552, 5.5521, 6.44).

Wittgenstein started with the second form of solipsism, which is to be found also in Nietzsche and Schopenhauer; but he had sufficient contact with the British to come to realize the importance of a language in which one could communicate with certainty. Russell, on the other hand, as was pointed out above, came to see a perfect language as contributing to some form of solipsism; and its solipsistic qualities are inescapable. We may differentiate the two men by saying that Wittgenstein did not abandon his solispsism, but extended it to include the whole human race. Even in *Philosophical Investigations*, even when the very structure of language has been very much broadened, it is still necessary for lions or gods to speak with human speech if they are to be understood.

But even in the very narrow definition of language which we find in the *Tractatus*, the broader definition of language which Wittgenstein assumed there is preferable to the almost Stirner-like position which seems to have been his when he came to England. That he did not completely abandon his older position can be seen in the propositions about the metaphysical "I" which begin at 5.62. Obviously, if there be a metaphysical "I", it can only be shown; nothing can be said about it, and there is always grave danger that the "I" and God will in some fashion become identified. Should that happen, and it seems that at times it did happen with Wittgenstein in the same way that it happened to Spinoza (6.45), then the world of our common experience becomes at best a shadow world, a dream. Iris Murdoch, in her novel *Bruno's Dream*, explicates the *Tractatus* in this fashion.[12] Since she had worked with Anscombe on the translation of the posthumous Wittgenstein papers,[13] we

[12] Iris Murdoch, *Bruno's Dream* (New York: Viking Press, 1969), 87-88.
[13] *Philosophical Investigations,* translator's note.

cannot assume that her work was a mere *tour de force*. Malcolm speaks of Wittgenstein's constant "amazement that *anything should exist at all*".[14] At his worst, one could never accuse Russell of identifying himself with God. Although there is very little of the Nietzsche or the Wagner about Wittgenstein, there is absolutely none about Russell.

The differences between the two men, the author of the *Tractatus* and the author of the 1918 lectures on logical atomism, may best be shown by explicating one narrow aspect of those lectures: their handling of the problem of modality. Portions of Russell's explication in Lecture Five read as follows:

A propositional function is simply any expression containing an undetermined constituent, or several undetermined constituents, and becoming a proposition as soon as the undetermined constituents are determined.

One may call a propositional function
  necessary, when it is always true;
  possible, when it is sometimes true;
  impossible, when it is never true.
Much false philosophy has arisen out of confusing propositional functions and propositions. There is a great deal in traditional philosophy which consists in attributing to propositions the predicates which apply to propositional functions, and, still worse, sometimes attributing to individuals predicates which merely apply to propositional functions. . . . In all traditional philosophy there comes a heading of "modality", which discusses *necessary, possible,* and *impossible* as properties of propositions, whereas in fact they are properties of propositional functions. Propositions are only true or false.

It will be out of the notion of sometimes, which is the same as the notion of possible, that we get the notion of existence. To say that unicorns exist is simply to say that "(x is a unicorn) is possible". . . . Existence is a predicate of a propositional function, or derivatively of a class. . . . To say that the actual things in the world do not exist . . . is strictly nonsense, but to say they do exist is also strictly nonsense.[15]

For Russell, existence means that it is the case that at sometime at

14 Malcolm, *Ludwig Wittgenstein,* 70.
15 Russell, *Logic and Knowledge,* 231-33.

least one value of "x" in the propositional function will transform the function into a proposition. He does not, however, believe it possible to transform the propositional function Ux (where U stands for unicorns) into Ua, i.e., into a proposition, because there are no unicorns.[16] For Russell it is false to say of the present king of France that he is bald. In fact, it is nonsense to speak of the present king of France. Russell is attempting to have it two ways at once. He wants to say that there is only logical existence; yet he equally wants to say that the last king of France was deposed in 1830, an empirical fact within a definite worldline. In the 1924 lecture on *Logical Atomism* he is less sure.[17] There may be various world-lines, each with its own time.

Although Wittgenstein's position is not metaphysical but linguistic, and follows from a linguistic frame of reference which has coherence and consistency as the criteria of meaning, it is fairly obvious that he would have held that Russell was being *unsinnig* in the quoted passages. If there are a large number of worlds which do have common characteristics, then the boundaries of these worlds are tautology and contradiction. Within those boundaries, it is quite possible that some of the worlds would have unicorns and some not. It would also be possible that there could be a present King of France, that he is bald, that he is not bald, that he wears a wig and does not wear a wig. There are a number of references in the *Tractatus* which could be quoted in opposition to Russell. A few will help us to see the wide gap that existed even though Russell felt that, in the 1918 lectures, he was being true to Wittgenstein.

Ein mögliches Zeichen muss auch bezeichnen können. Alles was in der Logik möglich ist, ist auch erlaubt. ("Sokrates ist identisch" heisst darum nichts, weil es keine Eigenschaft gibt, die "identisch" heisst. Der Satz ist unsinnig, weil wir eine willkürliche Bestimmung nicht getroffen haben, aber nicht darum, weil das Symbol an und für sich unerlaubt wäre.) Wir können uns, in gewissem Sinne, nicht in der Logik irren (5.473).

---

16 Russell, *Logic and Knowledge*, 233.
17 Russell, *Logic and Knowledge*, 341-343.

Das Einleuchten, von dem Russell so viel sprach, kann nur dadurch in der Logik entbehrlich werden, dass die Sprache selbst jeden logischen Fehler verhindert. — Dass die Logik a priori ist, besteht darin, dass nicht unlogisch gedacht werden *kann* (5.4731).

Wir können einem Zeichen nicht den unrechten Sinn geben (5.4732).

Die "Erfahrung", die wir zum Verstehen der Logik brauchen, ist nicht die, dass sich etwas so und so verhält, sondern, dass etwas *ist:* aber das ist eben *keine* Erfahrung. Die Logik ist *vor* jeder Erfahrung — dass etwas *so* ist. Sie ist vor dem Wie, nicht vor dem Was (5.552).

It seems most unlikely that Russell could have written any of these statements. He certainly could not have written the last. There is nothing illogical in there being a present King of France or a unicorn. That there is not a present King of France and that there are no unicorns in the common world in which we are living are historical or evolutionary accidents. "Alles Geschehen und So-Sein ist zufällig" (6.41). On other world-lines they may well exist. All we can really say is that there cannot both be and not be a King of France at the same moment of time in the same world-line (6.3611, 6.3751).

That Wittgenstein understood what Russell was trying to do: to give a highly generalized view of the world, can be seen in the discussion in the *Tractatus* of the generalized proposition. It must be noted, however, that Wittgenstein in talking about the generalized propositions, denies that the propositions can have anything but form (5.526). This is his way of speaking of propositional functions. In this sense the completely general proposition which appears finally at (6.) is a further internal limit on the possibilities within which there may be a very large number of actual worlds. These worlds may differ only slightly, but they do differ (5.5262). Schopenhauer would have had no quarrel with this. Russell should have had no quarrel, but he did. In any event, there is nothing in the *Tractatus* which would lend encouragement to men like Rimbaud with his *Drunken Boat* or to Joyce with *Finnegan's Wake,* but Wittgenstein would have approved of the earlier Joyce who wrote *A Portrait of the Artist as a Young Man.* In the later work, Joyce gives us incoherence; it is difficult to tell what *Finnegan's*

Wake is about. But we know that Joyce was, at least partially, under the influence of Mauthner.[18]

It is difficult, and probably unfair, to suggest that Russell did not understand his most promising pupil: Wittgenstein; but a review of the correspondence and a scanning of the *Tractatus* together with the "Introduction" which Russell provided can lead to no other conclusion. Despite his pretensions to objectivity, Russell was a solipsist, although not of the French variety. Wittgenstein, with Russell's help, had found a way out. It does not appear that Russell ever did. In contemporary British philosophy only J. L. Austin seems to have found where the problem lies.[19] After writing the *Tractatus*, Wittgenstein was not an isolated solipsist; the reader may judge about Russell with the help of the quotation below. Russell demanded too much and, in fact, got very little. Wittgenstein demanded little and got a great deal: the possibility of talking realistically with some of his fellow human beings. Russell concludes *Human Knowledge: Its Scope and Limits* with a discussion of non-empirical postulates which are necessary if an empirical theory of knowledge is to work. They need not be mentioned here, but his summary statement at the end of the book does show the inevitable trap into which he fell:

> But although our postulates can, in this way, be fitted into a framework which has what we may call an empiricist "flavor", it remains undeniable that our knowledge of them, in so far as we do know them, cannot be based upon experience, though all their verifiable consequences are such as experience will confirm. In this sense, it must be admitted, empiricism as a theory of knowledge has proved inadequate, though less so than any other previous theory of knowledge.[20]

Philosophy is science in the most general sense. If this be so, then, surely, there is no point in reading a philosopher since we do have scientists around who can write. Wittgenstein's position is quite

[18] Martin Esslin, *The Theater of the Absurd* (Garden City, New York: Doubleday, 1961), 5.
[19] J. L. Austin, *Sense and Sensibilia*, ed. by G. J. Warnock (Oxford: Clarendon Press, 1962), 144.
[20] Bertrand Russell, *Human Knowledge: Its Scope and Limits* (New York: Simon and Schuster, 1948), 507.

different. He is a linguistic phenomenologist, and he claims, quite correctly it would appear, that philosophy is not one of the natural or even the behavioral sciences (4.111-4.113). Surely it is not the generalization of all of the sciences. "Der Zweck der Philosophie ist die logische Klärung der Gedanken" (4.112). It is questionable whether Russell ever accepted this position; obviously he found it difficult to accept his pupil's later activities, about which he spoke with scorn.[21] He never really understood what philosophy must be about in the modern world: the clarification of language.

3

The failure to understand the *Tractatus* is the failure to understand what Wittgenstein was trying to do. That which gives the *Tractatus* its worth, even today, is not the logic, which in our time has become quite advanced, but the intentionality which unifies the whole. Mauthner's three-volume work is one work because of his emphasis on *Aufmerksamkeit*, the intentionality of individuals and corporate bodies which takes the raw materials of experiences and sensation and makes of them a world: *Das Wesen der Sprache*, of which the world of logic is only one part or region. Wittgenstein in the *Tractatus* explored the region of logic within the larger *Wesen der Sprache*; he knew that Rilke and others were exploring other regions. Wittgenstein knew, even at an early age, that the world did not need the forced unity of some *Übermensch*, but an artistic unity which, in the long run, only poetry can provide. And that artistic unity had to be based on realities, such realities as Rilke explored, not the disordered fancies of a Rimbaud or the reified myths of an out-moded Church. Some poets, the Pre-Raphaelites, the coterie which gathered around the Tiecks and the Schlegels, the romantics, could speak nostalgically about a past which could never be again. Yeats had said that the center did not hold and predicted a shambling, malformed Caliban as the new

21 Bertrand Russell, "Ludwig Wittgenstein", in Fann (ed.), *Ludwig Wittgenstein*, 31.

creation. Wittgenstein was hoping for something better: for a new center; and the *Tractatus* was as necessary for the new center, for the poetry of men like Rilke and Valéry, as the work of Saint Thomas Aquinas was necessary before we could have Dante, the poets of the Italian Renaissance, or Milton.

When one speaks of the *Tractatus* making the world safe for poetry one must have in mind the anagogic character of Rilke's *Elegies* and *Songs to Orpheus* or the majestic sweep of Eliot's *Four Quartets*. We are not speaking of wellmade jingles which, for a moment, catch the public's eye and then disappear. Surely, it was this understanding of his philosophic achievement which led Wittgenstein to read Tagore to the Vienna Circle when, according to Carnap, most of the Circle wanted to talk science.[22] Wittgenstein was not a scientist and made no pretense of being one; and surely most of what Carnap wanted to do seemed very silly. Although Carnap was never as close to Wittgenstein as Russell had been, it appears that he, also, thought of philosophy as a group of propositions of the utmost generality: a science of sciences.

Rilke's struggles with himself and his relations with others had led him, even before World War I, to recognize that if he were to create poems he must himself be a poet. Stated thus, the phrase seems an obvious truism; but much more was implied with Rilke: he had to choose between being a man who wrote poetry or a poet who wrote poetry. He chose. He made a choice for the latter life style; and it was to the poet's life that he gave himself. Whether Rilke's example influenced Wittgenstein cannot be determined; but both in Wittgenstein's life and in his writings there is the continual distinction between showing and saying. What can be said can be said clearly; what can be shown cannot be said (4.112, 4.1216). The *Tractatus*, as his penultimate statement says, is itself a *showing* rather than a *saying*, although surely some propositions in the earlier material are sayings rather than showings; but which? In an earlier section of this essay the later Wittgenstein is quoted as stating that it is the style of life which in fact determines the life and

[22] Rudolf Carnap, "Autobiography", in Fann (ed.), *Ludwig Wittgenstein,* 35, 37, 38.

what message that life is to convey to others (see above, p. 00). Obviously, a style of life must be lived twenty-four hours a day; it cannot be taken off and put on like a suit of clothes; and it can be talked about only obliquely. It is a major thesis of this essay that sometime during the latter part of World War I, even as he was finishing the *Tractatus*, Ludwig Wittgenstein chose to live his life as a Schopenhauerian saint. That he frequently failed is, on the whole, irrelevant. In contrast to saintliness, we may well speak of Schopenhauer and Spinoza living their lives out as philosophers: in the pursuit of truth rather than holiness; but, surely, there is some doubt about Spinoza. Was his the quest for truth or for holiness or did he identify the two? With Wittgenstein, his truth was always in the service of his holiness. But what is it to be a saint in the modern world when even truth is hard put for disciples?

4

He who has read this far in the essay is well aware that here an attempt is being made at a more radical interpretation of the *Tractatus* and of the early Wittgenstein than has been offered heretofore. Interpretations of the *Tractatus* have been many and varied. In the earliest period, the twenties, the general thesis seems to have been that Wittgenstein was a thoroughgoing Humean who was attempting to demonstrate that Hume's world still had a rigorously logical character. Miss Anscombe quotes one of the Austrians, Karl Popper, as follows:

> Wittgenstein tried to show that all so-called philosophical or metaphysical propositions were in fact non-propositions or pseudo-propositions: that they were in fact meaningless. All genuine (or meaningful) propositions were truth-functions of the elementary or atomic propositions which described "atomic facts", i.e. facts which can in principle be ascertained by observation.[23]

Miss Anscombe's comment is that there is a great deal about ob-

---

[23]   Quoted in Anscombe, *An Introduction*, 25.

servation statements in Popper, practically none in the *Tractatus*.[24] Although there is much to quarrel with in Miss Anscombe's *Introduction*, she is right at this point. Anyone reading the *Tractatus* with any care and without having prejudged it must be struck with the fact that this is not a Humean document. Unfortunately, Miss Anscombe falls into a ditch on the other side as she attempts to interpret the *Tractatus* for us. In a rather strange way, probably derived from her studies in Frege, she sees the *Tractatus* as attempting to find a way to mirror a Platonic world of pure forms.[25] According to her, the *Tractatus* is about logic and a picture theory of meaning in which the truth tables, elaborated in the middle sections of the *Tractatus*, are found, on the whole, to be a practical way of determining whether a complex proposition is true or false. The complex fact, to which the proposition refers, is composed of Platonic reals.

Her book is ingenious, and one can read it with profit as she talks about Russell, Frege, and Ramsey; but, despite her close association with Wittgenstein toward the end of his life and the apparent deep affection he had for her, one must come finally to the conclusion that she is not talking about the *Tractatus*. She has manufactured a Procrustean bed, and she is determined to make the *Tractatus* fit; but, to complete the metaphor, Wittgenstein sleeps very badly in the bed. We may be warned by the fact that she starts her analysis *in media res*.[26] In the end, she is forced to leave out much of the *Tractatus* (for practical reasons?).[27] The picture theory is an important contribution to logical theory, but, surely, Miss Anscombe never sees it as more than a Fregian elaboration of Russell's belief that for a name to have a meaning it must have a bearer.

Again one must state that Wittgenstein's importance in twentieth century philosophy cannot derive from his being an epigone of Russell and Frege. Wittgenstein is himself; and he used the tools which

24   Anscombe, *An Introduction*, 26.
25   Anscombe, *An Introduction*, 78, 81.
26   Anscombe, *An Introduction*, 18, 19.
27   Anscombe, *An Introduction*, 80n.

Frege and Russell had devised for his own purposes: to find a way
out of the trap into which Mauthner had fallen. Rs to the picture
theory and the truth tables; as Miss Anscombe describes them, they
are of very little value. Apparently Miss Anscombe herself recognized that there was something wrong, and it is most doubtful that
Wittgenstein would not have seen the impractical nature of the
picture theory if it is dependent ultimately on the observation of
logical simples. Miss Anscombe's statement reads as follows:

> It seems sure that the *Tractatus* account is wrong. This is partly because
> one cannot believe in the simple objects required by the theory; partly
> because it leads to dogmatic and plainly false conclusions about the
> will, about modality and about generalizations in infinite cases. But
> it is a powerful and beautiful theory: and there is surely something
> right about it — if one could dispense with "simples" and draw the
> limits of its applicability.[28]

Miss Anscombe is quite right in believing that there is something
magnificent about the picture theory and the truth tables. Her difficulty lay within herself and her belief that Wittgenstein was in
some way doing ontology rather than language criticism. If we
will think of the picture theory as a metaphor of what actually
happens when we use language, and think of the truth-tables as
means of preserving ourselves from incoherence when we do use
language we will begin to see the tremendous values involved.

In some respects, if not in all, the whole of the *Tractatus* may
be seen as an illustration of how the picture theory may be used:
images are thrown against images in the hope that the truth itself
will finally appear. Whatever this truth may be, it cannot be either
a contradiction or a tautology if it purports to refer to an experienced world. Contradiction and tautology can appear in a linguistic
world for they are means whereby one can move from one significant proposition to another. As was said above, although tautology
and contradiction are necessary for logic and for language, they
are the external boundaries of all possible worlds. No worlds include them. Contradiction and tautology are the internal boundaries
of the truth tables. "Tautologie und Kontradiktion sind die Grenz-

---

[28] Anscombe, *An Introduction*, 77.

fälle der Zeichenverbindung, nämlich ihre Auflösung" (4.466).
For Wittgenstein, the truth tables are a mechanical device to aid
in the avoidance of incoherence. Surely, neither he nor anyone
else has used them only when it was necessary to break up a complex proposition into its atomic parts. The intentionality of the
user is the determinant as to how the truth tables are used; and it
is the intentionality which determines whether a symbol is complex
or simple. As Miss Anscombe introduces us to the *Tractatus*, although we are given a great deal of meaningful information, there
is a way in which she also trivializes one of the contemporary
world's most important books. We are told how to play with a toy
and may expect to be amused after we have been given the
clues.[29]

The tragedy of Miss Anscombe's book is that she does not in
fact perform her self-assigned task: to introduce us to Wittgenstein's *Tractatus*. As his literary executor, as the person with whom
he spent many of the latter months of his life, she should have
been able to perform this task if anyone could; but she does not.
Her book is interesting in its own right and will be read for many
years by those who have grown to love the early Wittgenstein; but
the reaction to her book will normally be the negative one of disappointment. The reaction of various reviewers to her book is on
the whole the same: disappointment. Yet why are we disappointed?
Perhaps Miss Anscombe started with erroneous premises and was
never able to free herself from them? She obviously knows something is wrong, as do her reviewers; but what is wrong? This essay,
at least in part, attempts to demonstrate that Wittgenstein was talking about language. Miss Anscombe made his words apply to non-
linguistic things. Procrustes' bed does not fit. She knows it does
not fit and, almost honestly, she confesses that it does not fit. On
the page following the quotation given above, and in the quotation
itself, it is likely that the answer may be found. For Miss Anscombe, Wittgenstein's world is the mirror image of Plato's world
of forms except that there is, in fact, less substantiality to his

---

[29] Anscombe, *An Introduction*, 19.

world because there is no nurse or receptacle, which Plato provides for us in the *Timaeus*, and from which a world in time could be made.

In terms of space it may be wrong to use as much as a whole section of this chapter on Miss Anscombe and her *Introduction to Wittgenstein's Tractatus*; but Miss Anscombe's position as Wittgenstein's literary executor and her interesting, but disappointing, book have to be faced before one can go on. She cannot be right because her book does not hold together as a unity. One is tempted to use the word "incoherent" (*unsinnig*); yet Wittgenstein trusted her with his reputation and his papers. Surely she has been a jealous guardian as the following quotation from her letter to Engelmann reflects. Engelmann had written to her, as Wittgenstein's literary executor, to raise the question as to whether the letters Wittgenstein had written to him should be published. She wrote as follows:

If by pressing a button it could have been secured that people would not concern themselves with his personal life, I should have pressed the button; but since that has not been possible and it is certain that much that is foolish will keep on being said, it seems to me reasonable that anyone who can write a truthful account of him should do so. On the other hand to write a satisfactory account would seem to need extraordinary talent. . . . I am very sure that I did not understand him. It is difficult, I think, not to give a version of his attitudes, for example, which one can enter into oneself, and then the account is really of oneself.[30]

One may also conjecture that Miss Anscombe was the occasion for the following passage in *Philosophical Investigations*. In making this conjecture, the reader must be warned that Miss Anscombe was the translator of *Philosophical Investigations* and one of the editors. The passage in English reads:

We also say of some people that they are transparent to us. It is, however, important as regards this observation that one human being can be a complete enigma to another. We learn this when we come into a strange country with entirely strange traditions; and, what is more, even given a mastery of the country's language. We do not *understand*

---

30   Engelmann, *Letters*, xiv.

the people. (And not because of not knowing what they are saying to themselves.) We cannot find our feet with them.[31]

The German of the last sentence reads, "Wir können uns nicht in sie finden". The literal translation is, of course, "We cannot find ourselves into them"; and perhaps it would have been better had Miss Anscombe left it at that or invented a paraphrase including the word "empathy". The locution she did use is "unsinnig". When one reads her *Introduction* in the light of this passage, one becomes convinced that Wittgenstein was never able to make himself clear to her and was never really able to understand her. If one is interested in speculating, one can suggest that Wittgenstein found the whole donnish life exquisitely boring and was happy to flee it for the wilds of Ireland or Norway. Significantly, one of those who taught philosophy with Wittgenstein at Cambridge was Iris Murdoch, who fled the donnish life to write novels.

The last few pages about Miss Anscombe and her book are not really sufficient to show the extent of the disappointment which her book evokes. At the time it first came out (1959) it was widely reviewed. Some excerpts from those reviews reflect the common frustration and disappointment. George K. Plochmann compares the *Tractatus* to the *Republic*, the first *Critique* and *Process and Reality*, grouping them together as works requiring the study of a life time and justifying a life-time's study. He concludes his review with the faint praise that, although her study of the *Tractatus* had been helpful, it had by no means provided a key to the *Tractatus*. The definitive work had yet to be done.[32] Rush Rhees, who had been one of Wittgenstein's close friends[33] and had been associated with Miss Anscombe in the editing of Wittgenstein's posthumous works,[34] is quite scathing in his review.[35] He feels, ap-

---

[31] *Philosophical Investigations*, 223-23e.
[32] George K. Plochmann, "Review of Anscombe", *Modern Schoolman* XXXVII (1960), 242-46.
[33] Rush Rhees in "Symposium", in Fann (ed.), *Ludwig Wittgenstein*, 74-78.
[34] *Philosophical Investigations*, editors' notes.
[35] Rush Rhees, "Miss Anscombe on the *Tractatus*", *Philosophical Quarterly* X (1960), 21-31.

parently quite strongly, that she has completely missed the point of the *Tractatus*. He blames her errors, not on an error of vision, but on the fact that she had access to all of Wittgenstein's papers, including his notes for the *Tractatus*, and that she was unable to make necessary discriminations. Rhees' contention is that the *Tractatus* must be treated as a completed work and judged as such. He senses that Miss Anscombe's book is her book and does not necessarily have a direct correlation with the *Tractatus*. Rhees centers his criticism on the way that Miss Anscombe handles the problem of the relation between the picture theory of propositions and the truth-functional theory which he believes she handles rather badly. In fact, she does not bring them together at all.

If, as seems likely, Miss Anscombe was convinced that the early Wittgenstein was doing ontology rather than philosophical linguistics, her difficulties have a self-evident root. Surely, she should have known that a major difference between the early and the later Wittgenstein was the different meaning that became attached to the word "possible" as the implication of the Gödel theories became evident to him. When Wittgenstein wrote the *Tractatus* he was convinced that we could know a priori what was possible and what was not. When he wrote *Philosophical Investigations*, although he had by no means abandoned logic, he had accepted the consequences of the Gödel theorems: one can not know a priori what is possible. The *Investigations* are imaginative pragmatic constructions of possible worlds; the *Tractatus* is a syntactical investigation of what must be the substance of any possible world. Nevertheless, it is surely a misreading of the text to state that there is no concept of modality in the *Tractatus*. The text will not fit her view that the world of the *Tractatus* is that of an essentially static world. Nor will it fit her view that there is only one world. There is a range of possibilities and only the extremes and the structure defined by the general proposition (6) are fixed. In *Philosophical Investigations* the range is not so carefully delimited. The relevant quotations in the *Tractatus* are: 2.022, 2.027-2.063, 3.-3.0321, 3.5-4.04, 4.2-4.2211, 4.46-4.661, 5.4733. At 5.525 Wittgenstein recognizes the modalities in his own way:

Gewissheit, Möglichkeit oder Unmöglichkeit einer Sachlage wird nicht durch einen Satz ausgedrückt, sondern dadurch, dass ein Ausdruck eine Tautologie, ein sinnvoller Satz, oder eine Kontradiktion ist. In actual fact, *only the accidental is real* (6.41). The impossible and the necessary, as part of logic, are transcendental. It may be that when Miss Anscombe denies modalities for Wittgenstein, as she does specifically on page 81 and, by implication at many other places, she is speaking from within the framework of an Aristotelian metaphysics. In any event, she does not treat the *Tractatus* as an exploration of language in use.

None of the reviewers of Miss Anscombe's book who have been consulted has been in any doubt that she is very painstaking and that her book is a contribution to learning. But all who may have had the slightest personal relation with her seem to have been "ticked off" by her possessiveness and her apparent condescension to those who did not have the relation to "Ludwig" which she had had. She states: "Wittgenstein's *Tractatus* has captured the interest and excited the admiration of many, yet almost all that has been published about it has been wildly irrelevant."[36] One hesitates to write anything lest he be publicly whipped for being irrelevant; yet one must write as one must — especially if one is convinced that miss Anscombe is among those who fail to come to grips with the text. Her arrogance comes through again when she claims for herself a very superior knowledge of German.[37] Her German may be very superior, but Miss Cassirer, a native German speaker, in her review of Miss Anscombe's *Introduction* suggests that it is not as adequate as Miss Anscombe pretends.[38] Miss Cassirer suggests, however, that Miss Anscombe's failure, about which she has no doubt, lies not so much in her inability to handle the German prose as in her inability to lay aside the Frege-Russellian spectacles and to read the text as published. However, Miss Cassirer was nearer the truth in her closing statement where

[36] Anscombe, *An Introduction*, 12.
[37] Anscombe, *An Introduction*, 17n, 30n, 68n, 69n.
[38] Eva Cassirer, "Review of Anscombe", *British Journal for the Philosophy of Science* XIV (1964), 359-66.

she says that "language is the only intelligible thing for us in the world."[39] This, of course, is the thesis presented here: The *Tractatus Logico-Philosophicus* is a philosophical exploration of language, an attempt to answer some of the questions raised by Mauthner and others shortly before World War I broke out. Those same questions remain and become ever more pressing today.

---

[39] Cassirer, "Review".

IV

THE *TRACTATUS*: A MIRROR; NOT A RIDDLE

1

In the preceding chapters it was suggested that the clue to the unity and coherence of the *Tractatus* is to be found in the penultimate proposition which says, in part:

Meine Sätze erläutern dadurch, dass sie der, welcher mich versteht, am Ende als unsinnig erkennt wenn er durch sie — auf ihnen — über sie hinausgestiegen ist.

The propositions preceding this statement are thus not to be taken as absolutes, able to stand by themselves. Rather, they are necessary rungs on a ladder leading to a perspective which sees the several propositions as means to an end: "to see the world aright". From this perspective — which Wittgenstein hopes his readers will share — one will be able to see the limited value, even the falsity, of each proposition taken in isolation. The hope is that one will be able to see the whole of the *Tractatus* as a mirror of and for the world of men. The perspective is itself transcendent in Kant's sense, beyond even the transcendental world of logic and language — inexpressible, mystical, a possible "object" of religious experience.

One may compare the *Tractatus* to a very complicated musical score, particularly a long symphonic poem, in which the composer records his musings about life and the way things hang together in a whole. The apparent irregularities serve the purposes of the whole (4.013), and one must have the whole before him as he looks at or listens to the individual parts. Wittgenstein demands that we approach his work as one anagogic achievement: a poem for modern man which points to the way things are for men who live in language-worlds. In contrast to Mauthner he shows that these language-worlds do have some relation to the world of physical events (4.014-4.032, 5.5563-5.557), but we can see that this is so only if we approach our language-world by indirection. We must contrive a mirror for ourselves. The *Tractatus* is a kind of mirror; and the mirror shows us that there is a kind of order hidden in the flux of experience with which we seem to be surrounded.

Most commentators seem to ignore the penultimate proposition of the *Tractatus* and seek to find the meaning of the whole in one or more of the preceding propositions. Professor Finch, in his recent book on the early Wittgenstein, seeks the clue in a parabolic arrangement around proposition 4.0312.[1] The assumption here, as in so many other rearrangements of the materials, is that the *Tractatus* is a deliberately contrived riddle. But it seems most doubtful, in view of all that we know of Wittgenstein, that he would contrive a riddle which might deceive more than it would enlighten. That there is difficulty in understanding the *Tractatus* has been re-remarked on by many, but it is doubtful that the difficulty was compounded by Wittgenstein casting the whole into a riddle. The difficulty of the *Tractatus* lies in the compressed style and the attempts to make the work say things which the commentators want it to say.

If the penultimate statement is to be taken seriously, it can only mean that all which has gone before, and the penultimate statement itself, must be taken somewhat conditionally. Obviously, Wittgenstein did not think he had been talking nonsense or that he had been incoherent. He was very anxious to have the book published and was quite disappointed with Russell's "Introduction". Apparently, as Engelmann points out, he had not anticipated that there would be such a lack of comprehension of what he had written,

---

[1] Henry LeRoy Finch, *Wittgenstein – The Early Philosophy: An Exposition of the "Tractatus"* (New York: Humanities Press, 1971), 255-57.

and he finally gave up trying to explain.[2] In actual fact, the ladder simile probably explains the whole. Philosophical expressions are not genuine statements; only the elementary descriptive statements of the natural sciences are genuine statements (4.1, 4.11). Philosophy itself is an activity and not one of the sciences (4.111). It is concerned with showing, not with describing. Therefore, the *Tractatus*, which is a book in philosophy, is to a degree talking nonsense when it attempts to describe that which in fact can only be shown.

The propositions of the *Tractatus* are not, then, genuine propositions. They are pseudo-propositions; but they are nevertheless propositions which we must use, climb over, mount, if we are to see the world aright. The process itself is its own reason for being, and any attempt to base our understanding of the *Tractatus* on any group or congeries of propositions within it is foredoomed to failure. The *Tractatus* has legs and walks. It is because the *Tractatus* is an activity that it must, in a way, be its own commentary, and that all other commentaries are, at least to a degree, doomed to failure. No man can walk for another; and only he who has thought Wittgenstein's thoughts, as Wittgenstein himself points out in the Preface, can probably correctly understand him; but then, in a way, that person has become another Wittgenstein. To understand the *Tractatus* or the *Philosophical Investigations* we need to see that Wittgenstein was not, in fact, making a collection of positive statements in the form of an argument; rather, he was pursuing many metaphysical and logical possibilities to their self-defeating conclusions. He showed that we are trapped in language-worlds; but in the *Tractatus* he shows, as Mauthner could not, that the *Logos* is hidden within the several language-worlds.

Let us take a preliminary look at the nature of this *Logos*, which some have called a god,[3] and the relation of the *Logos* to the pseudo-propositions in which it lies hidden. The *Logos* makes its

---

[2]   Engelmann, *Letters*, 118.
[3]   Eddy Zemach, "Wittgenstein's Philosophy of the Mystical", in *Essays on Wittgenstein's Tractatus,* ed. by Irving M. Copi and Robert W. Beard (New York: Macmillan, 1966).

appearance in the central part of the *Tractatus* — the part concerned with the nature of the proposition. At 4.12 Wittgenstein says:

Der Satz kann die gesamte Wirklickeit darstellen, aber er kann nicht das darstellen, was er mit der Wirklickeit gemein haben muss, um sie darstellen zu können — die logische Form. Um die logische Form darstellen zu können, müssten wir uns mit dem Satze ausserhalb der Logik aufstellen können, dass heisst ausserhalb der Welt.

Der Satz kann die logische Form nicht darstellen, sie spiegelt sich in ihm. Was sich in der Sprache spiegelt, kann sie nicht darstellen. Was *sich* in der Sprache ausdrückt, können *wir* nicht durch sie ausdrücken. Der Satz *zeigt* die logische Form der Wirklichkeit. Er weist sie auf (4.121).

Wittgenstein's quarrel with Russell begins really at this point, but becomes most obvious shortly thereafter when he takes up the problem of internal and external, formal and proper relations (connotation and denotation). The problem of the disagreement becomes clearer if we remember that Mauthner's discussion of the same problem stands in back of Wittgenstein's observations. "Es wäre ebenso unsinnig, dem Satze eine formale Eigenschaft zuzusprechen, als sie ihm abzusprechen" (4.124). The issue is joined at the place where Wittgenstein, in his discussion about propositions, calls our attention to the folly of attempting to give a reference to the variable in a propositional function or even to name an object in a proposition (4.122-4.128). A proposition has a sense, but not necessarily a reference (4.121-4.1251), and "the variable name 'x' is the proper sign for the pseudo-concept" (4.1272). The variable name is at most a linguistic tool and actually has no reference even within language, let alone in the external world. Wittgenstein speaks similarly (at 5.461) about the signs for material implication and weak disjunction. They appear to be fundamental relations, but in fact they are not; and they may always be replaced by more fundamental expressions without loss of meaning. In a really fundamental language or logic, weak disjunction and material implication would not exist.[4] Failure to distinguish levels of meaning within language (which is surely different from establishing hier-

---

4 Anscombe, *An Introduction*, 164.

archies of languages as he suggests in the "Introduction") is why
Russell errs in his attempts to generalize propositional functions as
he talks about the modalities. This was discussed in the previous
chapter, but at this time we would like to suggest that Wittgenstein
was equally quarreling with Russell's belief that something in the
external world corresponds to the predicate of a proposition or a
propositional function (4.12721-4.24).
Wittgenstein has no objection to the generalization of the variable name. In fact, much of the central part of the *Tractatus* is
devoted to establishing a controlled way for generalizing the congeries of elementary propositions in such a fashion that the result,
although specious, would be a description of any world with which
we happened to be concerned.

It was suggested earlier that tautology and contradiction provide
boundaries, although they themselves lie outside of the possibilities, of any possible world. In Wittgenstein's discussion of the "proposition", which begins with 4.12 and continues through most of
the remainder of the *Tractatus*, he is concerned to find a general
proposition, not accidental in nature (6.1232), which will apply to
any object whatsoever. The general proposition satisfying these
conditions appears at 6. In the general proposition, which is derived by a series of successive negations of any given group of
elementary propositions, something quite definite is conveyed
about the structure of any world. In the simple sentential logic the
corresponding symbol would be "aRb", derived for example from
such a proposition as "Plato loves Socrates". The form has been
left; all else is denied. The general form of proposition is Wittgenstein's answer to Mauthner. There is a speciousness, but it is not
without its grounding in language and logic. It is not arbitrary,
and the lack of arbitrariness is the crucial issue. When the same
process is applied to numbers, which are members of a formal
series (4.1272-4.128), we find that the concept "number" is in itself the variable (6.022).

Evert W. Beth, while not making specific reference to the *Tractatus*, is aware of the kind of thinking which leads to the *physique
de l'objet quelconque*. It is the kind of thinking which lends itself

to contemporary work in quantum physics; and it is in radical divergence from any versions of the traditional Platonism such as those defended by Frege and Whitehead. Only such a system is "consistent with the present situation in logic, mathematics, and natural science".[5]

Significantly, the appearance of the general proposition follows immediately after Wittgenstein's discussion of solipsism and realism. Surely, this is not accidental. It is far more likely that Wittgenstein was attempting to show that even as pure solipsism coincides with pure realism (5.64) there is a common structure to any possible world which could be the correlate of the unknown and unknowable metaphysical "I". There are rules for the creation of worlds that are correlates to the many solipsistic "I"s, and any attempt to violate those rules, as in Rimbaud's *Drunken Boat*, can only result in incoherence. There is an ultimate structure to language. We are not left, as Mauthner thought, on a shoreless sea without a beacon. It is quite apparent that Wittgenstein believed that there is (are) metaphysical "I"(s). It is equally certain that he did not feel that it is possible to talk about it or them. Bradley, confronted with the same problem, developed the idea of Reality and finite centers. With Wittgenstein, the whole problem is left open. To use a Hindu analogy, the *Brahman* and the *Atman* may be one or many. Assuming, as we must,[6] that Wittgenstein was quite familiar with Schopenhauer and in many respects accepted Schopenhauer's view of the world, we are not trapped, as Schopenhauer was, by the problem of individuation. For Wittgenstein, what is one and what is many is determined by the way we intentionally use our language. Within language there are regularities. About that which is outside of language we cannot speak at all. Since both we and the world, apart from our language, are outside of language, we cannot speak about ourselves or about it at all; but we can show certain things about ourselves and the world. If we wish to discuss the basis of our action we can only respond with the word "faith".

[5]   Evert W. Beth, *The Foundations of Mathematics: A Study in the Philosophy of Science* (New York: Harper & Row, 1966), 625-26.
[6]   Anscombe, *An Introduction*, 12.

The reader will recognize the similarities with Kierkegaard and Santayana.

Metaphysically, Wittgenstein did not escape his solipsism; but by his exploration of language he showed that it is possible for two or more solipsistic entities to have reliable discourse with each other. Schopenhauer provided the Platonic forms as the basis for a common world; Wittgenstein showed that there is a logical ground for a common world in the general proposition which is the structure of any possible object. Individual worlds differ from each other even as individual languages vary while each retains the linguistic structure which lies at the base of *all* languages and all worlds (5.552, 5.5563-62). All individual languages, all particular worlds, are contingent, accidental, and so are the "I"'s correlated to them (5.63-5.641).

2

In the third chapter it was pointed out that Russell wanted to make the propositions of logic into very general propositions about the nature of the one world which we all share. Russell wished to ground his logic insofar as he could in empirical experience. He knew that a purely Humean position provides no basis for logic at all; he recognized that there might indeed be many worlds; but he nevertheless stayed as close to Hume as he could, believing that empiricism provides the most sensible way of dealing with the world. Frege, who is also mentioned by Wittgenstein in the Preface, was not so much an empiricist as a Platonist;[7] and, as a Platonist, he wanted his ideas to have very sharp and clear boundaries. In *Philosophical Investigations* Wittgenstein is concerned to point out that in certain language games it is not possible to have clear and distinct ideas, that to require clear and distinct ideas would be to falsify the inquiry. In the *Tractatus* Wittgenstein's quarrel with Frege and Russell is that they do not in fact take their own

[7]   E. D. Klemke, "Frege's Ontology: Realism", *Essays on Frege,* ed. by E. D. Klemke (Urbana: University of Illinois Press, 1968), 158.

ideas as seriously as they should. Logic is a language with a definite symbolic structure. The symbols are themselves quite arbitrary (3.33, 3.342, 3.3421), but once having been adopted, logic requires that the symbols be manipulated in a definite way (3.342). Logic itself precedes experience (5.552). If we are to understand the thinking which is embodied in the *Tractatus* we must assume that the author was in search of a logic which is self-consistent and which would hold for all possible worlds. The logic is prior to the worlds and not abstracted from the worlds; nor is there any reference in logic to a super-mundane world of pure forms. The only reference is to language itself.

To arrive at his understanding of a logic embedded and hidden in all languages, Wittgenstein used a rather elaborate process. The whole of the *Tractatus* is an explication of that process: the establishment of a mirror whereby the logic is revealed. The particular method is identified at 6.121 as a zero-method (*Null-methode*); but there are other names: zero-premise and zero-sum. In effect, the logician starts with any premise taken at random and draws necessary conclusions by *modus ponens*. If an inconsistency occurs or if the dependent proposition is falsified by this particular world, we then know that the premise is not valid for every possible object — for any possible world. It is suggested that the penultimate proposition of the *Tractatus* serves as the negation of all earlier propositions, turns all of them into *modus tollens*. The doubt is not complete, nor is the *modus tollens*; but we are warned that the propositions of the *Tractatus* are not self-evident truths.

Throughout the *Tractatus*, Wittgenstein is determined to demonstrate that the language with which he is concerned — the language of the *Principia* with a few corrections (3.325) — becomes a language which applies to all possible worlds. It must be internally consistent; there can be no such thing as accidental generality (6.1231); nor can there be any appeals to self-evidence (6.1271). The actual world with which one has to do, i.e. the correlate to the acting and knowing metaphysical self, is fortuitous (6.41); but the fundamental skeleton of that world is known a priori (6.124). The nature of that skeleton is shown in the language which all human beings share. Insofar as I have a private language, I have a private world (5.5563-5.63), but my private language is quite limited. Obviously, as will be discussed in a later chapter, there are striking similarities in this understanding of the *Tractatus* and the *Critique of Pure Reason*. At this place, it is probably justifiable to bring out the similarities with one of Wittgenstein's contemporaries: Henri Poincaré. For Poincaré it was possible to vary the axioms of any system for the exploration of nature and to examine the consequences. Objectivity, then, becomes an agreement between two or more persons. In his own words nothing "is objective except that which is identical for all."[8] The *Tractatus* shows us quite rigorously that all attempts at a traditional metaphysics or a "unified science", such as the Vienna Circle and Russell wanted, are foredoomed to failure. In his "Autobiography" Carnap speaks of Wittgenstein's total lack of interest in a "unified science".[9] Wittgenstein lacked this interest because he did not believe that any projects looking toward a unified science could be brought to a successful conclusion. Although Wittgenstein did not condemn the sciences, he placed them within the category of useful heuristic devices (6.343-6.372). Descriptive propositions which are phenomenologically true are the roots of our knowledge of the world (4.1-4.111) and provide the bases for the constructions, which are our sciences (5.555-5.5661, 6.3-6.361).

[8]   André Lalande, "Henry Poincaré: From *Science and Hypothesis* to *Last Thoughts*", *Roots of Scientific Thought: A Cultural Perspective,* ed. by Phillip P. Wiener and Aaron Noland (New York: Basic Books, 1957), 626.
[9]   Rudolf Carnap, "Autobiography", in Fann (ed.), *Ludwig Wittgenstein,* 37.

V

WITTGENSTEIN AND SPINOZA

1

Anyone studying the *Tractatus* must be struck with the similarities and sharp contrasts with Spinoza's *Ethics*.[1] Surely, these likenesses and differences cannot be by chance. The ordered propositions of the *Tractatus* remind one of the ordered propositions of the *Ethics*. The discussions of substance and of the nature of the world at the beginning of the *Tractatus* have their parallels in Part I of the *Ethics* where Spinoza makes an argument for there being but one substance to which we may without hesitancy give the name God. Again the discussion at the end of the *Tractatus* about *das Mystische* has its parallels with the concluding sections of Part V of the *Ethics*. In his distinction between two types of mysticism, Wittgenstein is able to affirm the kind of mysticism which Spinoza calls the intellectual love of God, and to point to another mysticism which is concerned with a Wholly Other. Finally, the title *Tractatus Logico-Philosophicus* has its parallel, both in the English and German editions, with a work of Spinoza's early manhood *Tractatus Theologico-Politicus*.

At first sight both Spinoza and Wittgenstein seem to be using an axiomatic method, although Spinoza's is much more explicit; but

---

[1] Garver sees the relation between the *Tractatus* and the *Ethics* as very close. He demonstrates this relation in an article in a recent group of essays. Newton Garver, "Wittgenstein's Pantheism: A New Light on the Ontology of the Tractatus", *Essays on Wittgenstein*, ed. by E. D. Klemke (Urbana, Ill.: University of Illinois Press, 1971).

as we begin to investigate their actual approaches we find that the axiomatic method is not, in fact, the method which either of them used to obtain the results which they put in writing. Both Spinoza and Wittgenstein were dialecticians; and this becomes obvious when we look at Spinoza's unfinished essay *On the Improvement of the Understanding* and Wittgenstein's *Philosophical Investigations*. The differences between Spinoza and Wittgenstein are marked, but three centuries and Kant lie between them. Spinoza had believed that an adequate idea had a necessary correlate in the objective world (extension); Wittgenstein confined his discussion to language itself, although, with Spinoza, he was convinced that only our constructions can really be trusted (5.555, 6.002, 6.111, 6.113, 6.12). Empirical knowledge is untrustworthy because it normally will not give us a picture of the world as it really is, but only ephemeral fragments. Spinoza came to believe that there could be only one substance. Wittgenstein starts out with the hypothesis that there are many substances; but he ends by confining his investigation to language alone.

It may be that the similarities between Spinoza and Wittgenstein have been obscured by the nature of the subjects with which they deal. In his various treatises, and in his correspondence, Spinoza, although a recluse, takes up many varied topics. Wittgenstein, on the other hand, pretty well confines himself to language, the foundations of mathematics, and limited digressions into the fields of esthetics, ethics and the verification principle. Nevertheless, each of them was quite confident about what he had accomplished; and each felt that he had achieved a final solution of the vexing philosophical and religious problems of his day; both were prepared to live their lives in terms of their solutions. It may be that Spinoza, like his famous successor, was determined to say what he thought could be said, to show what could be shown and to be silent about the rest. Their differences lie in the much narrower compass which Wittgenstein allowed himself. Since my purpose here is primarily theological, it is, perhaps, important to point out their differences in this area.

In Spinoza's case, the problem is the more easily seen because he spells it out in the *Political-Theological Treatise*. A limited, but certain, natural theology is possible; and there are some who can proceed to a knowledge of God in no other way; but there is also a way of revelation. There is no natural theology in Wittgenstein, although the possibility of special revelation is held open. In Wittgenstein's *Tractatus* reason cannot save because it has very limited power; the possibility of revelation is very doubtful; and the facts of revelation are at best ambiguous. In any case, revelation must always be private and special, for the facts of revelation are not facts about which we can talk (7). In other words, if another person has had an experience of God, he cannot communicate it to me. Spinoza believed it possible to communicate the results of special revelation and reason. Most people, however, can accept only the results of revelation and are forced therefore blindly to obey some prophet or institution which claims to have received a revelation or to be the guardian of one. For Spinoza, the results of correct reasoning and true revelation are identical because both speak of a world which is one; yet true revelation is inferior to correct reasoning because its language is the language of imagination rather than the language of logic and mathematics. Wittgenstein, on the other hand, having rejected reason as in any way capable of investigating the nature of God (Reality, *das Mystische*) would have believed it possible that good poetry, which, by definition, could not be incoherent, might show something of the nature of God to those who are capable of receiving the intuition.

Having stated that both Spinoza and Wittgenstein were dialecticians, it is important to recognize that each was concerned with the possibilities of a priori knowledge and the axiomatic method. Both Spinoza and Wittgenstein were logicians; both were recluses accustomed to solitary meditation on the necessary consequences which follow from varied premises, axioms, and definitions. The differences between the two men are less a matter of style or interest than of the times in which they lived. For Spinoza, logic was that discipline which had been worked out in connection with the Galilean science. As Spinoza recognized, it was a new logic and not the logic of the schoolmen. Although Spinoza found a place for the Aristotelian logic at the lowest levels of human consciousness,[2] the Spinozistic logic is essentially self-contained and axiomatic, a priori rather than a posteriori. Wittgenstein's logic is also self-contained, axiomatic; and the knowledge with which he wrestles in the *Tractatus* is a priori. But Spinoza lived before Kant; Wittgenstein after. Both men believed reason to be competent within her domain; but Wittgenstein found it necessary to limit that domain to a much smaller compass: human speech. For Spinoza, reason's domain was the whole universe: the mind of God.

It will help us to understand Wittgenstein if we recognize that he is not an empiricist. With Spinoza, he is a rationalist and very far from Locke and his "plain historical method". Like Spinoza, he has a new logic to work with which is very similar to the new mathematics of his time, even as Spinoza's logic was related to the Cartesian and Galilean mathematics. Wittgenstein's logic was developed by two of the significant mathematical philosophers of the twentieth century, Frege and Russell; and Wittgenstein was as confident in his use of that logic as Spinoza had been in the use of his logic. A further confirmation of the similarities in the two men can be seen in an examination of Spinoza's unfinished *On the Improvement of the Understanding*. There Spinoza shows us how the mind works with itself and needs no other reference. Wittgenstein's *Tractatus* is the record of such a process. It may well be read and studied as the record of a mind struggling with itself for a truth which is certain because it is a priori.

One reason for comparing Wittgenstein and Spinoza is their common concern for *necessary* as contrasted with *accidental* generality. As an empiricist, Russell had not been very deeply concerned with the problem; Wittgenstein makes this clear in his discussions of the axiom of reducibility and the theory of classes (6.031, 6.1232). Even Frege had resorted to self-evidence as providing sufficient warranty for a certain procedure. Wittgenstein felt this to be a serious error (6.1271). It was an illegitimate yielding to empiricism.

When discussing imagination and the emotions, Spinoza claims

---

[2] *Ethics,* Pt. II, Proposition XL, Notes.

that apparent external evidence is our largest source of error. His most important break with the medievalists is at this point. General notions, as the medievalists understood them, are *at best* abstractions of essential form, *at worst* images of conglomerate forms; and there was no way, on the basis of empirical evidence, to distinguish the essential from the purely imaginative. Adequate ideas are those we construct for ourselves and which we know are not inconsistent either internally or in relation to other constructed ideas. Spinoza distinguished common notions, such as we find in Plato's "Sophist", from general notions. The common notions are the necessary presuppositions of all thinking and are the very substance of the axioms and adequate ideas. The assumption of common notions underlies much of the argument of Wittgenstein's *Tractatus*. Without common notions there could actually be no argument; and there would be no way out of the empirical trap into which Mauthner had fallen. We would be as Mauthner states at the end of his monumental work, adrift on a shoreless sea without a beacon.

Whenever one begins seriously to think about the meaning of human existence and his particular place in the world, he is inevitably faced with the problem of solipsism. Are there one or many worlds; are there one or many minds; how is communication possible?[3] The empiricist actually has no answer. He, as a matter of faith, believes in one or many worlds. The rationalist handles the problem somewhat differently. Since he believes in common notions, he is able to offer them as an ultimate ground of meaning against which he is able to handle the problem of his solipsism. In the case of Spinoza, we have the argument in the beginning of the *Ethics* for the existence of only one substance. As he demonstrates in both Part II and Part III of the *Ethics*, Spinoza is deeply aware that as soon as we begin to think at all we must start with an assumption of solipsism. Wittgenstein's problem is both more

---

[3] For the best contemporary analysis of the problem of solipsism, the reader is referred to M. Merleau-Ponty, *Phenomenology of Perception*, trans. by Colin Smith (London: Routledge and Kegan Paul, 1962), Part Two, Chapter Four.

complex and also simpler than is Spinoza's. He is unable to quarrel with his experience of aloneness (the reader is reminded that three of his brothers committed suicide);[4] but he is equally aware that some form of communication is going on between the world(s) and men and between men and men. Mauthner confessed himself hopeless before the problem; Wittgenstein found a way to affirm that at the core of all language lay a single root: logic. This being true, it is possible for even monadic entities to talk meaningfully with each other and to have a dialogue with the world(s). Some of the propositions which set out this particular position are to be found in 5.552-5.556 and 6.3432-6.41.

It will be noted, of course, that Wittgenstein's world, although still a rationalist's world, is quite different from Spinoza's. If there is a god identifiable with the rational structure of the world he (or it) is at most a very inferior deity, far removed from the God of Spinoza. That Wittgenstein's world is neither Spinoza's nor Leibnitz' does not make him any less a rationalist. He is still very far from empiricism. Nor is Wittgenstein committed to any one of many possible worlds. What he has to say applies to all possible worlds, and goodness or badness is an extrinsic matter (6.41-6.44). Wittgenstein recognizes how impossible it is to say that this world of my experience is the best of all possible worlds. He can say, however, that the world of my experience has some similarities with the world of your experience. Otherwise we could not communicate meaningfully. We cannot go beyond this minimum statement because we are, as Spinoza did not realize, confined to a language-world and we dare not, as Spinoza did, assume that our ideas necessarily stand for things. Spinoza's arguments at the beginning of the *Ethics*, particularly those concerning the qualitative unity of the one unique substance, depend on an unconscious reification of certain key words.

---

4 Malcolm, *Ludwig Wittgenstein*, 94.

2

In drawing a parallel between Spinoza and Wittgenstein, we may find it to be not insignificant that each had a Jewish background. Wittgenstein's grandfather converted to Christianity;[5] and Spinoza was excluded from the synagogue for his heretical views on the authorship of the biblical books. Neither Wittgenstein nor Spinoza was prepared to accept the given answers of any religious community as adequate for his personal salvation; although one has the impression that his inability to accept the answers of the Roman communion was a source of some pain to the later Wittgenstein.[6] It would be improper to push the Jewish background of the two philosophers into extreme prominence; but one can say that each carried into his philosophy something of the activism which permeates the Bible. In neither instance is the end of thought an eternal stillness. Rather, the end of thought is activity itself; and thought is itself an activity, eternally creating and re-creating. Spinoza has so frequently been interpreted in either a Plotinian or a pantheistic way because men have not seen that the God of the *Ethics* in all of His attributes is activity. Spinoza's attribute of extension is not Descartes' extended substance, but a way of talking about an aspect of God's existence in and through Himself. The sections of the *Ethics* on human emotions and knowledge accent the fact that for Spinoza action rather than passivity is the secret of the world's being and, therefore, of God's Being. *Natura naturans*, which is God as He is in Himself, acts by the necessity of His own Being; but the action and the necessity are one. And that oneness is dynamic rather than static; it is surely false to equate Spinoza's extension with Descartes': God, as substance, is His own eternal cause. Insofar as we are in fact the cause of our own actions, we share in the Being of God's eternal activity; insofar as we are only reacting to external causes, or rather reacting to our imaginative construction of external things, we do not share in the Being of

---

[5] Georg Henrik von Wright, "Biographical Sketch", in Malcolm, *Ludwig Wittgenstein*, 2.

[6] Von Wright, "Biographical Sketch", 72.

God, at least as He is in Himself. In this sense God as *Natura naturata* is not identical with *Natura naturans;* and Spinoza is demonstrated to be not the pantheist he is usually thought to be. Wittgenstein's God is beyond the world of the individual, knowing, philosophical "I", and He is beyond the totality of all worlds. There is a great chasm between God and the world. God is the inexpressible, the mystical (6.532). The categories of logic and fact do not apply to Him (6.432-6.44). We may be able to learn something about *Natura naturata*: the world; but we may not assume, as Spinoza did, that logic can be used to penetrate into that which is beyond the world of experience.

At this point it is again important to draw some distinctions. According to the *Tractatus* logic is transcendental (6.13); but this

does not mean that the propositions of logic state transcendental truths; it means that they, like all other propositions, show something that pervades everything sayable and is itself unsayable.[7]

On the whole one can say that Wittgenstein uses "transcendental" in the Kantian sense as developed in the *Critique of Pure Reason*. Kant uses the word "transcendent" to apply to that which is beyond all possible worlds; and it is apparent that Wittgenstein is aware of the distinction, although the word "transcendent" does not appear in the *Tractatus*. Nevertheless, transcendence is implied in the whole doctrine of the expressible mystical. As with the early Mahayana doctrine of *nirvana* we can say nothing about it, not even that it exists; but it is the source of all values and possibly of existence itself (6.44). "Possibly" must be used in this connection because Wittgenstein seems to have two different attitudes toward the mystical: that in 6.45 and that in 6.522. There is apparently a mystical which can be known in the direct experience of one who has climbed up out of the world; this mystical is beyond all logic and therefore beyond all words. Then there is the mystical which is the experience of the world as a limited whole. Sometimes this whole is larger than at other times, depending on our moods (6.43); but this mysticism is dependent on our emotions.

---

[7] Anscombe, *An Introduction*, 166.

The transcendent mysticism is beyond everything that is or can be in the world. Nevertheless, the *Tractatus* is itself written from the perspective of the transcendent, the inexpressible. This is why it can be a mirror. The mission of the *Tractatus* is to help us who are still pilgrims to see the structure of the world, particularly as that world is described by logic and language. The mirror, of course, cannot show us that which is beyond the worlds because that which is beyond the worlds is also behind the mirror.

As for logic — and this is the most significant difference with Spinoza — it cannot tell us whether anything exists or not (6.1261-6.1264), although it can tell us what is impossible in the world (6.375). As the development of the general proposition shows, we know what must be the most general structure of any possible world; and a structural arbitrariness does not exist, although the factual content of any world, including its very existence, is arbitrary — at least from the viewpoint of the *Tractatus* (6.41) and the foundations of logic and mathematics. Spinoza's arguments for the necessary existence of *Natura naturans* would have fallen much more quickly under Wittgenstein's dissection than under Kant's. Existence itself is a mystery which we cannot penetrate. Insofar as we come to know existence, we find it accidental (6.41); but we must assume a willing (God, ourselves) which has some connection with that which does occur. But to talk in this way is to be incoherent (*unsinnig*), is to talk beyond the possibility of any knowledge (6.362-6.374).

Those who attempt to make Spinoza into either a Plotinian or a pantheist forget that for Spinoza *Natura naturans*, God as He is in Himself, acts with a different causation than does *Natura naturata*, God or the world as we know Him or It. In the first case, the causation is vertical: God out of the necessity of His own Being creates the Infinite and finite modes. In the second case, the modes work against each other in what we must presumably call causal efficacy. The actual aggregates produced by the second form of causation are not known by *Natura naturans*,[8] but they exist con-

---

[8]   *Ethics*, Part II.

tingently, thrown into existence by the ceaseless activity of the ultimate finite modes.[9] *Natura naturans* does not know them because *Natura naturans* knows only adequate ideas; and the objects of the contingent world are physical exemplifications of inadequate and confused ideas. We find an echo of this very sophisticated thinking of Spinoza's at 6.362 where Wittgenstein says:

Was sich beschreiben lässt, das kann auch geschehen, und was das Kausalitätsgesetz ausschlissen soll, das lässt sich auch nicht beschreiben.

We describe what happens in terms of the law of causality, and we really cannot imagine anything happening which we do not in some sense feel is caused; but we know in fact that the law of causality is part of the structure of our minds (6.36-6.361) or, more carefully, of our language. The world of *Natura naturata* is as it is; things happen as they do (6.41); and my will and this world are independent of each other (6.373).

Finally, it would be possible using Spinoza's understanding of God as both *Natura naturans* and *Natura naturata* to understand why *Natura naturans*, God as He is described in Part I of the *Ethics*, would be indifferent, because unaware, of what went on in *Natura naturata* (6.432). For Spinoza, salvation consists in the purifying of our confused ideas so that they become identical with the true and adequate ideas in *Natura naturans*. The following propositions from the *Tractatus* reflect this view of nature. But for *Natura naturans* Wittgenstein can only offer the *Unaussprechliche*. The way of salvation is the same; but for Wittgenstein there is no expressible end.

The Spinozistic propositions in the *Tractatus* which show Wittgenstein's ladder are:

Die Tatsachen gehören alle nur zur Aufgabe, nicht zur Lösung (6.4321).

Nicht *wie* die Welt ist, ist das Mystische, sondern *dass* sie ist (6.44).

Die Anschauung der Welt sub specie aeterni ist ihre Anschauung als —

---

[9] *Ethics*, Part IV, Definitions III and IV.

begrenztes — Ganzes. Das Gefühl der Welt als begrenztes Ganzes ist das Mystische (6.45).

It may very well have been Wittgenstein's studies in Spinoza, combined with his knowledge of Mach and Avenarius, which led him to propound the doctrine of logical atomism of the first part of the *Tractatus*. For Mach, the world of our experience is ultimately made up of the "elements". The comparable ultimate finite modes in the Spinozistic system seem to have been something to which we today might give the name of warps in Space-Time. One could probably call these ultimate finite modes particles if the word "particles" could be shorn of its Democritean overtones; but Spinoza's one world had no place for a void. With Mach, and Wittgenstein, the problem of whether there is or is not a void is left open. Neither is doing metaphysics. But like Spinoza's ultimate finite modes, Mach's "elements" may be said to have some sentience and some extension, although only potentially. They become actual only by becoming linked with other elements in a fact. Wittgenstein expresses the nature of reality (*Wirklichkeit*) at its most atomistic level in the description of the "atomic fact": "Im Sachverhalt hängen die Gegenstände ineinander, wie die Glieder einer Kette" (2.03). The subject-predicate way of describing things is denied. Worlds come to be and pass away out of the potentiality to which the name "die empirische Realität" (5.5561) is given. At any one instant of duration in a world whose totality is timeless, there may be one or more existing worlds, each coordinated with a philosophical "I" (5.64). It is within this framework that we must understand the phrase: "die Gesamtheit der bestehenden Sachverhalte ist die Welt" (2.04).

It is crucial at this point that we do not fall into the temptation of giving logic any sort of ontological status. Logic is not an aspect of *empirische Realität*, but neither is logic an aspect or quality of the several philosophical "I"s. Logic is the core of language; and language is an inter- and intra-personal relation. This is why there cannot be an intrinsic hierarchy of elementary propositions (5.556, 5.5561). Hierarchies of propositions can exist in language alone. But the *application* of logic determines what elementary propositions there will be and thus determines in some manner the nature of any particular world or any congeries of worlds (5.557). *"Die Grenzen meiner Sprache bedeuten die Grenzen meiner Welt"* (5.6); and the worlds may wax and wane in terms of our moods and their constraining and expanding effect on our use of language (6.43). Wittgenstein is by no means proposing any sort of idealism, although Lenin had seen a crypto-idealism in the work of Mach and Avenarius. What Wittgenstein is attempting to do with his analysis of language, his discussion of "empirische Realität" and "Welt", his recognition of philosophical "I"'s is to bring to our attention that reality (*Wirklichkeit*) as we come to know it is the result of dialogue.

Die "Erfahrung", die wir zum Verstehen der Logik brauchen, ist nicht die, dass sich etwas so und so verhält, sondern, dass etwas *ist;* aber das ist eben keine Erfahrung. Die Logik ist *vor* jeder Erfahrung — dass etwas *so* ist. Sie ist vor dem Wie, nicht vor dem Was (5.552).

If we can understand that *Logos* plays a creative role in our several worlds and that there is a potential matrix out of which all worlds arise, statements such as the following will no longer appear self-contradictory: "Es können alle Kombinationen der Sachverhalte bestehen, die andern nicht bestehen" (4.27). And it is because Wittgenstein is aware of how crucial propositional language and coherence are that he attempts, by means of the truth tables, to provide an alternative and artificial matrix which we can use instead of referring to an *empirische Realität* which in its essence is necessarily beyond our finding out. It was the same sort of helpless feeling about our experience of the phenomenal world which led Spinoza to develop his theories about the ontological and interrelated status of constructed, true, and adequate ideas.

Finally, like Spinoza's *Ethics*, the *Tractatus* is a soteriological document. Neither Spinoza nor Wittgenstein believed in an individual eternal life (6.4311-6.521), at least not, if by eternal we mean an endless duration. In the *Ethics*, Spinoza shows us that salvation is the continuing to gain ever more clear and adequate ideas as to the nature of both *Natura naturata* and *Natura naturans* until one finally becomes one with *Natura naturans*. Spinoza was a recluse because it was only by being a recluse that he could free his thought from the distracting influences of the flux within *Natura naturata*. With Wittgenstein, the problem of the meaning of life, and of individual salvation, vanishes in the recognition that the meaning of my life is not to be found in the understanding of my world (6.522). Only by the attainment of the inexpressible (in contemplation? may I possibly find joy. As has been suggested earlier, salvation for Wittgenstein seems to be analogous to that described for Schopenhauer in the closing section of the first volume of *The World as Will and Idea*.[10] In denying the world and the struggle to be, *conatus*, one is thrust by virtue of the double negation into a different and higher realm than is apparent in the worlds brought into being by the *Logos*. Spinoza would not have approved of this denial of *conatus*, for the essence of *Natura naturans* is "to be". The purpose of the *Ethics* is to show how, by the substituting of positive for negative emotions we may rise to the intellectual love of God. Spinoza would not have approved of the austerity with which Wittgenstein lived his life even though he would have approved of the retirement from the world. It is apparent that Wittgenstein, in terms of his religious life, took his direction from Schopenhauer rather than Spinoza. Perhaps his reason for doing so was not only the problem of the suffering he saw around him in World War I, and the deep sense of sin which Russell remarked before the war,[11] but his recognition that the path which Spinoza had chosen was no longer open. Spinoza would never have uttered the words at 6.52:

Wir fühlen, dass selbst, wenn alle *möglichen* wissenschaftlichen Fragen beantwortet sind, unsere Lebensprobleme noch gar nicht berührt sind.

Nevertheless, when we recognize the limitations Wittgenstein places on human thought, we recognize that the concluding portion of the *Ethics*[12] and the concluding sections of the *Tractatus* are not real-

---

[10]   Schopenhauer, Vol. I, Book IV, sec. 71.
[11]   Russell, "Philosophers and Idiots", in Fann (ed.), *Ludwig Wittgenstein*, 32.
[12]   *Ethics*, Part V, Propositions XXXIX, XL, XLII.

ly very different once we understand that for Wittgenstein it was impossible to talk about or to probe into the nature of Being or beings. At the last we must be silent (7). If there is a merger with the inexpressible Sense of the universe (6.41), it is not something which can be talked about.

3

We cannot move from the world of the *Tractatus* to *Natura naturans*, or to the traditional God of western theism; yet the nature of the existence of the world, *Natura naturata*, proclaims that in itself it is not self-explanatory (5.552, 6.44). There is a fundamental arbitrariness in all that happens, including the very existence of the world itself (5.552, 6.362-6.372, 6.41). We cannot say of this or that which happens that the events are caused by God, ourselves, or some other being (6.362-6.375). To think in causal terms is to think as men think (6.362-6.375). How God thinks is unknowable to us, as it is equally unknowable whether there is a God. But whatever the world is, it is not a big machine moving in terms of the inexorable laws of mechanics. Fundamentally, except for the logical structures imposed on the world by our logic, the world and our selves are mysteries. Wittgenstein's world and Wittgenstein's God are not the world and the God of Aristotle; but neither are the world and the God of Spinoza. Both Wittgenstein's and Spinoza's world are Jewish worlds permeated with a ceaseless activity. The difference is that Spinoza believes that, by the use of logic, he can penetrate to the very heart of Being; Wittgenstein hopes only to demonstrate that the worlds of our experience have a certain order and that this order is expressed in the languages we speak. It is by our careful study of our language and the *Logos* hidden within it that we are able to discover not only the *cosmos* hidden within the *chaos*, but the very organizing principle of the world (6.321-6.361). Logic is the scaffolding of the world (3.42, 6.341-6.361). Without the scaffolding there would be only *chaos:* Mach's "elements" in unceasing movement. Language (logic) creates the worlds; but language and logic are not able to go beyond the particular world which is mine (5.5563-5.62, 6.431) except to lay out the limits and structure that must obtain for any possible world: tautology, contradiction, and the general proposition. The truth-tables are the means whereby I examine the structure of any proposition which is not elementary. They are the means whereby I prevent my language from becoming incoherent, whereby I prevent myself from maintaining two or more contradictory statements at the same time. The truth-tables are part of the internal and axiomatic character of the system of the *Tractatus*.

However, the purpose in this section of the essay is not to repeat what may have been said immediately above, nor to anticipate what may be said in the last two chapters. Rather, the purpose is to unfold something of the working of Wittgenstein's mind at the time he wrote the *Tractatus* by examining the thought processes of a fellow Jew, Spinoza. As was said above, Spinoza has left us a record in *On the Improvement of the Understanding*[13] of how his mind worked. It seems most likely that the *Tractatus* was worked out in a similar fashion during World War I while Wittgenstein was in the Austrian Army. War, although it has its periods of excitement, is mostly tedium. We may easily assume that Wittgenstein filled those periods of tedium by trying to work through, on the basis of the new logic, his thoughts about the world, himself, and God. War provides both a place and a time to work through fundamental questions; and one is never far from the stimulus to consider them. Marcus Aurelius worked through his *Meditations* while leading his army against the Goths; and Descartes wrote his *Meditations* almost immediately after leaving the army in which he had been serving.

At the beginning of the essay *On the Improvement of the Understanding*, Spinoza gives us his reasons for devoting his life to philosophy and for giving up any hope of significant riches, honor, or sensual pleasure. Although the philosopher's hope of obtaining

---

[13] The text used in the examination of the essay *On the Improvement of the Understanding* is that appearing in *The Chief Works of Benedict de Spinoza*, trans. by R. H. M. Elwes (New York: Dover Publications, 1951).

or participating in a Supreme Good may be frustrated; riches, honor, and sensual pleasure, considered as ends in themselves, are self-defeating, carrying in their train ills for which there is little compensation. The major difficulty, however, is not so much with riches, honor, and pleasure in themselves as it is in our desire to possess. As did Gautama, Jesus, and Socrates, Spinoza found the root of human ills in the desire to live for and to possess that which is transient. Pleasure, honor, and riches may be quite useful; but they may never be more than means in furthering an end which is the Supreme Good. Spinoza did not visualize this Supreme Good as a transcendent deity who could only be approached through ecstasy. Rather, the Supreme Good is an activity: the union of the individual with God conceived both as *Natura naturans* and *Natura naturata*. Only if we know both the structure and substance of God can this be possible; and our first responsibility, having come to see what the end of our life should be, is to devise a way to think rightly about nature, man, God, and human emotions. We must find a way to free ourselves from the bondage to bad (passive) emotions by substituting good (active) emotions; the *Ethics* describes the method for doing this. The end of the philosophical life is to become increasingly intuitively aware of what is true and thereby to become one with the Truth. In Part V of the *Ethics* this process is called the "intellectual love of God".

However, it is not immediately possible for us to know what is true. The world presents itself to us as an unceasing flux; and it is evident that men's understanding of the world is more frequently in error than it is correct. If we are to understand the world aright, we must devise intellectual tools which will serve to strengthen our minds. Subsequently, the strengthened mind can devise ever more rigorous tools. In the essay, Spinoza saw this process as a four-rung ladder, reminiscent of the ladder in Plato's *Republic*; in the *Ethics*, a more precisely reasoned book, he reduced the rungs to three. One may legitimately ask whether the truth-tables were not such intellectual tools for Wittgenstein. If they were, the range of their usefulness was much more limited for Wittgenstein than the essentially Galilean tools which Spinoza emulated. In devising his tools, Spinoza does not abstract from sense impressions. In the essay and the *Ethics*, he is most careful to point out that his way is not the way of the schoolmen nor of Aristotle. Rather, as he begins to construct his tools, he finds that self-consistency is the necessary criterion and that he cannot, in fact, rely on any tools except those of his own construction. Although most of his illustrations are taken from Euclidean geometry, not all are; but the principle is the same. A constructed triangle always has its interior angles equal to two right angles. A square circle is obviously self-contradictory and false. It cannot be constructed; and we have here only a playing with words or, as in the case of a flying horse, contradictory images. In addition to their truth, which is built into them, true and adequate ideas lead to others, and, finally, the whole of the world is disclosed in the attribute of mind. The world is disclosed in two ways: *Natura naturans*, which has maximum intensionality; and *Natura naturata* which has maximum extensionality. The way to union with *Natura naturans* is through the scientific study of *Natura naturata*; but the proper study of *Natura naturata* is by means of the kind of logic which Galileo developed, which seeks to discover finite modes of some complexity, such as the law of falling bodies.

As stated above, Spinoza's method appears simple and non-dialectical, but in fact it is not so, as we shall demonstrate below; nor were Galileo's demonstrations simple and non-dialectical. To clarify ideas when they move beyond the simplest level of complexity, we must throw them against each other. We can see this method in the *Ethics* where Spinoza demonstrates that the relations between the ideas that he is talking about are what will later be called formal or internal relations. Infinity, for instance, was for Spinoza a quality and not a quantity, and could not be divided. Miss Anscombe remarked on the fact that Wittgenstein would not, or could not, distinguish between finite and infinite quantities;[14] but the whole discussion of formal and proper relations in the *Tractatus* which begins at 4.122 surely owes something to Spin-

---

[14] Anscombe, *An Introduction*, 146.

oza's discussion of the matter. Wittgenstein's solution of the problem to which we will turn shortly is radically different from Spinoza's. It is nevertheless important to recognize that Wittgenstein thought of himself as a constructionist (5.555-5.556).

The dialectical nature of Spinoza's thought can probably best be shown by the following quotation from *On the Improvement of the Understanding*:

I have been forced so to arrange my proceedings, that we may acquire by reflection and forethought what we cannot acquire by chance, and that it may at the same time appear that, for proving the truth, and for valid reasoning, we need no other means than the truth and valid reasoning themselves: for by valid reasoning I have established valid reasoning, and, in like measure, I seek still to establish it. Moreover, this is the order of thinking adopted by men in their inward meditations.[15]

In considering Spinoza's method it is important to recognize that he is doing an essentially intensional analysis. Relations for him are all formal and internal, and all true ideas are necessarily adequate ideas because the universe is one. In turn, all true and adequate ideas lead eventually to a recognition that God is both *Natura naturans* and *Natura naturata* and that within these two phrases all reality is included. In fact, to believe that something is discrete is to believe falsely; for that which is discrete, if there could possibly be such a thing or idea, is unknowable.[16] A good example of Spinoza's intensional analysis may be seen in the *Ethics*[17] where he argues for the indivisibility of substance, of extension, and even of such a finite mode as water.

In the *Tractatus*, Wittgenstein is obviously exploring the contrary thesis: that there is an ultimate atomism in which all relations are external, proper, and extensional. His solution to the problem of relations is both radical and linguistic. He draws back from making any ontological commitment, finding that a satisfactory solution to the problem of formal and proper relations can only be

15 Elwes, *Chief Works*, II, 16 (see note 13 of this chapter).
16 Elwes, *Chief Works*, II, 15 (see note 13 of this chapter).
17 *Ethics*, Part I, Propositions XII-XV.

found if we regard the intention of the language user and confine ourselves to language in use (4.122-4.128): "There is no philosophic monism or dualism, etc." It must be recognized, however, that Wittgenstein's position rests ultimately on the prior thought of Mach and Mauthner.

THE CENTRAL EUROPEAN PHILOSOPHICAL
BACKGROUND

1

Wittgenstein's fundamental approach to the philosophical problems with which he was concerned can be seen most clearly in his handling of the question of whether the world in its essence is one or many. In the chapter on Spinoza, this approach was touched upon as an attempt was made to compare and contrast Wittgenstein's and Spinoza's approach to the problem. Spinoza was a monist, although a monist of a very complicated kind; it is false, for instance, to say that for Spinoza all distinctions were blurred. Rather, Spinoza recognized that in differentiation there is equally a negation; but the negation can not be so complete as to make a discrete entity of anything. Anything which is completely discrete would necessarily be unknowable, and there would be no possibility of such a discrete entity participating in anything else: there could be no process. In some respects, Spinoza's analysis reminds one of the discussion in Plato's "Parmenides". If one is going to do ontology at all, one must recognize some kind of an ultimate unity before one can begin to talk about separateness.

Since Hume, we have seen many philosophers who have seemingly proposed a radical pluralism, which the doctrine of logical atomism appears to presuppose. At the time when Wittgenstein was coming to maturity in Vienna, the great intellectual struggle in central Europe was between the materialists and the idealists, although the epistemological complications introduced by the Neo-Kantians, particularly of the Marburg School, cannot be ignored. Mach and Avenarius, in attempts to free science from any involvement in the prevailing epistemological and metaphysical questions, proposed an ultimate psychological pluralism which would be neutral with respect to the metaphysical controversy. The attempt to substitute a form of psychology for metaphysics may be seen in the titles to their chief works: *Kritik der reinen Erfahrung* (Avenarius) and *Beiträge zur Analyse der Empfindungen* (Mach). It is most likely that Wittgenstein's concern to dissociate himself from both psychology and epistemology is related to the new factors which Mach and Avenarius had imported into the philosophical scene (4.1121, 5.541, 5.5421, 5.641, 6.423). Logic is itself not an epistemology; and the purpose of the earlier portions of the *Tractatus* is to determine by analysis and dialectic what may and what may not be said about logical or linguistic atoms. Finally, it must be recognized that the doctrines of Mach and Avenarius came to be interpreted in various ways. Lenin saw the doctrines as a crypto-idealism (*Materialism and Empirio-Criticism*), but others interpreted the sense impressions in an almost materialistic way (Ayer). In any event, Mach's phenomenalism was quite widespread in pre-World War I Vienna and led directly to the thought patterns of the Vienna Circle, with which Wittgenstein's name will always be conjoined.

If we study the *Tractatus* as an exercise in dialectics and against the philosophical developments in Central Europe referred to in the previous paragraphs we find that Wittgenstein rejected idealism (4.0412) and that he nowhere affirmed materialism. The issue in the *Tractatus* is with the "elements" which Mach had affirmed and which Wittgenstein, in accordance with the Marburg School, calls *Gegenstände*.[1] But if there are elements, then it should be possible to know them and to make predications about them. Otherwise, they are at most constructions which we must assume if we are to operate in terms of Mach's intent. The dialectic of the *Tractatus* is to determine the legitimacy of talking about these proposed

---

[1]   William H. Werkmeister, *Cassirers Verhältnis zur Neukantischen Philosophie,* herausgegeben von Paul Arthur Schilpp, Sonderdruck (Stuttgart: W. Kohlhammer, n.d.), 534-47.

elements. In a phrase borrowed from Avenarius,[2] Wittgenstein, near the end of the whole discussion of monism and pluralism, internal (formal) and external (proper) relations, says:

Die logischen Formen sind zahllos. Darum gibt es in der Logik keine ausgezeichneten Zahlen und darum gibt es keinen philosophischen Monismus oder Dualismus, etc. (4.128).

In Wittgenstein the problem of discreteness and monism, intensionality and extensionality, formal and proper, and internal and external relations, is carried back to an examination of intent, and above all to the intent with which language is used. Our intentionality in using language, both in groups and alone, determines whether we are talking about objects intensionally or extensionally (4.1213-4.2). Wittgenstein is equally convinced that our recognition of the existence or the non-existence of a state of affairs is dependent upon the intentionality with which the language is used. This is why he can state that

Jeder mögliche Satz ist rechtmässig gebildet, und wenn er keinen Sinn hat, so kann das nur daran liegen, dass wir einigen Bestandteilen keine Bedeutung gegeben haben (Wenn wir auch glauben, es getan zu haben) (5.4733).

Die Anzahl der nötigen Grundoperationen hängt nur von unserer Notation ab (5.474).

In these two passages, as well as in others, Wittgenstein is distinguishing his position from that of Frege, who talks about an a priori legitimacy (5.4733) — surely a form of Platonism. But he is equally distinguishing his position from Mauthner's assumption that language is always, at least to a degree, a betrayal. For Wittgenstein, language contains within itself a quality of self-consistency and a reliable relation to the external world.

Alle Sätze unserer Umgangssprache sind tatsächlich, so wie sie sind, logisch volkommen geordnet. — Jenes Einfachste, was wir hier angeben sollen, ist nicht ein Gleichnis der Wahrheit, sondern die volle Wahrheit selbst. (Unsere Probleme sind nicht abstrakt, sondern vielleicht die konkretesten, die es gibt.) (5.5563).

[2] Frederick Copleston, *A History of Philosophy* (8 vols.; Westminster, Md.: The Newman Press, 1955-1966), VII, 359.

Die *Anwendung* der Logik entscheidet darüber, welche Elementarsätze es gibt. Was in der Anwendung liegt, kann die Logik nicht vorausnehmen. Das ist klar: Die Logik darf mit ihrer Anwendung nicht kollidieren. Aber die Logik muss sich mit ihrer Anwendung berühren. Also dürfe die Logik und ihre Anwendung einander nicht übergreifen (5.557).

The reliability of language in its relation to the external world and, at the same time, a recognition that the quarrel between monism and pluralism is a false one, may be seen in the following quotation:

Die Grammophonplatte, der musikalische Gedanke, die Notenschrift, die Schallwellen, stehen alle in jener abbildenden internen Beziehung zu einander, die zwischen Sprache und Welt besteht. Ihnen allen ist der logische Bau gemeinsam. (Wie im Märchen die zwei Jünglinge, ihre zwei Pferde und ihre Lilien. Sie sind alle in gewissem Sinne Eins.) (4.014.)

Wittgenstein's position vis-à-vis Frege and Mauthner is by no means a compromise, but it can only be understood properly if we realize that for Frege there is a qualified, but nevertheless sharply defined, ontological structure to the world of which legitimately constructed propositions are a reflection; Mauthner, on the other hand, sees only a chaos in which language carves out worlds which are necessarily false as they are more and more sharply defined in the socalled language of abstract thought. Consider the following quotation from Mauthner against both Wittgenstein and Frege. Wittgenstein's own unique synthesis will then become more easily apparent.

Nur die Richtung der Aufmerksamkeit gibt den Einleitungsgrund nach Modalität und Relation, nach Qualität und Quantität. Wie es in der Welt der Wirklichkeiten keine Bejahung und Verneinung, keine Möglichkeit und Gewissheit gibt, sondern nur eben Wirkliches, dessen wir bejahend gewiss sind, so gibt es in der Natur auch keine allgemeine und keine partikulare Sätze.[3]

Shortly before this quoted statement, Mauthner says that our pictures of the world are composed of sentences (*Sätze*) which in turn are built of words which refer ultimately to sense impressions (*Emp-*

---

[3] Mauthner, *Beiträge*, III, 337-38.

findungen) and are the more inaccurate the further they are from sense impressions.[4] Wittgenstein obviously had Mauthner's understanding of language in mind when he wrote:

Das angewandte, gedachte, Satzzeichen ist der Gedanke (3.5).

Der Gedanke ist der sinnvolle Satz (4).

Die Gesamtheit der Sätze ist die Sprache (4.001).

Der Mensch besitzt die Fähigkeit Sprachen zu bauen, womit sich jeder Sinn ausdrücken lässt, ohne eine Ahnung davon zu haben, wie und was jedes Wort bedeutet. — Wie man auch spricht, ohne zu wissen, wie die einzelnen Laute hervorgebracht werden. . . . Die Sprache verkleidet den Gedanken (4.002).

In the *Tractatus*, and for that matter, in *Philosophical Investigations*, Wittgenstein is showing that Mauthner's chaotic conclusions do not follow from Mauthner's premises. He is equally showing that the kind of sharpness of definition for which Frege was looking can be found only in a mirrored reflection of the hidden structure of language itself. For Wittgenstein, as for Mauthner, language thus carves worlds of understanding out of the strangeness of multifarious sense impressions; but there is one logic hidden within all language, as Frege and Russell have demonstrated; and that logic, although not internal to the world's structures, is not false to them. However, our recognition of the existence or non-existence of a particular state of affairs depends on the intentionality of the language itself.

2

In his handling of the use of language Wittgenstein demonstrated that the age-old problem of individuation is not, in fact, a reflection of the world, or of human minds, but of language itself and of the intention with which language is used. We need not, nor can we, step outside of language to a world of thought or matter, to a world which is pluralistic or monistic, and find there an ultimate

---

[4] Mauthner, *Beiträge*, III, 337-38.

reference for the symbols of our language. We have what symbols we have; and the language of the *Principia Mathematica* provides, on the whole, a proper syntax for the symbols. It is with this understanding of semiotic that the first part of the *Tractatus* begins to take on a new meaning.

We must recognize, if we are to understand the *Tractatus*, that Wittgenstein deliberately conflated the meaning of the word *Gegenstand*, which can be used for an object of thought as well as for something more substantial, with *Sache*, an affair with overtones of activity, and *Ding*, thing (2.01). The conflation is crucial to our understanding of the *Tractatus* if we can recognize, as Wittgenstein uses the word, that *Gegenstände* do not have an empirical existence until they are a part of, or are members of, a fact. If we were being Aristotelian we would be tempted to speak of *Gegenstände* as being the potential of that which in the world of our experience becomes a *Sache*, a state of affairs, or a *Ding*. Wittgenstein does not want to deny existence to *Gegenstand*; but neither does he wish to affirm it unconditionally. We can see this shifting of meaning at 4.1272; and 4.2211 becomes really coherent if we think of *Gegenstände* as sharing in the kind of being-non-being that Plato talks about in the *Sophist*. In *Philosophical Investigations* (I, 46), Wittgenstein, using a quotation from the *Theatetus*, makes the same point about the objects of the *Tractatus*. They are the references of names at most, and their ontological status is indeterminate. It seems most likely that Wittgenstein chose *Gegenstand* as a substitute for Mach's and Mauthner's *Empfindungen* to avoid prejudging the whole matter of the ultimate constitutents of reality. *Gegenstand* can include the objects of thought as well as sense impressions. Nevertheless, *Gegenstand* does not exclude the possibility of something quite material, as Wittgenstein is attempting to show us at 2.01.

It seems most likely that Wittgenstein was attempting by his use of the word *Gegenstand* to indicate that the several worlds are each carved out of a very large, perhaps infinitely large, range of possibilities. Nevertheless, there is no world until the *Gegenstände* have been arranged into chains (2.03, 2.04) or facts. It is quite possible that these chains or facts are most complex (5.5541), but this cannot be decided a priori. At most one can say that there is no hierarchy of forms of the elementary propositions. Hierarchies, as in the sciences, are internal to language and heuristic in nature (5.556, 5.557, 6.361, 6.343). One final clue will help our understanding of *Gegenstand* as a translation device for *Empfindung*. At 5.5561, Wittgenstein uses *Realität* instead of *Wirklichkeit* for one or two times in the entire *Tractatus*. The proposition reads:

Die empirische Realität ist begrenzt durch die Gesamtheit der Gegenstände. Die Grenze zeigt sich wieder in der Gesamtheit der Elementarsätze. Die Hierarchien sind, und müssen unabhängig von der Realität sein.

There are many worlds and many realities *(Wirklichkeiten)*, but there is only *Realität*. Consider the following early propositions from this point of view:

Die Struktur der Tatsache besteht aus den Strukturen der Sachverhalte (2.034).

Die Gesamtheit der bestehenden Sachverhalte ist die Welt (2.04).

Die Gesamtheit der bestehenden Sachverhalte bestimmt auch, welche Sachverhalte nicht bestehen (2.05).

Das Bestehen und Nichtbestehen von Sachverhalten ist die Wirklichkeit. (Das Bestehen von Sachverhalten nennen wir auch eine positive, das Nichtbestehen eine negative *Tatsache*) (2.06).   (Italics added.)

Die Sachverhalte sind von einander unabhängig (2.061).

Aus dem Bestehen oder Nichtbestehen eines Sachverhaltes kann nicht auf das Bestehen oder Nichtbestehen eines anderen geschlossen werden (2.062).

Die gesamte Wirklichkeit ist die Welt (2.063).

Die Welt ist die Gesamtheit der Tatsachen, nicht der Dinge (1.1).

Was der Fall ist, die Tatsache, ist das Bestehen von Sachverhalten (2).

Der Sachverhalt ist eine Verbindung von Gegenständen. (Sachen, Dingen.) (2.01).

If Mach was doing metaphysics, then the point of view which has just been displayed is metaphysics and probably the only metaphysics which really takes Spinoza seriously. But Mach claimed he was not doing metaphysics; he was clearing the scientific enterprize from the metaphysical taint in order to get on with the scientist's job. The effort of the *Tractatus* is certainly partly an attempt to finish the job which Mach had begun by turning to a linguistic and dialectical analysis of the whole problem of the one and the many.

We could leave the *Tractatus* as an essay in linguistic and dialectical analysis, which it certainly is; but it is important to recognize that Wittgenstein was not content with such a limited view. Like Spinoza, he wanted to know both the nature of the world and how he might find salvation. As to what the world is in itself, this is beyond our knowing; but there is something in the world corresponding to the core of our language. Salvation comes from denying both the world and ourselves; but there is no blindly striving, unconscious Will.[5] In the next chapter Schopenhauer's metaphysical system will be discussed insofar as it can be shown to have had an effect on Wittgenstein's thought. The last chapter, in connection with a discussion of Wittgenstein's religious life, will show the apparently dominating influence of Schopenhauer's understanding of the saintly man.

Like Spinoza, Schopenhauer placed *conatus* at the center of his metaphysical system. *Conatus* in Spinoza's system is the creator of existence itself and, if we are to make a moral judgment, we will proclaim it a good. Schopenhauer saw *conatus* as primarily evil because, in its blind striving to become, it frequently creates more ill and pain than good. For Spinoza, salvation is the "intellectual love of God"; for Schopenhauer, since the Will is beyond all intellectual comprehension and yet, by its effects, known to be the occasion of pain, salvation has to come about by the denial of striving and therefore of life. It is obvious that Wittgenstein did not believe it possible to attain to God by intellectual means; it is equally obvious that he did not attribute the existence of the

---

Anscombe, *An Introduction*, 11.

many worlds to the lust of an unknown will. The existence of a world, such as Wittgenstein's or any other man's, is the result of accident. "Alles Geschehen und So-Sein ist zufällig" (6.41). Necessarily, that world disappears equally fortuitously; but as long as that world exists there is a metaphysical 'I-correlate" to the world and bounding it (5.6-5.641, 6.43-6.4311). At death, both the metaphysical "I" and the world cease to be (6.431-6.4312). This understanding of the world and the self is very close to Schopenhauer's; but the purpose of the *Tractatus* is by no means solely religious.

The *Tractatus* demonstrates that there is a basic correlation between all possible worlds (*empirische Realität*) and language, and that by an examination of language we can discover the limits and the minimal structure of any possible world. The fact that there are languages unique to individuals and groups (5.62), as well as common language patterns, accounts both for much of the commonality in our several worlds and for their particular uniqueness. In the *Tractatus* the problem of the One and the Many is solved through an examination of the primary role played by language. Language is the explanation for both the One and the Many; and we need not look for a metaphysical explanation. The issue, however, is not the symbols of the language, which is where Mauthner got lost, but the syntax: the fundamental structures of *language* which demand that once a symbolic system is chosen its implications be carried forward with rigor. The important quotation is almost immediately before the reference to *Realität*:

Es ist klar, wir haben vom Elementarsatz einen Begriff, abgesehen von seiner besonderen logischen Form. Wo man aber Symbole nach einem System bilden kann, dort ist dieses System das logisch wichtige und nicht die einzelnen Symbole. Und wie wäre es auch möglich, dass ich es in der Logik mit Formen zu tun hätte, die ich erfinden kann; sondern mit dem muss ich es zu tun haben, was es mir möglich macht, sie zu erfinden (5.555).

It is equally important that Wittgenstein closes his discussion about solipsism, private worlds, and private languages with his second mention of *Realität*. There is a *Wirklichkeit* which comes into being and passes away in correlation with the extensionless "I" which bounds it. That *Wirklichkeit* or *Welt* and its corresponding "I" arise out of and pass back into the matrix which is *Realität*. The propositions are:

Das hängt damit zusammen, dass kein Teil unserer Erfahrung auch a priori ist. Alles, was wir sehen, könnte auch anders sein. Alles, was wir überhaupt können, könnte auch anders sein. Es gibt keine Ordnung der Dinge a priori (5.634).

Hier sieht man, dass der Solipsismus, streng durchgeführt, mit dem reinen Realismus zusammenfällt. Das Ich des Solipsismus schrumpft zum ausdehnungslosen Punkt zusammen, und es bleibt die ihm koordinierte Realität (5.64).

Obviously, the "coordinated reality" is not all of reality, but only that portion which is coordinated with the "I". Nor can we speak of that reality, which is the "empirical reality" of 5.5561, as having an existence apart from all knowers and actors. It is because of this close connection between men's knowing and acting, on the one hand, and their several worlds, each carved out of *Realität*, on the other, that we can speak of synonymity in language and a correlation between the logic of language and the common logic of the worlds.

A *caveat* must, however, be entered at this point. There is nothing in the *Tractatus* which tells us where the philosophical "I"s come from. They may arise from the matrix, which was suggested above; they may be only points of view; or they may be implanted into the world by *das Höhere*. Finally, they may be aspects of *das Höhere*. Wittgenstein would have regarded the question as unanswerable; therefore, there is no question (6.5).

VII

WITTGENSTEIN AND SCHOPENHAUER

1

Anyone reading through the three volumes of Schopenhauer's *World as Will and Idea* is inevitably struck by the great pessimist's affection for Kant, for Spinoza,[1] for some of the early Christian heretics and for the Vedantists. He expressed an undisguised contempt for most other philosophers and theologians; and this was particularly so with respect to the German idealists who, he felt, had sold out to the Church and to the State for the sake of personal security. If one thought in terms of the facts of experience, he had no choice except to be a pessimist; and anyone who thought otherwise was either not thinking clearly or was a charlatan. Schopenhauer's contempt for Hegel is well-known. His contempt for the Protestant theologian Schleiermacher is less well-known. Schleiermacher, who had translated the Platonic dialogues into German and who occupied the chair of theology at the University of Berlin while serving as chaplain to the King of Prussia, maintained that philosophy is a necessary step on the way toward true religion. In fact, his major work, *The Christian Faith*, is incomprehensible to one who does not have some fairly detailed knowledge of the currents within German thought at the beginning of the nineteenth century. Schopenhauer, while the two of them were at the University of Berlin, is reported to have said to Schleiermacher that a truly religious man needs no philosophy.[2] Whether Schopenhauer

---

[1] Schopenhauer, *The World as Will and Idea*, II, 13n.
[2] Copleston, *A history of Philosophy*, 262.

really understood what Schleiermacher was trying to say is questionable; but there is no question that Schopenhauer had a deep reverence for what he called "a saint", and little patience with anyone who claimed to be religious and at the same time affirmed the world. A saint must be a world denyer; and Schleiermacher certainly did not fit into that category even though he had spoken about our absolute dependence on the infinite totality, on *Natura naturans*.[3] Schopenhauer had as little patience as had Kierkegaard, his contemporary, with academic philosophy or theology.

Chapter V sought to illuminate the *Tractatus* by making comparisons and contrasts with Spinoza's chief works. The last chapter will do the same with Kant and the *Tractatus*. It must be accepted, however, that in each case the comparisons are made on the basis of internal evidence alone. With Schopenhauer the situation is otherwise; in addition to the internal evidence, there is a considerable amount of external evidence that Schopenhauer exercized a great deal of influence on the young Wittgenstein and that this influence continued until Wittgenstein's death. Miss Anscombe's references have already been noted; but Carnap, in his *Autobiography*, is at pains to state that Wittgenstein strongly defended Schopenhauer within the Vienna Circle.[4] Although Schopenhauer was not, himself, a mystic, in the *World as Will and Idea* he speaks most strongly in favor of mysticism as the real answer to the problems of life. Carnap was very conscious of the mystical streak in Wittgenstein.[5] It is possible that Wittgenstein could have obtained his knowledge of Spinoza and Kant from a close reading of Schopenhauer; but it is most unlikely. The coincidences are too striking. What is most likely, as has been mentioned earlier, was that the young Wittgenstein was led by his reading of Schopenhauer, and the generally pessimistic tone of upperclass Viennese life at the turn of the century, to turn to the other philosophers whom Schopenhauer and Nietzsche mentioned,[6] mining them for those argu-

---

3   Copleston, *A History*, 154.

4   In Fann (ed.), *Ludwig Wittgenstein*, 35-36.

5   In Fann (ed.), *Ludwig Wittgenstein*, 38.

6   Erich Heller, "Wittgenstein: Unphilosophical Notes", in Fann (ed.), *Ludwig Wittgenstein*, 89-106.

ments which would aid in his own philosophical and religious development.

It is significant that when we examine the nature of Schopenhauer's influence, we find that Wittgenstein's own writing style betrays nothing of the baroque or the vanity which is so characteristic of Schopenhauer's style. Nor do any of Wittgenstein's works show the repetitiveness which we find in the *World as Will and Idea* or in most of Schopenhauer's mature works. Wittgenstein's writing is compressed, elliptic and parsimonious. On the basis of style alone, and possibly on the basis of tone, one would be more apt to choose Nietzsche than Schopenhauer as mentor.[7] On the whole, the chief influence of Schopenhauer on Wittgenstein seems to have been more emotional than intellectual, and it is probably to Schopenhauer that he owed both his mysticism and his early anti-Christian bias.

Wittgenstein's cynical, anti-Christian, anti-metaphysical temperament in the years immediately before the first World War[8] could have arisen from various experiences other than the reading of Schopenhauer and Nietzsche. The family was nominally Roman Catholic; and there could have been a negative reaction to the Church. There was the anti-metaphysical bias in Mach and others both in and out of the University. His temperament could have resulted from certain problems of psycho-sexual development. We do know that Wittgenstein had a great respect for Otto Weininger[9] who finished his major work on sex and temperament only a few months before his suicide. There is actually no way for us to know what were the determining influences on the young Wittgenstein, although Russell does remark that his student friend was frequently very depressed and that he had not yet firmly fixed his attitude on many things.[10]

Russell was apparently both surprised and disappointed that his

[7] E. Heller in Fann (ed.), *Ludwig Wittgenstein*, 89-106.
[8] Russell, "Ludwig Wittgenstein", in Fann (ed.), *Ludwig Wittgenstein*, 31.
[9] Von Wright, *Biographical Sketch*, 21.
[10] Russell, "Philosophers and Idiots", in Fann (ed.), *Ludwig Wittgenstein*, 31-32.

friend came home from the war a deeply committed Christian.[11] Russell used the word "Christian" with both a lack of precision and a pejorative intent; but it is important to recognize that a radical change did take place in the young Wittgenstein at some time during the war years. The nature of this change will be part of the subject matter of Chapter X. For the moment let us assume that the change occurred as the result of a fundamental reassessment of the nature of the Schopenhauerian Will and Wittgenstein's acceptance of the role of both genius and saint in the Schopenhauerian sense.

Schopenhauer had made an excellent case for the life of genius as the life of a man who not only creates artistic objects but also contemplates the eternal forms (*Gegenstände?*) which are the first objectification of the Will. We know that after Wittgenstein gave up the life of a school teacher he occupied himself both with sculpture and as codesigner of a house for his sister in Vienna.[12] Again, in accordance with the Schopenhauerian definition, he lived, or tried to live, as a saint. He gave away his large fortune at the end of the war and lived thereafter in the most austere manner.[13] Nevertheless, he is a yea sayer rather than a nay sayer.

Schopenhauer's intellectual influence on the young Wittgenstein is most easily detected in those references to solipsism and the will which crowd the last pages of the *Tractatus*; but there is also some influence of Schopenhauer in Wittgenstein's hardheadedness with respect to what may be counted as real. Many have attributed this hard-headedness to the influence of Hume, but Miss Anscombe states that Wittgenstein never read more than a few pages of Hume.[14] Wittgenstein's grounding in the here and now may also be attributable to the influence of Mach, his own studies in engineering, and the war.

Schopenhauer was led to his doctrine of the "world as will and idea" through his study of the Kantian philosophy, his rejection

11 Russell, "Ludwig Wittgenstein", in Fann (ed.), *Ludwig Wittgenstein*, 31.
12 Von Wright, *Biographical Sketch*, 11.
13 Von Wright, *Biographical Sketch*, 10.
14 Anscombe, *An Introduction*, 12.

of the Hegelian attempt to ground the empirically observable world on reason, and his own careful and somewhat pessimistic observations of the world around him. Like Spinoza, he saw the will to exist (*conatus*) not only in all of empirical nature, but even in the realm of the pure Platonic forms which he saw as the patterns of the fundamental forces in the world and, at a higher level, of the species. The patterns and species are represented in any empirical world by an indefinitely large number of individuals whose coming to be and passing away is a matter of indifference to the Will. The doctrine of the forms and the individual (numerically different) exemplifications, although reminiscent of Plato is actually closer to Spinoza's.

The difference between Spinoza and Schopenhauer lies in their respective analyses of the ultimate. For Spinoza, although *Natura naturans* is ceaselessly active, It is active in a totally rational fashion. Schopenhauer also sees ultimate reality as ceaselessly active; but It is active as a blind, irrational Will objectifying Itself, no matter how. The order we see in our worlds is there only because the Will in objectifying Itself necessarily first objectifies Itself in the Platonic forms. Insofar as there is an order in the worlds of the individual knowers, that order is there because of the forms; but the Will is not bound to the forms. The Will brings into being every possibility, and some possibilities are only passing dreams.[15]

Does this argument of Schopenhauer's stand in back of the Tractarian discussion of from? "Nur wenn es Gegenstände gibt, kann es eine feste Form der Welt geben" (2.06). Schopenhauer believed that men necessarily think in terms of sufficient reason; but this is so because such a way of thinking is an accidental character of the human mind. Sufficient reason is not a characteristic of the Will which is beyond all form and all reason (6.41, 6.432). Wittgenstein, in his attempt to make sense of the world, struggles against both Mauthner and Schopenhauer, and possibly Nietzsche. Wittgenstein's discussion of the problem of an ultimate irrationalism may be seen in the following set of propositions:

[15] Schopenhauer, *The World as Will and Idea*, III, 296-298.

Der Gedanke enthält die Möglichkeit der Sachlage, die er denkt. Was denkbar ist, ist auch möglich (3.02).

Wir können nichts Unlogisches denken, weil wir sonst unlogisch denken müssten (3.03).

Man sagte einmal, dass Gott alles schaffen könne, nur nichts, was den logischen Gesetzen zuwider wäre. — Wir könnten nämlich von einer "unlogischen" Welt nicht *sagen*, wie sie aussähe (3.031).

The reference here is to the traditional theology of the Roman Communion which affirms that the essence of God's nature is reason. The major break that Luther made with the medieval Church was at this point. He spoke of "that whore Reason". The criterion by which truth came to be judged in the Reformed tradition is the Bible, an utterance of a God Who in His essence is hidden (*Deus Absconditus*). It is interesting and significant that, in the *Philosophical Investigations*, Wittgenstein repudiated his earlier position, affirming that the question of what is logical and what is not is dependent on the imagination of the thinker.[16] Although his later position was different from the much narrower position of the *Tractatus*, it must not be inferred that the later Wittgenstein had fallen into either irrationalism or empiricism. Rather, he was refining his earlier position and accepting the full consequences of his Schopenhauerian solipsism. There may be other worlds very much unlike the one we apparently share; but it may not be said of such worlds that they are senseless (*unsinnig*). Anticipations of the later point of view are already evident in the two propositions of the *Tractatus* about the lack of a logical necessity for the axiom of reducibility (6.1232, 6.1233). At no time in his life did Wittgenstein choose the irrational empiricism so characteristic of Mauthner's work. In fact, Wittgenstein's life may be seen as one long attempt to recognize the legitimacy of Mauthner's work while drawing a line beyond which Mauthner's conclusions are not valid.

It is obvious that Mach, Mauthner, and Russell are the background against which the propositions which conclude the following paragraph may be thrown. It is Wittgenstein's intent to show that,

---

16 *Philosophical Investigations*, Part II, Section xii, 230.

although there may be an indefinitely large number of elements out of which worlds may be constructed, all worlds demonstrate, to one who looks in the proper mirror, that they have been constructed in terms of one rather than many logics; and that logic may be found hidden within the totality of all languages. It will help our understanding of the *Tractatus* if we can come to think of the work as a great mirror which in itself exists outside of the world and is therefore *unsinnig*. But this mirror is capable of showing us the picture of the world as it is in its ultimate structure. That structure is logic. The key words in the *Tractatus* are "Spiegel" and "Spiegelbild". The mirror is transcendent, and the propositions which make up the mirror are *unsinnig*; but the logic which is revealed by the mirror is only transcendental (6.13).

Except as elements of thought, the elements out of which any particular world is made are also transcendent. We must presume their existence; we cannot demonstrate it (4.2211). We cannot meaningfully discuss their origin or dissolution. In this sense we may compare the elements of *empirische Realität* with *das Höhere*. They are both transcendent and defy any rational explanation for their existence, their quasi-existence or any quality they may be presumed to possess. Nevertheless, we may speak of that which is impossible in the case of the elements. An element, for instance, cannot be of two contrasting colors (4.123, 6.3751). But the impossibility is a matter of thought and not a matter of empirical investigation. The *Gegenstände* of the *Tractatus* correspond to the Platonic forms of the *World as Will and Idea,* even as *das Höhere* corresponds to the Will; but in each case most, if not all, of the meaning (*Bedeutung*) has been eroded away. The propositions referred to here are these:

Etwas "der Logik widersprechendes" in der Sprache darstellen, kann man ebensowenig, wie in der Geometrie eine den Gesetzen des Raumes widersprechende Figur durch ihre Koordinaten darstellen; oder die Koordinaten eines Punktes angeben, welcher nicht existiert (3.032).

Im Satz drückt sich der Gedanke sinnlich wahrnehmbar aus (3.1).

Wir benützen dass sinnlich wahrnehmbare Zeichen (Laut- oder Schriftzeichen etc.) des Satzes als Projektion der möglichen Sachlage.

Die Projektionmethode ist das Denken des Satz-Sinnes (3.11).

Zum Satz gehört alles, was zur Projektion gehört; aber nicht das Projizierte. Also die Möglichkeit des Projizierten, aber nicht diese selbst. Im Satz ist also sein Sinn noch nicht enthalten, wohl aber die Möglichkeit ihn auszudrücken. ("Der Inhalt des Satzes" heisst der Inhalt des sinnvollen Satzes.) Im Satz ist die Form seines Sinnes enthalten, aber nicht dessen Inhalt (3.13).

Das Satzzeichen besteht darin, dass sich seine Elemente, die Wörter, in ihm auf bestimmte Art und Weise zu einander verhalten. Das Satzzeichen ist eine Tatsache (3.14).

Nur Tatsachen können einen Sinn ausdrücken, eine Klasse von Namen kann es nicht (3.142).

Although the argument of these propositions is primarily against Mauthner, it must be noted that Wittgenstein is also rejecting the extreme position of Mach and the set and class theory of Russell. Language is the *Logos*; and the *Logos* can be trusted to create worlds which are empirically grounded and which are not irrational. If there is such a Will as Schopenhauer attempts to prove, that Will is not open to the inspection of speaking beings. Nor is the will as ethical subject open to empirical investigation (6.423, 6.43).

2

Several pages above, it was brought out that Schopenhauer developed his doctrine of the Will through an observation of the world, a rejection of ontological reason, and a study of the Kantian philosophy — to which he believed himself to be the true heir. Kant's *Ding-an-sich* became, in Schopenhauer's system, the Will randomly creating a plenitude of worlds, some of which were correlates to human centers of consciousness: "I"s. For Schopenhauer, the commonality of the many human worlds was obtained by the fact that all human minds function in terms of the "Fourfold Root of the Principle of Sufficient Reason": Kant's category of causality in its several manifestations in the human world. For Schopenhauer, the principle of individuation is the human under-

standing of space-time; the Will itself knows no principle of individuation and is completely indifferent to the numerically different
worlds which exemplify the same kind of world. Is it not this view
which stands in back of 6.432: "Wie die Welt ist, ist für das Höhere
vollkommen gleichgültig. Gott offenbart sich nicht *in* der Welt"?
In this case, however, Wittgenstein elevates the Will to the status
of *das Höhere*. In addition, as the second sentence reads, *das Höhere* does not reveal itself in the world. *Das Höhere*, unlike the
Will, cannot be discovered either by introspection or by empirical
investigation and hypothesis. Schopenhauer claimed that the Will
could be so discovered if we would only really look; although the
Will is actually revealed only in an a posteriori investigation of our
own acts and their meaning,[17] and in the study of the world of
our experience.[18] Although we shall return to the problem of individuation in the last chapter, it is important to note that, for Schopenhauer, numerical distinction is not in fact a distinction.[19] But
Schopenhauer did hold out hope for the Saint, as a numerically distinct member of the human species, finally becoming *sui generis:*
a species unique from all others.[20] To a lesser extent this is also
true of the man of genius, but only when he is functioning as a
genius;[21] at other times he falls back into the generality of the
species. It is interesting that Kierkegaard, a contemporary of Schopenhauer's, could have come to much the same conclusion. In *Fear
and Trembling*, particularly, Kierkegaard points out that he who is
able to suspend the ethical in a religious manner becomes something different from all other men: an individual. Against the
Schopenhauerian and Kierkegaardian thought we must place Wittgenstein's outer boundaries: contradiction and tautology, and his
formula for the general proposition. There cannot be any objects
or worlds which evade these limitations, at least in terms of the way
men think and talk; and we cannot escape the fact that we are
human beings. How animals talk is unknown, but lions cannot talk

---

17 Schopenhauer, *The World as Will and Idea*, 390-395.
18 Schopenhauer, *The World as Will and Idea*, 390-395.
19 Schopenhauer, *The World as Will and Idea*, III, 298.
20 Schopenhauer, *The World as Will and Idea*, I, Sec. 71.
21 Schopenhauer, *The World as Will and Idea*, III, 144.

to us, unless they become human beings; and gods cannot understand us, unless we speak and they are able to hear us.[22] Schopenhauer's intellectual influence on the *Tractatus* shows up at a number of places. The doctrine of atomism with its genera of logical, colored, temporal, and spatial atoms has its roots in *The World as Will and Idea* (Book I). Wittgenstein's use of *Wirklichkeit*, in contrast to *Realität*, as an expression for the activity of material bodies in an individual world goes back to the *Four-Fold Root of the Principle of Sufficient Reason* (Section 21). The propositions beginning with 5.62, where Wittgenstein talks about solipsism and realism, and ending with 5.64, where he distinguishes between the phenomenal and the philosophical "I", are pure Schopenhauer. Again at 6.1233, Wittgenstein suggests the likelihood of many worlds. The proposition reads:

Es lässt sich eine Welt denken, in der das Axiom of Reducibility nicht gilt. Es ist aber klar, dass die Logik nichts mit der Frage zu schaffen hat, ob unsere Welt wirklich so ist oder nicht.

Again at 6.34, although Wittgenstein appears to be talking about the propositions of the natural sciences, it is the many, possible Schopenhauerian, worlds that provide the background for the statement. But, in terms of the logic of the *Tractatus*, although not that of *Philosophical Investigations*. Wittgenstein has proved that there are boundaries — contradiction and tautology — for all possible worlds, and that any possible object, or world, must have the structure described by the general proposition. The proposition reads:

Alle jene Sätze, wie der Satz vom Grunde [the principle of sufficient reason], von der Kontinuität in der Natur, vom kleinsten Aufwande in der Natur, etc., etc., alle diese sind Einsichten a priori über die mögliche Formgebung der Sätze der Wissenschaft.

The sentences of the sciences are themselves only linquistic tools reflecting the logical character the world must have for us (6.3, 6.32). For Wittgenstein's own system, at least when he published the *Tractatus*, it is important to recognize that he believed that only

22 *Philosophical Investigations*, Part II, xi, 217, 223.

elementary sentences or propositions have ontological validity. Complex or compound propositions, if they are true, have their ultimate roots in the elementary propositions which make them up; but complex propositions, before analysis, as for example through the truth-tables, are only linguistic symbols without necessary ontological reference.

Ist der Elementarsatz wahr, so besteht der Sachverhalt; ist der Elementarsatz falsch, so besteht der Sachverhalt nicht (4.25).

Es ist klar, wir haben vom Elementarsatz einen Begriff, abgesehen von seiner besonderen logischen Form. Wo man aber Symbole nach einem System bilden kann, dort ist dieses System das logisch wichtige und nicht die einzelnen Symbole (5.555).

Eine Hierarchie der Formen der Elementarsätze kann es nicht geben. Nur was wir selbst konstruieren, können wir voraussehen (5.556).

Die empirische Realität ist begrenzt durch die Gesamtheit der Gegenstände. Die Grenze zeigt sich wieder in der Gesamtheit der Elementarsätze. Die Hierarchien *sind,* und müssen unabhängig von der Realität sein (5.5561).   [Italics added.]

Wissen wir aus rein logischen Gründen, dass es Elementarsätze gebe, dann muss es jeder wissen, der die Sätze in ihrer unanalysierten Form versteht (5.5562).

It is difficult to see how anyone reading these statements could insist that Wittgenstein was an empiricist. Elementary propositions are a necessary consequence of logical rather than empirical analysis. We can, however, determine certain empirical matters from this analysis if we can demonstrate the logical impossibility of certain states of affairs (4.123, 6.3751). Perhaps it is this knowledge which stands in back of Wittgenstein's assertion that positive knowledge can come even through false propositions (4.023). Finally, causality, for Wittgenstein, is not so much a structure of the knowing mind (as it was for Schopenhauer) as a structure of language.

Was sich beschreiben lässt, das kann auch geschehen, und was das Kausalitätsgesetz auschliessen soll, das lässt sich auch nicht beschreiben (6.362).

Einen Kausalnexus . . . gibt es nicht (5.136).

3

Wittgenstein rejects both the Kantian statement of the categories and the Schopenhauerian canon of sufficient reason. The *Tractatus* may be thought of as an attempt to establish a new canon of reason on a minimal basis. At first sight, as many have assumed, Wittgenstein seems to have grounded his canon on Hume, but our investigation has already shown that Hume is irrelevant to the *Tractatus*. Wittgenstein is saying both more and less than Hume. The objects of the world are both empirically real and transcendentally ideal; language (logic) ties the objects together into chains or facts, and it is the facts so arrived at that give me and others like me a world or a congeries of similar worlds. There is, however, nothing in the external world which justifies my assuming that one state of affairs will necessarily follow from another (5.132-5.141, 6.36311-6.37). "Der Glaube an den Kausalnexus ist der *Aberglaube*" (5.1361). Lord Russell's elucidation of Wittgenstein's attack on the causal nexus is illuminating. His attack is justified because all propositions are constructions from elementary propositions, tautologies or contradictions. Nothing may be deduced from elementary propositions because they are independent of each other (2.061, 3.21, 5.134); and from a tautology only a tautology may be derived; from a contradiction, anything may be derived.

There cannot, in Wittgenstein's logic, be any such thing as a casual nexus. "The events of the future", he says, "cannot be inferred from those of the present. Superstition is the belief in the casual nexus". That the sun will rise tomorrow is a hypothesis. We do not in fact know whether it will rise, since there is no compulsion according to which one thing must happen because another happens.[23]

Wittgenstein states that logical research is no more than the investigation of *all regularity* and that outside of logic all is accidental. Existence itself is accidental (6.3, 5.552).

Wittgenstein does not attempt to tell us why there is a world. In fact, his effort is spent in telling us that this is an illegitimate ques-

---

[23] Bertrand Russell's original "Introduction", to Wittgenstein's *Tractatus Logico-Philosophicus* (1922), 15, 16.

tion. All he is prepared to grant is that if there is to be a world, that world must conform to the general proposition. In such a world "only *lawful* connections are thinkable" (6.361). Using the traditional school logic we find that the sentence converts to "all thinkable connections are lawful". Mauthner would have had no difficulty in making that statement. Frege and Russell could not have made it; it is very doubtful if Kant would have felt easy with it; but Schopenhauer would have been in agreement with Wittgenstein.

The influence of Schopenhauer can be seen at 6.373 also; but at this place Wittgenstein is distinguishing his position from Schopenhauer's. For Schopenhauer, the ultimate was the Will. The Will in its metaphenomenal fecundity creates all things, including the worlds; and the Will expresses itself in the several subjects that are correlates to those worlds. There is only one Will, but its phenomenal expression is significantly varied because of the worlds correlated with it which, for all practical purposes, make It into many wills. We can thus say that even as there are inevitably all kinds of worlds, there are all kinds of will correlated to those worlds. Nevertheless, at 6.373 Wittgenstein says, "Die Welt is unabhängig von meinem Willen". In other words, I do not sense any necessary relation between the world as I experience it and the world as it is. My own willing, insofar as I am a metaphysical "I", cannot change the facts of the world (6.4321). As an empirical ego I am a part of the world (6.423). The facts of the world are ultimately grounded in *empirische Realität*. At best they represent a task (6.4321). It all sounds much like the ancient heresies, the Gnostics, in which there is a *psyche* implanted or fallen into the world from on high.

There is an ambiguity in the last pages of the *Tractatus*. Wittgenstein had stated that his theory of language had done away with monism, dualism, and pluralism (4.128); yet his doctrine of the soul and of the Mystical, on the one hand, and his doctrine of empirical reality, on the other, imply a most radical dualism. However, he is consistent at this point: before both the mystical and the empirical reality one must be silent. They are each beyond the possibilities of being talked about. We can live out our lives only in the middle ranges, although we may have intimations of something beyond which is also the source of the ethical and the esthetic (6.41-6.422). Several quotations from the last pages of the *Tractatus* will support the short summary statement which thus argues for a radical dualism in the *Tractatus*.

Wenn das gute oder böse Wollen die Welt ändert, so kann es nur die Grenzen der Welt ändern, nicht die Tatsachen; nicht das, was durch die Sprache ausgedrückt werden kann (6.43).

Die Tatsachen gehören alle nur zur Aufgabe, nicht zur Lösung (6.4321).

Wir fühlen, dass selbst, wenn alle *möglichen* wissenschaftlichen Fragen beantwortet sind, unsere Lebensprobleme noch gar nicht berührt sind. Freilich bleibt dann eben keine Frage mehr; und eben dies ist die Antwort (6.52).

Die Lösung des Problems des Lebens merkt man am Verschwinden dieses Problems (6.521).

Es gibt allerdings Unaussprechliches. Dies zeigt sich, es ist das Mystische (6.522).

But, surely, the unspeakable is equally true of *empirische Realität*. We can, like Rilke, explore into both "empirical Reality" and *das Höhere*, but our explorations are connotative at best.

The *Tractatus*, at least during the early portions where the author talks of objects, things, and states of affairs, appears to be speaking denotatively. What Wittgenstein is actually doing, however, is showing that denotation has an ultimate arbitrariness within its procedures. All we can, in fact, do, is explore syntax and establish a congeries of arbitrary symbols. But, having created our symbols, logic requires that they be manipulated in a certain way. The fact that there seems to be a correlation between the way in which the symbols are manipulated and the way in which the empirical world goes indicates that we have here a clue about the world. But logic is not the structure of the world. The crucial proposition is 5.557:

Die *Anwendung* der Logik entscheidet darüber, welche Elementarsätze es gibt. Was in der Anwendung liegt, kann die Logik nicht vorausnehmen. Das ist klar: Die Logik darf mit ihrer Anwendung nicht kollidieren. Aber die Logik muss sich mit ihrer Anwendung berühren. Also durfen die Logik und ihre Anwendung einander nicht übergreifen.

Logic is not the structure of the world, but, in a persistent figure (3.42, 4.023, 6.124), Wittgenstein says that logic is the scaffolding of the world. Logic is prior to the world (5.552). It is necessary that there be logic if there is to be a world for human beings (the form of any object whatsoever), but we cannot go from logic to the world in any Platonic or Aristotelian fashion. "Nicht nur muss ein Satz der Logik durch keine mögliche Erfahrung widerlegt werden können, sondern er darf auch nicht durch eine solche bestätigt werden können" (6.1222). Our best figure, however, is to suggest that logic and language are mirror-images of the world. "Die Logik ist keine Lehre, sondern ein Spiegelbild der Welt" (6.13). This was also a famous Gnostic figure.[24]

---

[24] Gnosticism took many forms during the lower Roman Empire. A work which had a tremendous influence during the Middle Ages and the Renaissance and even appealed to Leibnitz was Martianus Capella's *De Nuptiis Philologiae et Mercurii*. In a volume entitled *De Nuptiis Philologiae et Mercurii: A Literary Re-evaluation* (to be published by The Medieval and Renaissance Institute, (Munich) (*Muenchner Beiträge zur Mediavitik-und-Renaissance Forschung*), Professor F. J. LeMoine of the University of Wisconsin examines in considerable detail the use of language in mirroring the world. Significantly, the maiden *Philologiae* (Language) as she prepares for her marriage with Mercury, the Egyptian *Thoth*, finds it necessary to go to the limits of the world, there to encounter *Ignotus Pater*. Surely this is the equivalent of Proposition Seven.

VIII

THE ANAGOGIC THEOLOGY
OF THE *TRACTATUS*

1

The title of this essay is *The Anagogic Theory of Wittgenstein's 'Tractatus'*. The use of the unfamiliar word is to point to the fact that the *Tractatus* itself is not a saying but a showing or a pointing, a fact which Russell completely missed in his "Introduction". During the Middle Ages certain words came to describe ways in which literary works were to be studied and understood. At the lowest level, the level of immediate experience, texts are to be taken literally. It is only at this level that we can understand a work as a "saying". At all of the other levels of interpretation, the text is a "showing". The second level of interpretation is the "allegorical". The text stands in a one-to-one relation with that which is being described. In English, our best example of an allegorical work would probably be *Pilgrim's Progress*. At the third level, the tropological, the intent of the text is to convey a moral message. Most New Testament parables are to be read tropologically rather than allegorically, although some of the described visions, such as those in the Apocalypse, must be read anagogically. To read them otherwise is to destroy both the author's intent and the meaning of the passage.

At the anagogic level, the literary work becomes a great poem creating and sustaining a world which is peopled and structured by the poet's imagination. Yet this new world is not cut off from the world in which the poet lives. Rather, the anagogic piece of literature points beyond itself to things in the world which otherwise might not be seen if the poet had not written. In antiquity, Virgil's *Aeneid* is probably the best example of an anagogic work. Commissioned by Augustus, it was an attempt to show the inner heart of Roman history and to provide a base on which that history could go forward. Dante's *Divine Comedy* is an anagogical way of talking about the world which Saint Thomas attempted to describe in his theology. Milton's attempt to justify the ways of God in his dealings with men is almost as great an achievement. In each of these three examples, the poet is attempting to point out that there is an order in the world which makes sense; but the poet is pointing to this order in an oblique way. If his poem were taken literally, it would collapse from internal inconsistencies; but he who is able to read the poem anagogically may find a way to see the world aright.

It is not the intent of this essay to suggest that Wittgenstein was a poet and that the *Tractatus* is a poem. Nevertheless, as Wittgenstein pointed out in the Preface, the *Tractatus* was not intended as a textbook in logic or to correct some trifling errors in Frege and Russell. Rather, as Engelmann points out in his *Memoir*, the *Tractatus* is an attempt to place a boundary around the "sayable" and to point beyond the "sayable" to that which is really important.[1] Normally, what Wittgenstein was attempting to do in the *Tractatus* would have been done by a poet; but by the beginning of the twentieth century all of the categories of literary expression had become very much confused: poets and theologians spoke about the "unsayable" in literal language; and scientists attempted to extrapolate from their experiments to the whole of the universe, an equally illegitimate enterprize. It is true, however, that at least three of the twentieth century poets, Yeats, Eliot, and Rilke, have chosen to speak poetically about the "unsayable". Each was tremendously influenced by the French symbolists; and none of them can be understood if their language is read in the literal fashion of the scientist.

Wittgenstein chose a different task than the poets: to explore the

---

[1] Engelmann, *Letters*, 143.

"sayable" so that those who wished to go beyond would have some rules as to the nature of coherence. The issues can be set out in a spatial metaphor: only over the middle ranges, between "das Höhere" and "empirische Realität" is it possible to *say*. All else must be *shown*, and only he who can understand poetry can understand what it means to talk anagogically. He who cannot understand is either a philistine or a barbarian. An illuminating remark of the later Wittgenstein illustrates this point: "About a don who criticized Blake he said, 'He can't understand philosophy; how could you expect him to understand a thing like poetry?' "[2] As he wrote the *Tractatus*, Wittgenstein was undoubtedly aware that at the highest level of *das Höhere* only the *via negativa* was usable in the exploration of the real; but there seems little question that he felt the mythopoetic was legitimate for the lower slopes of Mount Carmel. The danger, of which we have been made aware by the *Tractatus* (and works inspired by the *Tractatus*), is that we reify our poetic figures and try to say what is not "sayable". The anagogic always points beyond itself. Unlike the literal, it is never a depiction.

2

There are many ways in which things and ideas may be shown and not said. Wittgenstein, himself, records that the rigid distinction he made in the *Tractatus* between saying and showing was broken up, at least partially, by the vulgar Neapolitan gesture of Professor Piero Sraffa, a colleague at Cambridge.[3] The whole of *Philosophical Investigations* is an endeavor to come to grips with the fact that the boundaries between "showing" and "saying" are not as precise as Wittgenstein leads us to believe in the *Tractatus*. Nevertheless, if we look at Wittgenstein's life from about the middle of World War I and pursue the correspondence between him and Engelmann and read the notebooks from that period, we become aware

---

[2] D. A. T. Gasking and A. C. Jackson, "Wittgenstein as a teacher", in Fann (ed.), *Ludwig Wittgenstein*, 55.
[3] Fann, *Wittgenstein's Conception of Philosophy*, 48.

that his life itself was a showing forth of a deep religious experience which he had sometime during the war years.

Earlier in the essay it was pointed out that Rilke was forced at one point in his early manhood to make a choice between being a man who wrote poetry or being a poet. Wittgenstein did not have to make this choice, but, apparently, he was confronted with the necessity of choosing to be a religious man or continuing to be a man who was at times religious. The evidence seems to point to the fact that at some time in 1916 he made the choice to become a religious man. Russell saw the change as that of one who moved from being anti-Christian to Christian. Von Wright reports:

The period of the war was a crisis in Wittgenstein's life. To what extent the turmoil of the time and his experiences in war and captivity contributed to the crisis, I cannot say. A circumstance of great importance was that he became acquainted with the ethical and religious writings of Tolstoy. Tolstoy exercised a strong influence on Wittgenstein's view of life, and also led him to study the Gospels.[4]

We know that in later life Wittgenstein's favorite philosopher was Søren Kierkegaard,[5] and, surely, there is some similarity in Kierkegaard's custom of approaching life's problem obliquely by the use of pseudonyms and Wittgenstein's distinction between the "sayable" and the "showable". Kierkegaard also made his life a showing, as did Pascal and Augustine, all men whom Wittgenstein admired.[6]

Wittgenstein was interested in the same kind of problems with which the existentialist writers were concerned, and it was the great existentialists of earlier periods whom he read in preference to more formal philosophy; but he was a logician and not an existentialist. Insofar as the existentialists showed him something, he was interested in looking; he had problems when they tried to say something: "Was gezeigt werden *kann, kann nicht* gesagt werden" (4.1212). Philosophy's job is to make clear thoughts which otherwise are blurred (4.122), but in doing so philosophy points beyond itself

4 Von Wright, *Biographical Sketch*, 9, 10.
5 M. O'C. Drury, "A Symposium", in Fann (ed.), *Ludwig Wittgenstein*, 70.
6 Von Wright, *Biographical Sketch*, 21.

to the "unspeakable" (4.115). It is in this sense that we can speak of the *Tractatus* as an anagogic document. It points beyond itself to that which in itself is the inexpressible. "Es gibt allerdings Unaussprechliches. Dies *zeigt* sich, es ist das Mystische" (6.522). In a conversation with Drury, Wittgenstein summed up his own life by means of a quotation from Bach which appears on the title page of the latter's *Little Organ Book*: "To the glory of the most high God, and that my neighbor may be benefited thereby." Pointing to his own pile of manuscript, Wittgenstein said "That is what I would like to have been able to say about my own work." Drury felt that this wish must have been granted to Wittgenstein because "he made wonder secure".[7] The pretensions of a rationalist explanation of the world were thoroughly undermined (6.37-6.372).

It would be possible to multiply many incidents which showed Wittgenstein as a deeply religious and philosophical man. Rudolph Carnap reports that even in his conversations with the Vienna Circle Wittgenstein frequently appeared to be a seer or a mystic, one deriving his answers from some higher sphere.[8] It is consistent with the view here expressed that Wittgenstein gave away his large fortune at the end of the war[9] and that he lived out the balance of his life as austerely as possible.[10] Malcolm reports that "what made him an awesome and even terrible person, both as a teacher and in personal relationships, was his ruthless integrity, which did not spare himself or anyone else".[11] The English philosopher Stephen Toulmin has attempted to demonstrate that it is impossible to separate Wittgenstein the philosopher from Wittgenstein the man.[12] He further states that if we consider Wittgenstein's statements against the background of his person, we will come to the necessary conclusion that most of that which has been ascribed to Wittgenstein is simply not the case. Toulmin states:

---

[7]   Drury, "A Symposium", 71.
[8]   Carnap, "Autobiography", Fann (ed.), *Ludwig Wittgenstein*, 37.
[9]   Von Wright, *Biographical Sketch*, 10.
[10]   Von Wright, *Biographical Sketch*, 10.
[11]   Malcolm, *Ludwig Wittgenstein*, 27.
[12]   Stephen Edelston Toulmin, "Ludwig Wittgenstein", *Encounter* XXII (January 1969), 58-71.

(1) Wittgenstein was never a positivist.
(2) He was never deeply concerned with epistemology.
(3) He was not a linguistic philosopher.
(4) There were not "two Wittgensteins", having different philo-
     sophical questions and concerns — the author of the *Tractatus*
     and the author of the *Investigations*.
(5) There were not even two distinct Wittgensteins — one the tech-
     nical philosopher, the other the "thinker".

Toulmin summarized Wittgenstein's attitude toward metaphysics
in this way:

> Wittgenstein's opposition to metaphysics had a great deal in com-
> mon with Schopenhauer's, and nothing at all with Comte's. For him,
> the word "metaphysics" was no blanket term of denunciation, to be
> used cavalierly to sweep aside whatever was not "meaningful", or
> "factually verifiable", as of no importance. Rather, he used the word
> in a highly specific sense — to designate the kind of philosophical dis-
> cussion which "obliterates the distinction between (i.e., confuses) fac-
> tual and conceptual investigations".

In his most interesting article Toulmin is concerned to point out
that there is a continuity which ran from Kant through Schopenhauer to Wittgenstein. There is an implicit linguistic concern in
Kant which became more open in Schopenhauer; and Wittgenstein's
overwhelming concern for language reveals a deep concern for the
transcendental tasks which were the concern of his predecessors.

   In the preceding chapter it was suggested that Schopenhauer's influence on the young Wittgenstein was more emotional than intellectual. Had there been a significant intellectual influence, Wittgenstein's own literary style would have been different — more
ornate, more diffuse. But anyone reading the great pessimist with
the concentration which we know Wittgenstein possessed must have
been influenced and impressed in the deeper reaches of his own
being. Schopenhauer's ethical theory is very far from any form of
eudemonism or utilitarianism; but it is equally far from the ethics
of prudence or the categorical imperative. Schopenhauer claimed
that most of us are under the domain of selfish lust and that there
is no relief from an eternal round of births and rebirths, untold
suffering, until we realize that the sufferer and he who causes the

suffering are, in fact, identical. If there is to be an ethics at all, ethics must be grounded on the principle of sympathy (*Mitleid*) and austerity and, at its highest levels, on the calm acceptance of apparent nullity (*nirvana*) as the only meaningful completion of our lives.

The emotional appeal of Schopenhauer's ethical system is very great; and it must have been particularly great for a young man caught up in the agony of the mindless fury of trench warfare in World War I. Surely, if there was ever an experience of helplessness before large, mindless forces, the men of World War I experienced it. Before such forces, one can run; but that is to convict oneself of cowardice and a lack of a sense of duty to one's fatherland. In any event, the likelihood of being shot is almost complete. One can do one's duty; but what is one's duty in the midst of a pandemonium? All that is left, if one wants to live morally at all, is to make the little world around oneself somewhat better for one's being there. Engelmann tells us that Wittgenstein had the reputation of being a *guter Kamerad*.[13] Sympathy becomes the only source of ethical action because everything else is a "tale told by an idiot, full of sound and fury, signifying nothing". Sympathy, as the ground and source of ethical action is Schopenhauer's position as well as the position of the New Testament; and it is even more the position of Hinduism and Mahayana Buddhism. Sympathy was also the position which Tolstoy accepted for himself toward the end of his life; and we know that Wittgenstein, quite by accident, discovered Tolstoy in 1916 in eastern Moravia.[14] Schopenhauer uses the word "Mitleid"[15] rather than the more common German words for sympathy which accent feeling. Tolstoy would have spoken similarly in Russian when he gave up his estate and began to live as a member of a peasant community, a *sobernost*. "Mitleid" is removed as far as possible from the sentimental overtones which accompany all of the western European tongues when they speak of "sympathy".

13   Engelmann, *Letters*, 142.
14   Von Wright, Biographical Sketch, 9.
15   Schopenhauer, *The World as Will and Idea*, 485.

A minor thesis of this essay is that Wittgenstein made a decision for sainthood (as Schopenhauer defines the term) sometime in the middle of World War I. It is impossible, however, to say that he made such a decision since we have no letters or other written works which point to such a decision; but it is not a decision which one could announce for the very fact of announcing would be a denial. Rather, the decision to be a saint is a decision which would have to be lived out; and one's own life would be a testimonial both to the decision and to the completeness with which one had carried through with the decision. Later, in Chapter X, when we discuss the relation between Engelmann and Wittgenstein, we shall find it necessary to return to this question. At this moment let us treat the question of sainthood as a surmise, knowing that Wittgenstein, if he had made such a decision, did not attain to sainthood. His relations with other human beings were too "touchy". Nevertheless, in one of his letters to Malcolm, who was then teaching at Princeton, he talks about the great need for people to "live quietly, in a sense, and be in a position to be kind and *understanding* to all sorts of human beings who *need* it".[16] This is a truly Schopenhauerian statement. In sum, Wittgenstein seems to have achieved a Schopenhauerian view of the world during World War I, but was never able to convert the decision into the total acquiescence in the world's sorrows which both Schopenhauer and the New Testament demand.

3

In the first three chapters of this essay it was shown that, although many scholars have studied the *Tractatus*, each has come up with a different interpretation. Conceivably, there may be some truth in each interpretation; but, in concluding his review of Anscombe's *Introduction*, Plochman said that the "key to the *Tractatus* had not been found".[17] Perhaps there is no one key, but several, and the

---

[16] Malcolm, *Ludwig Wittgenstein*, 37.
[17] Plochmann, "Review", 246.

Tractatus is not the unified whole which its author believed it to be when he established his decimal notation. Surely, this lack of unity is a major claim of those who seek to find a riddle in the *Tractatus* or who claim that the present order has been artificially imposed on a number of aphorisms written at different times. Perhaps again, the *Tractatus* is a literary work, like some kinds of great poetry, that has a truth at several levels of interpretation which, though consistent, are distinct from each other. Perhaps also, there is a key to the *Tractatus,* but those who have looked have not looked for it in the right places or from the right perspective. It is the contention of this essay that the *Tractatus* is, as its author claimed in his letter to Ficker, a literary work in which the secret of its construction is to be found in the Preface and the conclusion.[18] As an anagogic work, the *Tractatus* points beyond itself to the real truth of the universe, but if we are to see the blinding truth of the universe, it is necessary that we go through the process of considering and dismissing all other claims to Truth. "Meine Sätze . . . als unsinnig erkennt . . . wenn er . . . über sie hinausgestiegen ist" (6.54).

When one comes across this phrase toward the end of the *Tractatus*, if one has done anything other than glance at the preceding arguments and aphorisms, one is shocked. The *Tractatus* has obviously said a great deal; yet its author now claims that the propositions are *unsinnig*. Does he mean for us to dismiss his book as some sort of bad dream? Hardly. Yet, if this is not to be the case, what must we make of this book, its propositions and its aphorisms? The crucial word is "hinaussteigen". We must, by the use of the propositions and aphorisms, climb completely out of the world of ordinary discourse. Only from this vantage point outside of the world can we see the world aright; but we are no longer in the world when we can see the world aright; and the world's languages no longer apply to what we do see. We must be silent and contemplate, although we may, at a later time, act in accordance with the vision which we have experienced. We may be able to show

18 Engelmann, *Letters*, 143-44.

by our actions something of what we have experienced; but we can never "say". The figure is not new with the *Tractatus*. We find the figure in that of the charioteer in Plato's *Phaedrus;* and it appears constantly in both the Christian and Gnostic literature of the late Roman Empire: one climbs the "steep ascent of Heaven" and on, through "the Heavenly spheres", until one is caught up in the blinding awareness of that which is "unspeakable". The world depicted in the *Tractatus* is itself transcendental to the world of our daily experience; and the *Tractatus* points beyond itself to that which is purely transcendent. The *Tractatus* points to "the beyond"; it does not tell us what the beyond is like. In fact, the *Tractatus* claims that it is impossible to tell what the beyond is like. In this sense, the *Tractatus* is an exercise in "revisionary metaphysics" — to use Strawson's phrase.[19]

The relation between Wittgenstein and Kant will be explored in Chapter X. At this point, the reader is cautioned on the distinction which Kant made between the transcendental and the transcendent. Wittgenstein uses these two words in the Kantian sense. Logic and mathematics are transcendental disciplines for Wittgenstein even as they were for Kant; and, with Kant, Wittgenstein rejects the possibility of talking about the ideas of the reason as if they referred to actual entities. The actual entities, if they do exist, would be transcendent. Wittgenstein's intent is to say that we must be silent before any experience of transcendence. To attempt to talk about the transcendent, even in a negative way, as Kant does, is to be incoherent; but to talk about the transcendental is not so much to be incoherent (*unsinnig*) as to talk about entities that do not exist (*sinnlos*). A great portion of the *Tractatus* is concerned to talk about that which is *sinnlos,* but not necessarily incoherent. That which is *sinnlos* exists in language; it does not have an external correlate. The distinction between *sinnlos* and *unsinnig* must be maintained if the *Tractatus* is to make sense.

Max Black's *Companion to the Tractatus* is as invaluable for the study of the *Tractatus* as is a concordance for the study of a biblical

---

[19] Quoted in Black, *A Companion*, 386.

text. The book stands within the traditional way of understanding the *Tractatus*; and it is obviously a labor of love and a labor of deep and wide-ranging scholarship. Yet, from the point of view of this essay, the *Companion*, like Miss Anscombe's *Introduction*, lacks a unity and imposes that lack of unity on the *Tractatus* itself. The failure is owing to the fact that Professor Black is unable to see that the *Tractatus* is pointing beyond itself to some wordless faith, the thesis of this essay. It is not that Professor Black does not try, for he tries very hard. Yet there is a deep blindness, as for instance when he conflates *Wirklichkeit* and *Realität* in his glossary, as if Wittgenstein's use of *Realität* in only two places in the *Tractatus* was the result of arbitrary choice and had no relevance beyond that. Nevertheless, Black sees the *Tractatus* as doing a necessary job of language clarification by pressing so hard against the limits of language that we finally know that nothing of any further value may be found either by pressing harder or by twisting words to any further use. In the essay's first chapter, it was suggested that this job was primarily a poet's. Black thinks that the job is one for a logician. It is the contention of this essay that the two jobs, that of the poet and that of the logician, are actually inseparable. Much poetry is gibberish; but a good poet knows logic both in its intensional and extensional senses. That is part of the reason why his work is good poetry. Lewis Carroll, although not a great poet, knew what he was doing from a logical point of view. He illustrated much of his logic with his poetry. To paraphrase: in the *Tractatus* and in his life Wittgenstein was trying to make the world safe for poetry.

Black is honest. Like Maslow,[20] Stenius,[21] and Pitcher,[22] he has no hesitancy in admitting that there are many sentences in the *Tractatus* which he does not understand; and he methodically and exhaustively explores every possibility which is within his own

[20] Alexander Maslow, *A Study in Wittgenstein's 'Tractatus'* (Berkeley: University of California Press, 1961).

[21] Erik Stenius, *Wittgenstein's Tractatus: A Critical Exposition of Its Main Lines of Thought* (Oxford University Press, 1960).

[22] George Pitcher, *The Philosophy of Wittgenstein* (Englewood Cliffs, N.J.: Prentice-Hall, 1964).

frame of reference. Black's sympathy with what he believed Wittgenstein was trying to do is shown in the following quotations:

No philosophical classic is harder to master. According to Wittgenstein himself, it was misundertood by Russell, Moore and Frege; and even Ramsey, whose critical notice in *Mind* is the best short study of the text, sometimes went badly astray. . . . A serious reader must labour strenuously to reconstruct Wittgenstein's thoughts from cryptic and elliptical suggestions, getting what help he can from a succession of images that dazzle as much as they illuminate.[23]

The major difference between Black's thesis as to the meaning of the *Tractatus* and that of this essay is that Black sees the young Wittgenstein being driven by certain "fundamental questions in the philosophy of logic and mathematics",[24] whereas the theory here presented is that Wittgenstein, although concerned with logical problems, was driven more by a transcendent faith than the problems of logic. Black, of course, is aware of the fact that Wittgenstein held very strongly to the belief that logic is a basis for metaphysics and that logic is important because it leads to metaphysics. For Wittgenstein this was necessarily so; for, his nature being what it was, he needed a tool which would enable him and others so minded, to separate sense from nonsense. His studies in logic enabled him to see that there was some nonsense in Russell and Frege, as for example in the axioms of reducibility and infinity (5.535, 6.1232, 6.1233); and we know that at the end of his life he found a great deal of nonsense in the reified myths of the Church of his baptism.[25] In a very real sense, as both Stenius and Black point out, Wittgenstein is a Kantian philosopher attempting a century and a half after Kant to determine how knowledge is possible, what are its grounds and limits, and what must be left to faith, even a wordless faith.

In his study of language, to which Mauthner's *Beiträge* must always be remembered as a foil, Wittgenstein found the key to his solution of the Kantian questions. Black's peculiar importance is

23   Black, *A Companion*, 1-2.
24   Black, *A Companion*, 3.
25   Malcolm, *Ludwig Wittgenstein*, 72.

that he recognized Wittgenstein's starting place as language. Miss Anscombe's failure to recognize this fact is her most fundamental error. Black writes:

Truths of logic can be certified "from the symbol alone" — here there is an important shift of interest from thought to language. Any number of philosophers had previously held *a priori* propositions to be verifiable by inspection of their meanings alone . . .; it was one of Wittgenstein's distinctive innovations to consider thoughts only as embodied in what he calls the "significant proposition" *(der sinnvolle Satz)* and so to transform the question of the relation of thought to reality, which Anscombe considers a "principal theme of the book" *Introduction,* p. 19) into the more promising question of the relation of language to reality. . . . Wittgenstein hoped that comparison of alternative symbolisms, without explicit reference to the reality they represented, might serve to reveal their necessary features, their invariants, and so indirectly to reveal the form of the world. His ontology is on the whole suggested by his views about language, rather than the reverse, although the interaction between semantics and metaphysics in the book is too complex to be reduced to a simple formula. . . . Whatever the order of composition, the final conceptions of language, logic and reality are virtually inseparable.[26]

That Wittgenstein is a metaphysician Black does not doubt. It may be suggested, however, that the importance of language for Wittgenstein may not be so much its being a key to reality as its being a means of bridging the gaps between what otherwise would be private worlds. Language is both a means of escaping from the inevitable solipsism of one who must say that "the world is my idea" and demonstrating that there is a fundamental similarity in the nature of all possible worlds. Wittgenstein states it thus: "Man sagte einmal, dass Gott alles schaffen könne, nur nichts, was den logischen Gesetzen zuwider wäre" (3.031). For Saint Thomas Aquinas it was part of God's nature to be logical. Both Luther and Calvin denied this, placing God's will in a superior position within the divine nature to His intellectual qualities. Therefore, God as He is in Himself is unknown *(Deus Absconditus)*; we can know Him only as He reveals Himself, particularly as He reveals Him-

---

[26] Black, *A Companion*, 7-8.

self in the Scriptures (*Deus Revelatus*). Wittgenstein's is a mediating position. He does not attribute a logical nature to God; but neither does he permit us to make illogical statements about the world or ourselves, insofar as we are parts of the world. "Wir könnten nämlich von einer 'unlogischen' Welt nicht sagen, wie sie aussähe" (3.031). Logic, as Mauthner had said, is an aspect of language (3.032). What we, God or the world are, considered as objects in themselves, is impossible for us to say, although it might be possible for us to show (3.032, 4.1212).

Like Kant, Wittgenstein in the *Tractatus* was breaking with every dogmatic form of metaphysics or theology; but he was not substituting a hidden metaphysics for one whose possibilty he had denied. In one sense he was welcomed by the positivists because he was one with them in their denial of metaphysics; but in another way he equally denied their faith in the sole reality of sense experience and mathematics. Maslow, writing in 1959 of his experience of writing *A Study of Wittgenstein's Tractatus* in 1933, states:

My study was written very largely from the point of view of logical positivism, a view I no longer hold. Quite appropriately, as it seems to me now, my struggles with the obscurities of the *Tractatus* gradually forced me to reconsider many of my own philosophical convictions (some of which, previously, I had not been aware of), and by the time I had finished my essay, I had pretty well finished with my positivism as well. I climbed through it, over it, and threw away the ladder.[27]

Although speaking from another point of view than Maslow's, Black believes that much of the difficulty in interpreting the *Tractatus* comes from an inability to distinguish *sinnvoll* (which refers to empirical propositions), *sinnlos* (which refers primarily to 'formal' statements, such as we see in pure mathematics and logic — i.e. transcendental propositions) and *unsinnig*. The Ogden translation, for instance, thoroughly confuses the last two. Tautologies and contradictions are *sinnlos*, but they are not *unsinnig* (4.461-4.4611). According to Black, only statements which we would characterize as *unsinnig* (incoherent) are truly nonsense; but Black

[27] Maslow, *A Study*, vii-viii.

defends their use in the *Tractatus*.[28] They are the means which Wittgenstein uses to explore the limits of language and the world. The truth-tables are means whereby their range is limited to possible statements rather than incoherent sounds. Significantly, *unsinnig* is the adjective used in the penultimate statement of the *Tractatus*.

Black's treatment of the *Tractatus* is in some respects the direct result of the carefulness with which he has written the *Companion*. He considers each word and proposition within the *Tractatus* with great care; he does not, however, see the work as the whole it is. Nevertheless, Black's summing up of Wittgenstein's efforts is most important for its recognition of the value of the *Tractatus* even from a somewhat limited point of view. Black writes:

> Wittgenstein's book cannot be held to "say" anything, for it would be a howler to take it as consisting of empirical statements. But there remains the alternative of treating many of his remarks as formal statements, "showing" something that *can* be shown. Then they will be in no worse case than logical and mathematical statements and there will be no theoretical barrier to their use in rational communication. A great many of Wittgenstein's remarks can be salvaged in this way — indeed all those that belong to "logical syntax" or philosophical grammar. For all such remarks are *a priori* but involve no violation of the rules of logical syntax. . . . The expression and communication of statements belonging to philosophical grammar is as reputable an activity as mathematics. Wittgenstein is not rallying us to the destruction of the *a priori* disciplines; he will be satisfied if we understand them and their "peculiar" position in contrast to the sciences. This line of defense applies to all cases in which Wittgenstein is seeking the "essence" of something. In all such cases, his investigations, whether successful or not, result, in an *a priori* statement that ought to be treated, on his principles, as the expression of a certain rule.[29]

Black's defense of the *Tractatus* is excellent as far as it goes, yet throughout his valuable work, there seems to be the same assumption which he had criticized in Russell: the assumption that at least to some degree Wittgenstein is talking about some aspects of

---

[28]   Black, *A Companion*, 385.
[29]   Black, *A Companion*, 382.

"reality" which are other than language itself.[30] The last two propositions were not put in the *Tractatus* merely to mystify. They were placed there to prevent anyone using the book and its thoughts as a means of deriving any kind of metaphysics or antimetaphysics from an examination of the empirical world. If we are to make sense out of the world we must make the attempt by some other method than the sciences, the philosophy of science, or dogmatic metaphysics and theology. The world is my idea, and, except for language, I am forever isolated within the world which is mine. It was perhaps this knowledge which caused Miss Cassirer to question the fundamental premises of Miss Anscombe's *Introduction* and to state near the end of her review that "language is the only intelligible thing we have".[31] Perhaps it needed someone with an insight borrowed from *The Philosophy of Symbolic Forms* to recognize in the *Tractatus* a neo-Kantian document.

4

An increasing number of scholars have come to realize that Wittgenstein was not merely echoing or developing thoughts of Frege and Russell and that similarities to Kant are not accidental. Those who have seen this similarity have normally also qualified their statements with the suggestion that the Kantianism probably came through Schopenhauer and not from a direct reading of the *Critiques*. The first widely read commentator on the *Tractatus* to try to make an approach through Kant was Stenius who devoted a whole chapter to "Wittgenstein as Kantian Philosopher".[32] Most people seem to read Stenius with mixed reactions. There are many extremely interesting insights; but one is never quite sure whether Stenius is dealing with the text of the *Tractatus* or is off on a tangent of his own. Possibly the reason for the mixed reaction can

---

[30]   Black, *A Companion*, 12-13.
[31]   Cassirer, "Review", 66.
[32]   Stenius, *Critical Exposition*, 11.

be found in the conclusion of the preface to his book.[33] He takes Wittgenstein's own Preface quite literally where the latter says that very likely no one would really be able to understand the *Tractatus* unless he personally had thought similar thoughts. Black does a very workmanlike job. It may be, however, that he stood too close to the text. Stenius, on the other hand, stands almost in the tradition of Dilthey. He uses the *Tractatus* as the starting point, the occasion, for the development of his own thoughts. If he thinks well, it will be because he has had thoughts which are similar to those which Wittgenstein had when the latter was writing the *Tractatus*. Stenius attempts to look beneath the words of the *Tractatus* to the philosophical vision which brought it into being. Whether he is successful, only the reader can judge. The author of this essay is obviously closer to Stenius than to Black, but he has Black's reverence for the text. Perhaps Black would have written a better book had he been willing or able to approach the *Tractatus* with the kind of inquiry which, since Dilthey's days, we have known as *Verstehen*. He would not then, as has been indicated, have assumed that Wittgenstein's use of the words "Wirklichkeit" and "Realität" was purely arbitrary. Nevertheless, Black's book more trustworthy than Stenius', even though there are insights in Stenius' book which are not even considered in Black's.

It is from Stenius' philosophic vision that we see why Wittgenstein says that the world divides into facts rather than into things. Human beings do not find the world divided into things. The Gestalt psychologists have shown us that our perceptions are of a field which we analyze in different ways in accordance with our intention. "What things and predicates are perceived depends on what facts are relevant."[34] The value of Stenius' book is considerably diminished by his continuing to see Wittgenstein as one who used a subject-predicate form in his analysis of elementary statements; but Stenius grasps, as few commentators have, the importance of the perceiving subject, of the intentional arc, for an understanding of the *Tractatus*. It is possible to force many of the state-

---

[33]   Stenius, *Critical Exposition*, x.
[34]   Stenius, *Critical Exposition*, x.

ments of the *Tractatus* into a subject-predicate form; but it appears to have been Wittgenstein's intention to do away with this form except in the case of pseudo-propositions, the propositions of generality. Nevertheless, if we persist in our use of the subject-predicate form, which we have inherited from the schoolmen, the following statement by Stenius would have been accepted by both Wittgenstein and Black:

The role of things in the world picture is to act as "bearers" of predicates and that is their *raison d'etre*. If a "thing in itself" means a "thing" without predicates then the assumption of a thing in itself has no purpose; indeed such a thing cannot be thought of as a thing: it is inconceivable. That is why we can never really say what a thing is in itself. The same is true of a "predicate in itself".[35]

It is doubtful if either Black or Wittgenstein would have accepted Stenius' Proposition II.3 as necessarily derivative from Wittgenstein's propositions, 1, 1.1, and 1.2. Stenius' proposition reads:

Things and predicates are complementary. Things enter into the world (whether this i s understood as a "thing" or as a "fact") as elements of facts.[36]

This proposition is a kind of playing with words. In the first part of the *Tractatus*, Wittgenstein is trying to show that any attempt to get outside of the language world is certain to end in incoherence (*unsinnig*). In the quoted proposition from Stenius the incoherence is obvious as soon as we look at what is being said. What could possibly be meant by the statement that "things and predicates are complementary"? Stenius is trying both to have an ontology and not have it at the same time. Only when we realize that we are confined to language worlds do we realize that to look for referents to our words is to be caught in a hopeless chase. The purpose of the first part of the *Tractatus* is not to demonstrate a logical atomism, a fact which Stenius assumes, but to demonstrate that logical atomism begins to fall apart of its own weight as soon as we attempt to examine it closely. At most, logical atoms can

---

[35] Stenius, *Critical Exposition*, 27.
[36] Stenius, *Critical Exposition*, 28.

have only a formal existence and that within language itself. Their existence is required by our analysis of language and the existence of the possibilities of such artificial languages as Rosser's in which objects exist without any necessary or even supposed existence with a corresponding empirical world (4.211, 4.122, 4.123, 4.126, 4.127, 4.22). Wittgenstein's whole handling of the question of Occam's razor presupposes the same confinement to language and the language world of each speaker or group (3.328, 5.47321). The propositions at the beginning of the *Tractatus* must, as a group, be seen as *unsinnig*; the attempt to build a world out of logical atoms is a vain task. Similarly, Pitcher claims that the simple objects are semantic absolutes. Their ontological existence is incoherent,[37] is impossible.

Stenius' chapter on "Wittgenstein as a Kantian Philosopher" is interesting and insightful. Stenius is of the opinion that Wittgenstein probably knew Kant only through Schopenhauer, an impression he probably received from his stay with Miss Anscombe; but to make this assumption is to assume that the boyish Wittgenstein would not have pondered the three *Critiques* before he went off to England. Even until very recently, a knowledge of the three *Critiques* was thought likely in every lad who had been to a *Gymnasium* or *Realschule*. Nor is it likely that the relation between Kant and Wittgenstein which Stenius tentatively explores would have come about without an awareness of the Kantian philosophy and Schopenhauer's criticism of it. Schopenhauer reduced the Kantian categories to causality. Stenius says: *"What Kant's transcendental deductions are intended to perform: this is performed by the logical analysis of language."*[38] "Wittgenstein moves the limits of theoretical reason to the limits of language."[39] "The *Tractatus* could be called a 'Critique of Pure Language'."[40]

---

37   Pitcher, *The Philosophy of Wittgenstein*, 120-24.
38   Stenius, *Critical Exposition*, 218 [italics in original].
39   Stenius, *Critical Exposition*, 218.
40   Stenius, *Critical Exposition*, 220.

IX

THE *TRACTATUS* AND POST-SYMBOLIST POETRY

1

Stenius arrived at his various positions as the result of a continuing dialogue between the *Tractatus* and himself. His book is a report of that dialogue. If one stands where Stenius did when he wrote the book, one will very likely come to similar conclusions. Nevertheless, as is true with all internal criticisms of a text, there will always be some doubt as to whether the report is of a true or an imaginary conversation. Stenius, at least, was aware of both the advantages and disadvantages of his method of exposition. This has been less true with others. Surely Russell believed that he was being faithful to the text, and there is little doubt that Miss Anscombe tried to be. Yet Wittgenstein disapproved of Russell's interpretation, and a minor thesis of this essay suggests that Miss Anscombe's *Introduction* is of limited value. Stenius, like the others, sees the young Wittgenstein primarily concerned to solve certain logical puzzles. It is obviously the case that Wittgenstein wished to solve certain puzzles and that he was concerned to correct his old mentors, Frege and Russell, at certain points; but it is the contention of this essay that Wittgenstein's interests were far more fundamental: that he was concerned to lay out the possibilities for what we might well call metaphysical poetry: the kind of poetry which in our time has been written by Rilke, Yeats, and Eliot. Mention has already been made of Wittgenstein's relation with Rilke. Less well-known is that Eliot was deeply aware of the problems and relations between poetry and logic. To a captious critic who suggested that some of his incursions into the new poetry were illogical, he replied with a defence taken from the *Principia Mathematica*.[1]

It is significant in calling attention to the relation between symbolic logic and contemporary poetry that one of the articles in the Fann anthology ,that by George Pitchere is called Wittgenstein, Nonsense and Lewis Carroll". A similar anthology about T. S. Eliot contains an article by Elizabeth Sewell entitled "Lewis Carroll and T. S. Eliot as Nonsense Poets".[2] An explication o fthis relation, to which attention has been called before, may be seen in the following selection:

Analogy is indeed the very name of our characteristic poetic logic. No doubt the attraction for analogy for us is in the fragmentation of faith and the diversity of logics and the divisiveness of our minds generally. These fragments, says Eliot, I have shored against my ruins. . . . To the medieval mind the unity of things was insistently present, and had to be interpreted; to us unity is what we only seek by all the machineries of desperation and longing, sometimes longing without hope; and the means of our search is by analogy or collateral form. . . . Collateral or analogical form is as near as we are likely to come to the organic. . . . It was a similar perception that led St. Augustine to say that in every poem there is some of the substance of God. My point had perhaps better be pushed a little further and by an analogy taken from mathematics and physics thought of besides poetry and morals. In mathematics it is not necessary to know what one is talking about; in physics it is, since the test is knowledge. Yet the mathematics (creating out of the rigor of *formal* relations) generates the physics, and often does so without being itself understood. Mathematics is theoretic form for the *feeling* of the relation of things. Poetry is like mathematics. . . . Poetry is the rebelliousness and the pang of what is alive. . . . The Poetic impulse is . . . toward creation. . . . Reason likes the finished job; but poetry *likes* the new job — the living process.[3]

Reason must control the poetic work, prevent incoherence (*unsinnig*); but "nonsense is how the English chose to take their Pure

[1]   Hugh Kenner, "Bradley" in *T. S. Eliot: A Collection of Critical Essays*, ed. by Hugh Kenner (Englewood Cliffs: Prentice Hall, 1962), 56n.
[2]   Kenner (ed.), *T. S. Eliot*, 65.
[3]   R. P. Blackmur, "Irregular Metaphysics" in Kenner (ed.) *T. S. Eliot*, 60-61 [formal has been italicized].

Poetry, their *langage mathématique* or *romances sans paroles:* their struggle to convert language into symbolic logic or music."[4] Surely it is at the point of what we may call nonsense poetry that we begin to see a relation of what may be said and what can only be shown: the inexpressible and mystical of *Tractatus* 6.522. What is to be said must be said with rigor; but conflicting images, images divorced from time, make it necessary for the reader to climb up and out of the verses to the reality which transcends them and transcends even the transcendental expressions within the verses. The Reality referred to is that Reality which sublates *(aufheben)* and penetrates all. This Reality is surely that which Bradley had in mind; but it is not far from the Colossian statement which affirms of the *Logos* that "in Him all things consist". Despite the similarities, the Reality is not a Plotinian One past all finding out. Rather the similarities with Mahayana Buddhism are quite apparent. If we were to talk about the theological development of the West, we would be drawing analogies with the period in the development of Mahayana Buddhism which showed itself immediately before the appearance of *The Awakening of Faith in the Mahayana.* There is the same interest in logic, the same building of a significant faith on the ruins of an old, apparently demolished by nihilism. We can see the attraction of Buddhism for Eliot in the notes to *The Waste Land;* an even deeper attraction may be seen in Schopenhauer, surely one of the teachers of Wittgenstein's youth.

Yet, as we treat of the *Tractatus*, all of the evidence for a religious point of view seems to be internal. Both Russell and Anscombe knew Wittgenstein personally and had many opportunities to discuss things with him. If one is to disagree with the view that Wittgenstein was primarily concerned with logic and mathematics and their foundations, one must look for alliances wherever he may find them. In this essay alliances have been sought with Spinoza, Schopenhauer, and Eliot; and an attempt will be made to show Wittgenstein's dependence on Kant. But there is need for a contemporary source; for a statement from someone who knew Witt-

---

[4]   Elizabeth Sewell, in Kenner (ed.), *T. S. Eliot*, 65.

genstein well at the time when he was writing the *Tractatus*. That source surfaced in 1967 with the publication of Paul Engelmann's *Letters from Ludwig Wittgenstein with a Memoir*.

2

Paul Engelmann, who died in Tel Aviv, Israel, in 1965 before his work was quite finished, met Wittgenstein while the latter was at an artillery training center near Olmütz in Moravia in 1916. Engelmann was not in the army because of his pacifist leanings and because a serious illness caused his discharge shortly after he was drafted. Olmütz was Engelmann's home town, but he had studied architecture in Vienna under Alfred Loos, a friend of the Wittgenstein family. It was Loos who asked Wittgenstein to call on the Engelmanns. Dr. Josef Schächter, a friend of Engelmann's during his last years, describes him as follows:

Engelmann was a mystic in Wittgenstein's sense. To him the meaning of the world and the purpose of life lay outside the physical and psychological universe. At the same time, his cultural-philosophical investigations . . . are entirely based on rational argument, since the mystic element can only become manifest but never communicated in explicit statements.[5]

In other words, the mystical can be shown; it cannot be described, depicted, or talked about.

In the introduction to his *Memoir*, which was found by his friends among his papers after his death, Engelmann discussed both: why he finally chose to publish Wittgenstein's letters to him and his own memoir about Wittgenstein; and why he had delayed so long.

Posthumous fame is like the satyric drama following the tragedy of a life of genius. It was the peculiar manifestations of that kind of fame which induced me in 1958 to write to Miss Elizabeth Anscombe, whom I knew by name not only as the Editor of the *Philosophical Investigations* but also as a pupil of Wittgenstein's who was close to him during

[5]   Engelmann, *Letters*, x.

the last years of his life. I said in the course of my letter that I was not particularly keen on writing down and publishing my reminiscences of Wittgenstein . . . even though it might have led to a desirable and important rectification of the accepted account of Wittgenstein's views. I asked Miss Ascombe's advice, and she wrote in her reply:

If by pressing a button it could have been secured that people would not concern themselves with his personal life, I should have pressed the button; but since it has not been possible and it is certain that much that is foolish will keep on being said, it seems to me reasonable that anyone who can write a truthful account of him should do so. On the other hand to write a satisfactory account would seem to need extraordinary talent. — Further I must confess that I feel deeply suspicious of anyone's claim to have understood Wittgenstein. That is perhaps because, although I had a very strong and deep affection for him, and, I suppose, knew him well, I am very sure that I did not understand him. It is difficult, I think, not to give a version of his attitudes, for example, which one can enter into oneself, and then the account is really of oneself: if for example infected with one's own mediocrity or ordinariness or lack of complexity.

This on the whole encouraging reply was one of the reasons which eventually induced me to compile this book in its present form. . . . Nevertheless . . . the picture which my disposition enables me to give is entirely subjective, comparable to the likeness of an eminent man presented by a good portrait painter. . . . The period in which the letters here presented . . . [was] the period of the preparation and publication of the *Tractatus*. This is one justification for bringing out this book. Whether it remains the only justification for what I have to give will depend on whether I have succeeded in illuminating his life through mine as well as through his.[6]

Certain references to the fifty-four letters from Wittgenstein will appear later in the essay. Our concern at this point is with the *Memoir*, with Engelmann's understanding of what Wittgenstein was attempting to do in the *Tractatus*. Engelmann's observations are based on what was obviously a very intimate relation with the young Wittgenstein. Despite Engelmann's protestations, which were obviously encouraged by Miss Anscombe's remarks, there is an objectivity to his small treatise. He is fairly sure, for instance, that the *Tractatus*, despite its great worth, would not have been

---

6   Engelmann, *Letters*, xiii-xv.

published if Russell had not been willing to write the "Introduction".[7] Nor does he believe that those who saw Wittgenstein as a positivist were entirely to blame.[8] The reader will recall that a minor thesis of this essay is the assertion that Wittgenstein and the Vienna Circle had common roots in the phenomenalism of Mach. Russell's "Introduction" and the climate of opinion both in Vienna and England were such as to lead men to look either to Hume or to phenomenalism, for alliances and ancestry. Yet the Wittgenstein whom Engelmann knew was a religious and not a secular man. Engelmann and Wittgenstein were at one in believing that, although a person may be deeply religious, he must never surrender the reason to emotion or to dreams and fancy. This is surely equally the position of Rilke, Yeats, and Eliot as it is not the position of Rimbaud, on the side of secularism, or Gounod, on the side of religion. Rimbaud and Gounod are incoherent (*unsinnig*). Engelmann's own words for Wittgenstein's and his common position are summarized thus:

It is not a question of head *or* heart, reason *or* emotion: the watchword must be reason *with* emotion, head *and* heart. We cannot say: what we lack is feeling. But we shall be much nearer the truth in saying: what our reason lacks is feeling, we need reason endowed with feeling, indeed with the unspoken feeling that is manifest in our reason; it is what we call heart: feeling which does not pour freely outwards in emotional self-indulgence, but which is restrained, turned inward, thus suffusing the whole personality and bringing warmth even to its coldest part, the seat of reason.[9]

Eliot, Rilke, and Yeats would not have said it otherwise.

Engelmann begins his own observations on the composition of the *Tractatus* with two statements. Echoing Wittgenstein's own Preface, he states that there must be a psychological awareness on the part of the reader which is similar to that which Wittgenstein himself possessed at the time he wrote the *Tractatus*. If such a psychological awareness is present, the *Tractatus* will not seem

---

[7]   Engelmann, *Letters*, 117.
[8]   Engelmann, *Letters*, 97, 117-18.
[9]   Engelmann, *Letters*, 89.

such a mysterious and closed book to the reader.[10] Secondly, Engelmann points out that Wittgenstein came to philosophy as an
adult, a mature man similar to the mature Goethe.[11] What he
received from his teachers, Schopenhauer, Hertz, Frege, and Russell, were the tools with which to do his own job: to write out a
philosophical view of the world which would reflect his own mystical, personal experiences and conflicts.[12] Engelmann summarizes
Wittgenstein's intent and accomplishment in an admirable paragraph. He first states that the intent of the *Tractatus* was to elaborate a world picture and that logic was merely the tool which Wittgenstein had chosen to use. Then he continues, stating that the
elaboration of a world picture was accomplished

in sovereign fashion, ending up with implacable consistency by nulli-
fying the result, so that the communication of its basic thoughts, or
rather of its basic tendency — which, according to its own findings,
cannot on principle be effected by direct methods — is yet achieved
indirectly. He nullifies his own world of picture, together with the
"houses of cards" of philosophy (which at that time at least he thought
he had made collapse), so as to show *"how little is achieved when these
problems are solved"*. What he wants to demonstrate is that such en-
deavors of human thought to "utter the unutterable" are a hopeless
attempt to satisfy man's eternal metaphysical urge.[13]

The analogy with Kierkegaard is striking. Each had the same intent, the same destructive urge to attack pretentious metaphysical
systems. Kierkegaard, however, chose literary methods to accom-
plish the same end, the famous pseudonyms and their tendency to
wound from behind. In the usual sense in which the word is used,
neither Kierkegaard nor Wittgenstein was a mystic. Yet, if we think
of them as mystics in the way in which our three modern poets
would have used the phrase, we find that both were mystics. With
reference to Wittgenstein's mysticism, Engelmann says:

Irrespective of the process of growth of this system of thought, logic
and mysticism have here sprung from one and the same root, and it

10 Engelmann, *Letters*, 94.
11 Engelmann, *Letters*, 95.
12 Engelmann, *Letters*, 96.
13 Engelmann, *Letters*, 96.

could be said with greater justice that Wittgenstein drew certain logical
conclusions from his fundamental mystical attitude toward life and the
world. That he should have chosen to devote five-sixths of his book
to the logical conclusions is due to the fact that about them at least
it is possible to speak.[14]

In contradistinction to the positivists, and this must include Russell, Wittgenstein passionately believed

*that all that really matters in human life is precisely what, in his view,
we must be silent about.* When he nevertheless takes immense pains to
delimit the unimportant, it is not the coastline of that island which he
is bent on surveying with such meticulous accuracy, but the boundary
of the ocean. . . . God does not reveal himself *in* the world (6.432) (yet
he reveals himself *through* the world, *in that* the world exists). "There
is indeed that which is unutterable. This makes itself *manifest,* it is the
mystical" (6.522) (but not a "bluish haze surrounding things" and
giving them an interesting appearance (as Wittgenstein once said in
conversation)).[15]

At this point in our exposition of Wittgenstein's thought it is important to recognize several things about his mysticism. First, in
the parenthetical remark which Engelmann has given us, we must
recognize that for Wittgenstein mysticism does not imply an ecsta-
tic union of the "alone with the One". There may well be an emotional component; but the mysticism is not established by emotional means (a blue haze). Secondly, the objects of the mysticism
are never defined. They are "das Mystische", "das Höhere"
(6.632, 6.522). Thirdly, Wittgenstein has specifically divorced
himself from any form of monism or dualism or pluralism (4.128)
even though he may be read as a radical dualist, a position which
was affirmed earlier in our discussion. But he is still a mystic by
his own confession.

Of what then does his mysticism consist? Lord Russell is surely
on the right road to the understanding of this problem in the last
two pages of his "Introduction".[16] We can be honest mystics only
if we are persuaded that we can never actually stand outside of our

---

14   Engelmann, *Letters,* 97.
15   Engelmann, *Letters,* 97-98. [Italics in the original.]
16   Russell, "Introduction", 22-23.

own skins and that it is false to extrapolate from our limited experience, our private *Wirklichkeiten*, to the world as a whole and
as it is in itself. The middle ranges of life and experience are open
to us, and we can describe these middle ranges in a reliable way:
we can talk about them; we can depict them; the world as a limited
whole is open to us and to our feelings (6.54). But the totality of
the whole (*die Gesamtheit)* is not open to us either as a totality or
as it is in itself (4.52, 5.5262, 5.5561). It is foolish (*unsinnig*) to
pretend that it is (6.53). This problem of totality does not say that
we cannot say things about it. We can define its limits with our
understanding of contradiction and tautology; we can, as in the
general proposition, say what must be the general features of any
object which arises out of the totality. By means of the truth-
tables we can determine what is and what is not incoherent in any
statement we make; but what the *Gesamtheit* is *an und für sich*
we cannot say.

Nevertheless, in good poetry which, to a significant degree,
shows the world obliquely, it is possible to gain a glimpse of the
world as it is in itself. Good poetry does this, at least in our time,
by refining its images most carefully, even as Wittgenstein in the
Tractatus refined and polished his images, finally throwing the
images against each other to evoke in the mind of the reader or
listener a sense of that which in itself is beyond meaning *(Bedeutung)*. It is possible for us to speak of bearers of meaning within the
world of our experience; yet to say of the totality of all that is (*die
Gesamtheit*) that it has meaning in the way an object has meaning
is to commit an absurdity.

3

Before continuing the discussion of poetry as a means of extending
our vision, it may be well to pause for a moment over several
terms in the *Tractatus* which seem to have an ambiguous meaning.
To what degree Wittgenstein was aware of the ambiguity it is not,
at least not at this time, possible to say, although the following

exposition will try to be faithful to his thought and to the implications surrounding his use of *Wirklichkeit* and *Realität*. As was mentioned above, *Realität* occurs in only two places in the *Tractatus*, at 5.5561, where it is conjoined with *empirische*, and at 5.64. Obviously, although Black seems to think Wittgenstein's use of *Realität* is only an arbitrary substitution for *Wirklichkeit,* there is a clue to a considerably deeper meaning, perhaps to the implicit metaphysics which stands in back of Wittgenstein's thought. At 5.5561 Wittgenstein says:

Die empirische Realität ist begrenzt durch die Gesamtheit der Gegenstände. Die Grenze zeigt sich wieder in der Gesamtheit der Elementarsätze.

There are several peculiar things about this proposition. The *Tractatus* is an a priori study. Why then do we speak of empirical reality? Again, as has been indicated above, *Gegenstand* does not necessarily stand for an empirical Democritean atom. *Gegenstand* may only be an object of thought. Possibly we Anglo-Saxons have been trapped by the word "empirical". The empirical reality to which Wittgenstein is here referring must be a probable or possible state of being which is the ultimate limit of analysis. It really cannot mean anything more; and the same must be true with reference to the totality of elementary propositions: there must be an ultimate state of being in which all possible combinations of objects have some kind of existence. As with the discussion about *Gegenstände* we must assume a kind of meontic non-being for this kind of existence. It is more than nothing, but it is not yet something. *Wirklichkeit*, Wittgenstein's preferred word for reality, would not have this kind of being-non-being status. The very word implies in its nature the quality of action, of the pressure of activity.

The other recourse to "Realität" occurs in the midst of the discussion on the philosophical "I", which Wittgenstein carefully distinguishes from the psychological "I".

Hier sieht man, dass der Solipsismus, streng durchgeführt, mit dem reinen Realismus zusammenfällt. Das Ich des Solipsismus schrumpft zum ausdehnungslosen Punkt zusammen, und es bleibt die ihm koordinierte Realität (5.64).

Why is the last word not *Wirklichkeit?* Is it possible that what Wittgenstein is trying to say, what Schopenhauer certainly would have said, is that out of the womb which is *Realität* there arises simultaneously both the world and the "I" which is coordinated with that particular world? Only if there is a philosophical "I" can there be either a world or a *Wirklichkeit*. Up until the time they stimultaneously arise there are really only possibilities, potentialities. Why *this* rather than *that* world and "I" arise is beyond the possibility of our knowledge. However, as the analysis of the *Tractatus* demonstrates, we can show that if there is to be a world, it will have a certain settled character: the character of any object whatsoever.

If our analysis of the two uses of *Realität* and their relation to *Wirklichtkeit* is correct, many other obscure passages in the *Tractatus* begin to take their rightful place. Wittgenstein's use of the word "Welt" contains an ambiguity. Is he talking about some objective singular world out there? It sometimes appears that he is. But it is much more likely that he is talking about the *Welt* which is coordinated with the metaphysical "I" to which we affix the name "Ludwig Wittgenstein". This world is the *Wirklichkeit* which Wittgenstein knows, but it is not a *Wirklichkeit* under Wittgenstein's control (6.373-6.374). Nevertheless, at death, both the philosophical "I" and the world coordinated with it cease to exist (6.431-6.4312), fall back into the womb of *Realität,* from which they had arisen. Finally, *das Höhere, das Mystische* begin to assume some, if not all of the qualities of *Realität.* They both are and are not. They could, of course, be "parts" of *Realität;* but it seems that Wittgenstein wished to claim a different quality for *das Höhere,* even as he seems to have wanted to claim a different quality than the psychological for the philosophical "I". There is no warrant in the *Tractatus* for assuming that the philosophical "I" is part of *das Höhere.* If there is any dependence on Schopenhauer in this reconstruction, the answer must be an emphatic No! *Das Höhere* seems to be other than either *Realität* or any of an indefinitely large number of *Welten.* Nevertheless, and this demonstrates a qualitative difference from *Realität, das Höhere* is the sense of the world (6.41). "Der Sinn der Welt muss ausserhalb ihrer liegen." Can we then say that the meaning of the world is given to the world by *das Höhere*? This would seem to be denied by 6.432. *"Wie* die Welt ist, ist für das Höhere vollkommen gleichgültig." But this statement applies to events within the world; it does not necessarily apply to a world as a whole or to the totality of all worlds. God is outside of the totality of all worlds. He can, therefore, give meanings which we cannot because we cannot get outside of our worlds (5.6-5.63), and we are limited in our "saying" to what we can depict. We cannot depict the world as a whole or as it is in itself. Nor can we depict God, nor can we depict *Realität*. We are limited in our depicting, our "saying", to events which take place within our world. But, since all worlds share a common quality, that of any object whatsoever, we can converse with our fellows. Finally, the pure poet extends our common language toward ultimacy: God and *Realität*. Our worlds become larger because the poet has lived and written.

4

The way the poet puts his images together enables us to gain a glimpse of the world as it is in itself. The poet is not bound by the ordinary rules of syntax and of subject-predicate discourse. His is a connotative art in which the boundaries of the various images are determined by their place within the scheme of the verses and the poems as a whole. At first reading, the competent poet may appear to be uttering gibberish, to be incoherent; but as we study the words and the structure of his verses we may find a coherence in the whole and, equally, a refined pattern within the subordinate wholes. Black suggests that it is the logician who expands language;[17] this may be true of such a logician as Wittgenstein who in many ways provided a rationale for poetry; but it is surely not true of a man like Ayer or others who subscribe to any form of

---

[17]   Black, *A Companion*, 381-86.

the verification principle. In actual fact, it is the poet, who by his use of conflicting images, each of them carefully defined, leads us toward God, *das Höhere*, and the womb of things, *Realität*. The poet never completely describes ultimacy, but the world which he does describe is a larger one because he has written. As an example of the "showing" that a good poem can do, let us take "Mr. Eliot's Sunday Morning Service", a poem which many critics have proclaimed as bombastic nonsense, but which, in fact, is intricately designed to show both the falsity of reaching toward and believing that one has found ultimacy and the knowledge that in the middle ranges in man's proper place, a proper place particularly because the middle range has been transfigured by the knowledge that the fullness of life extends both toward ultimate heights and depths.

Although we have no means of knowing which Sunday Morning Service evoked Mr. Eliot's poem, we do know that it comes from his pre-Christian period and that he was living in London at the time. It is not unlikely that Eliot had gone to Saint Paul's Cathedral where Inge was Dean, and that the poem is a reaction to Inge's sermon. Inge was completely convinced that there was no fundamental difference between true Christianity and the mystical theology of Plotinus. He wrote and spoke in those terms and offered no alternative to his understanding of the worship and pursuit of the One and the gross animality of Sweeney in his bath. At the beginning of the poem we have a picture of the One and its neutered and powerless progeny: Christian theology; at the other end there is an undefined, anti-intellectual, gross life which has nothing outside of the immediate sensual gratification. Eliot rejected both in favor of a human, yet transfigured, Christ. We are human beings, and it is at the human level that we must live and speak. To attempt to be one with the Plotinian One is surely false; but to reject everything except the immediate pleasures of the senses is equally false.

The mysticism of the *Tractatus* is not Plotinian. Plotinianism attempts an escape from the world; the *Tractatus* makes no such attempt, although it may be so interpreted. The *Tractatus* reveals an attempt, impossible though it may be for anyone except a great poet, to stand outside of the world and to catch a glimpse of the world, to see its interconnections and to become one with the world in its totality. It is not by chance that Wittgenstein saw qualities of similarity between his work and Spinoza's. As Spinoza sought the intellectual love of God, he sought to be united with God in the adequacy of his thought. Wittgenstein knew that the mystic journey was not the one which Spinoza described in his *Ethics*; at best, Spinoza's way could bring one only partially to his goal.

Die Anschauung der Welt sub specie aeterni ist ihre Anschauung als — begrenztes — Ganzes. Das Gefühl der Welt als begrenztes Ganzes ist das mystische (6.45).

Although Spinoza saw a difference between *Natura naturans* and *Natura naturata,* God as an intensional and God as an extensional Being, he did not see a radical break. It is possible to go from one to the other. With Wittgenstein, on the other hand, there is a radical break, not in substance, as with Plotinus, but in attitude. He who has climbed up through the propositions is not in another world. Rather, he has a different attitude toward the world. He sees the world aright. When he is able to do this, to see the world aright, he is a true Mystic. It is significant that Wittgenstein spells the Spinoza type mysticism with a lower case "m"; the true mysticism, the inexpressible, with an upper case "M".[18]

---

[18] In the German text from which the Ogden translation is made, the word "Mystische" in 6.45 is spelled with a lower case "m". In the German text from which the Pears and McGuiness translation is made the word is spelled with an upper case "m". In the two other places where the word "Mystische" appears, 6.44 and 6.522, both texts agree in spelling the word with an upper case "m". In the *Prototractatus,* a manuscript found in Vienna in 1965, the "m" of 6.45 is upper case. It is an unresolvable question, at least at this time, to determine whether the lower case "m" of the 1922 edition was an accidental slip or a deliberate change. It is most likely the latter since it would not normally be the case that one would spell a German noun with a lower case first letter, and it is most likely that someone, knowing the rules for German orthography, deliberately corrected what he believed to be a slip. This will explain the fact that in the last translation of the *Tractatus* the word "Mystische" appears with an upper case "m" in all three places. It is more likely, however, that the lower case "m" in 6.45 in the 1922 edition is there by Wittgenstein's choice. The reference,

It is most unlikely that Wittgenstein had any experience with the religions of Asia before he wrote the *Tractatus;* but there is a fair amount about those religions in Schopenhauer, who found the religions of India particularly helpful in his understanding of the human condition. Nevertheless, there is a Zen flavor to the *Tractatus,* particularly its concluding portions. Zen Buddhism, a variety of the Mahayana, claims to have found a way to see the world aright without at the same time rejecting the world. The phrase which epitomizes Zen is: "Samsara is nirvana". Salvation, even of a mystical variety, is to be found within the flux of the world through being able to see the world aright. The fundamental issue is a change in attitude, and that can take place only after many years of effort; but to see the world aright is to see that the flux of the world is identical with that of the individual who is able to unite himself with that flux seen as a totality. When we look at the propositions from 6.43 to the end of the *Tractatus* we see this same Zen quality. It is how we see the world that determines its shape and limits for us; and if we are really at peace with the world and ourselves we know that there is a fundamental identity to all things. If I have experienced this unity, this identity, I cannot speak of the experience except poetically. I must be silent (7).

To those who find all of this quite mystifying, one can only recommend Mr. Eliot's *Four Quartets,* some of the Zen koans with their deliberate break with ordinary patterns and thoughts and some of the Japanese haiku. In many respects the *Tractatus* is like a very long koan: it makes many assertions and then at the end

---

unlike the other two references, is to feeling. To spell "Mystische" with a lower case "m" is to denigrate the word and to distinguish the word from its intellectual use in the other two places. If one will recall that the *Tractatus* comes out of a Viennese atmosphere and that Freud was one of the prominent intellectuals of the city in the immediate post-war years, one can see the reason for the change. To Freud, mysticism was a feeling of union with a totality. He called this feeling "the oceanic feeling". 6.45 refers directly to this sort of feeling; feeling is not necessarily involved in the cases of the other two uses of "das Mystische". The changes between the *Prototractatus* and the earlier edition of the *Tractatus* may represent a wavering on Wittgenstein's part between a subjectivist and an objectivist understanding of mysticism.

nullifies them all. The true meaning must be beyond both the assertions and their nullity. Again, like a Haiku, the *Tractatus* must be seen synoptically if it is to be seen correctly. Although expressed in exquisite and sparse German and in an apparently very orderly way, the *Tractatus* speaks with the still, small voice which the Hebrews attributed to God himself. There is no bombast, but one knows, after one has lived with the *Tractatus* for many months, that one has, in fact, been changed, has been helped, perhaps, to see the world aright.

According to Engelmann, Wittgenstein saw the intellectual malaise of our time as following from our inability to separate that which was utterable from that which was not. As a result of this inability, both the sciences and the humanities had become quite confused. Scientific laws which could be no more than heuristic devices (6.32-6.361, 6.363-6.372) had been given a metaphysical status; and those whose job it was to protect the realm of values had continued to compromise until there was very little left to the realm of values. Although Engelmann does not mention them by name, it is obvious that neither he nor Wittgenstein had much respect either for liberal theologians or for those theologians who reified myths. But neither did they have a great deal of patience with those who reified the formulae of the sciences. Wittgenstein's method in the *Tractatus* is to demonstrate that synthetic a priori propositions, no matter how derived, have no ontological status, although they may have a linguistic status (5.5561, 6.111-6.12). From Carnap's remarks in his *Autobiography*, it is obvious that for Carnap and other members of the Vienna Circle the so-called scientific laws had at least a quasi-ontic status: they are certainly more than heuristic devices.

Engelmann thought of Wittgenstein as one who was completing Kant's work:

It is meaningless . . . to talk about the sphere of the transcendental, the metaphysical. . . . In this way he [Wittgenstein] renders all attacks on the transcendental impossible, but at the same time he also frustrates all attempts to defend it by talking. Yet he adumbrates another way by which this can be done. Here the sublime emerges not only pure but naked, as it were. . . . This led to an attitude to life that comes nearest perhaps to that sought by Tolstoy: an ethical totalitarianism in all questions, a single-minded and painful preservation of the purity of the uncompromising demands of ethics, in agonizing awareness of one's permanent failure to measure up to them. This is the demand Wittgenstein makes on himself. But even the example of a life lived in this way was sometimes apt to confuse weaker spirits. . . . The view of the *Tractatus* . . . can be summed up briefly by saying: ethical propositions do not exist; ethical action does exist.[19]

It is apparent From Engelmann's *Memoir* that Wittgenstein saw in poetry and music a showing rather than a saying. "The poet's sentences, for instance, achieve their effect not through what they say but through what is manifest in them, and the same holds for music, which also says nothing."[20]

---

[19] Engelmann, *Letters*, 108-10.
[20] Engelmann, *Letters*, 83.

X

THE REVELATORY EVENT

1

Engelmann's recently released book opens up a perspective on Wittgenstein which differs profoundly from the interpretations hitherto given to him. When one sees Wittgenstein as a mystic in the great western tradition, one finds an explanation for his choices in literature. Tolstoy, Dostoyevsky, Kierkegaard, Pascal, Spinoza, even John Henry Newman had caught a similar vision of reality, made radical breaks with conventional ways of thinking and launched themselves on new and different careers.

Probably the closest analogy lies at the very fountainhead of philosophy itself. In the *Apology* Socrates says:

> You have heard me speak at sundry times and in divers places of an oracle or sign which comes to me and is the divinity which Meletus ridicules in the indictment. This sign, which is a kind of voice, first began to come to me when I was a child; it always forbids but never commands me to do anything which I am going to do.[1]

In the *Symposium* Alcibiades refers to Socrates' fantastic powers of concentration, and all who knew Wittgenstein personally have remarked on similar powers of concentration. It is obvious from his reading habits that Wittgenstein found those authors who stood in the boundary between religion and philosophy to be fellow pilgrims, with whom he could commune in the spirit if not in the flesh.

[1] Plato, *Dialogues* (31), trans. by B. Jowett (New York: Random House, 1937), I, 414.

Engelmann's *Memoir*, the letters from the young Wittgenstein to Engelmann and Wittgenstein's *Notebook 1914-1916* tell us of some of the changes which were taking place in Wittgenstein as the result of his thinking about logic and the riddle of life. Russell has remarked that Wittgenstein came back from the war a changed man.[2] Apparently, Wittgenstein did not talk very much about the war, but Engelmann tells us that he was a very competent soldier, both as an enlisted man and as an officer. Engelmann speaks of his having been decorated for bravery several times[3] and mentions that when he became an officer his men were able to lean on him for strength.[4] One must assume that the war had its effect and that it was probably the war with its message of random and meaningless death which forced Wittgenstein to come to grips with his former brash rejection of religion and to find a place outside of the world on which he could rest his own being. During many months of the war he served as an artillery spotter;[5] and this particular situation in the midst of battle may have contributed to his understanding of the effect of the human will on events, the essential meaninglessness of much that goes on in the world and the status of men's understanding of so-called scientific laws. If one can see the propositions from 6.3 to 6.3751 and 6.43 to 6.4321 being put into final shape by an artillery forward observer, they become much more concrete and less esoteric.

Even before World War I ordnance maps in Europe were very carefully drawn to insure that artillery fire would be accurate to the highest possible degree. The maps were the common possession of most armies, for it was assumed that ground which had once been fought over would be fought over again. In use, it would have been customary to overlay the map of the battle area with a mesh with numbered spaces so that the spotter (Wittgenstein) could send signals back to his batteries giving changed direc-

2   Bertrand Russell, "Ludwig Wittgenstein", in Fann (ed.), *Ludwig Wittgenstein*, 31.
3   Engelmann, *Letters*, 140.
4   Engelmann, *Letters*, 142.
5   Engelmann, *Letters*, 142.

tions for laying the guns. The common ground for the gunners and the spotters would have been the ordnance tables, the ordnance maps, and the overlying mesh. The tables, which were a common possession of all artillerymen, were calculated according to Newtonian mechanics. Given the muzzle velocity and the distance, it would have been possible to insure that the projectile would land in any given square or triangle by raising or lowering the gun by so many mills, or by changing its direction. From one perspective, everything which happened on the field of battle was entirely in accordance with natural law (6.372). From another perspective, who was killed and who was not was a matter of chance or Fate (6.37, 6.372). From the viewpoint of the observer who willed that the shell would land in this square rather than in another, the fact that it did land as intended was a favour granted by the fates since there was no necessary connection between the willing and that which happened subsequent to the willing (6.373, 6.4321).

The importance of the illustration of the ordnance map for the philosophy of the *Tractatus* is to demonstrate that the worlds external to ourselves are of such a character that they can be described in a formal way (6.342-6.361). What formal way is chosen is a matter of accident, is arbitrary or a matter of expediency. The point which Wittgenstein was trying to make was that the apparent arbitrariness of language or description hid a logic which was of the essence of language and which was manifested in the way things could be described. Mauthner could not have said this because for him there were no *uniform* connections, as there were for Wittgenstein (6.361). Whitehead recognized a similar position to that expressed by Wittgenstein, although he treats it as a matter of mathematics, which he does not subsume under logic and language. Mathematics, for Whitehead, is the study of possibilities. Whether or not mathematics is applied is the result of a decision.[6] Both Whitehead and Wittgenstein apparently conceived of the possibility of ultimate occasions, to use Whitehead's phrase, making a

---

[6] Whitehead, *Process and Reality*, 496-99; *Dialogues of Alfred North Whitehead, as recorded by Lucien Price* (New York: Mentor Books, 1954), 252.

decision for or against existence. Wittgenstein, as asual, does not permit the separation of the occurrence from the language describing it.

Die Wahrheitsmöglichkeiten der Elementarsätze bedeuten die Möglichkeiten des Bestehens und Nichtbestehens der Sachverhalte (4.3).

Die Wahrheit der Tautologie ist gewiss, des Satzes möglich, der Kontradiktion unmöglich (4.464).

Ein Satz ist an sich weder wahrscheinlich noch unwahrscheinlich. Ein Ereignis trifft ein, oder es trifft nicht ein, ein Mittelding gibt es nicht (5.153).

Die Logik der Welt, die die Sätze der Logik in den Tautologien zeigen, zeigt die Mathematik in den Gleichungen (6.22).

It will be seen, however, that for Wittgenstein as well as for Whitehead, mathematics is a study of possibilities and not of actualities; but Wittgenstein made a more careful distinction. Tautologies exist only in language and not in the world. Since mathematics is a form of tautology, it is the study of possibilities which have become certain. Both Wittgenstein and Whitehead believe in an open future, but Wittgenstein's is radically open in the sense that what is thinkable was possible (6.361); Whitehead's doctrine of the future is closed to the degree that relations between the eternal objects determine what can and what cannot be a possibility in any situation. There is a quasi-causal nexus in Whitehead; there is none in Wittgenstein since each *Sachverhalt* and each elementary proposition is independent of all the others. "Der Glaube an den Kausalnexus ist der *Aberglaube*" (5.1361). It appears likely that Wittgenstein is more faithful to the language of the *Principia Mathematica*, but this fact does not make him a Humean any more than Whitehead's constant reference to Hume makes him one.

Wittgenstein's experience as an artilleryman was of the inexorability not of the laws but of the structure of the world which made it possible for there to be physical laws (5.552, 5.5521, 6.342-6.361). The logical form is itself transcendental, but it is not, as it is with Whitehead, a hierarchical structure of logical simples which require a principle of concretion, a primordial nature of

God.[7] The logical form is itself transcendental, as are the logical simples; but the world of our experience is not merely a copy of some transcendental realm. The totality of the logical simples and the possibilities of their combinations constitute the *Realität* out of which this actual world comes to be (3.3421, 5.471, 5.4711, 5.555, 3, 3.001-3.05). The form and the possibilities are a priori; the actualization, at least as far as we are concerned, is accidental. An actual object, whether it be a world or something much less complex, is a thing with the form and structure of the general proposition, the structure of any object whatsoever (2.01, 2.012, 2.0121, 5.634, 6., 6.37, 6.375, 6.362, 6.41). Both the world of all possible worlds *(Realität)* and the world of my experience owe their structure to the formal principle, which is logic; and this is equally true of the picture and the pictured, for the picture is also a fact *(Tatsache)* (2.1-3.02). The difference between an actual world and a possible world lies not in the logic which, except for quantification, is the same for both, but in the quality of the objects. In a possible world, which is but a portion of *Realität* (5.5262, 5.64), the objects *(Gegenstände)* are without extension. In an actual world, the objects have become things *(Dinge)* and are extended (4.01-4.0141, 4.1211-4.1272).

It must be recognized that in speaking in this way about things and objects we are doing a double violence against the *Tractatus.* The *Tractatus* is concerned with facts and propositions, not with things and objects. *Sachverhalte* and *Tatsachen* are correlates of individual minds and are dependent on the individual mind for the reality they have. Is it not true that when the individual dies, his world dies with him (6.431)? *Sachverhalte* and *Tatsachen* are described in propositions, and it is in propositions that they become parts of language. As parts of language, they become accessible to many minds; and it is as parts of language that it becomes possible to make existential and universal generalizations, although such generalizations have no counterpart in the experience of either *Realität* or a personal external world (4.126-4.1272). They

---

[7] *Process and Reality,* 134.

are linguistic contrivances even as the series of whole numbers (4.1252). For Wittgenstein, there is no world "out there", independent of every knowing and acting subject. Objects may have a meontic status, a status of potentiality; but they do not become things except as correlates to an individual knower. As with Schopenhauer, my world is my idea. Because of language I know that my world is very similar to the worlds of other human beings, and, on logical grounds, I know that there is a common form for any object whatsoever. It may be that God (the Will) brings *Realität*, the totality of potentiality, into the quasi-ontic status that we find in *empirische Realität*, but we do not know this. It would have been natural for a disciple of Schopenhauer to say this, but we have Miss Anscombe's word for it that Wittgenstein, while accepting the Schopenhauerian doctrine of the world as idea, rejected the idea of the world as will.[8] In any event, the God of the *Tractatus* seems much closer to the *Natura naturans* of Spinoza's *Ethics,* a point discussed in the fourth and seventh chapters.

2

Although Wittgenstein's theology has been a major aspect of much of this essay, we must try to show how he moved from the very real pessimism of his youth[9] to the qualified optimism of his mature years. Russell says of the young Wittgenstein that he was afraid that he might commit suicide, and that he was continuously concerned about his moral integrity. Pitcher reports:

Some sort of curse must have been hurled by a wicked and jealous demon over the gifted children who played in the luxurious mansion of the Wittgensteins in Vienna. Ludwig's sister, like their father, died slowly of cancer after several operations. Three of his four brothers committed suicide. The fourth, Paul, a brilliant concert pianist, lost his right arm in the first World War, only a few months after his highly successful debut. Ludwig himself was a strange tormented person. He

---

[8]   Anscombe, *An Introduction,* 11.
[9]   Bertrand Russell, "Philosophers and Idiots," in Fann (ed.), *Ludwig Wittgenstein,* 32.

was miserably unhappy as a child and youth; when 23, he confessed to his friend David Pinsent that for nine years he had suffered terrible loneliness and that he had continually thought of suicide. He even felt ashamed at never daring to kill himself; he had "had a hint" that he was *de trop* in the world, but had meanly disregarded it.[10]

David Pinsent is the one to whom the *Tractatus* is dedicated. He was killed during World War I.

Perhaps optimism, no matter how qualified, is too strong a description of Wittgenstein's mature character, particularly if we refer to his letters to Engelmann; but he did not suicide out as his brothers had done, and his own view of his life at the time of his death was that it had been a good life.[11] That it became a good life must be attributed to Wittgenstein's own striving after meaning in the midst of horror. We are accustomed, probably because of the influence of Strauss, to think of pre-World War I Vienna as a happy place, but this was not, in fact, the case. The Austro-Hungarian Empire was falling apart from inner decay, and it put up a fairly decent show against the Russians and the Italians only because the decay had proceeded further in Italy and Russia than it had in the land of the Hapsburgs. We need only to mention Mayerling to epitomize a whole culture and a whole era. Suicides were very common in pre-war Vienna, and a bleak despair underlay the frenetic gaiety. David Abrahamsen, the psychiatrist, has tried to analyze the mood of pre-war Vienna in his study of the life and suicide of Otto Weininger.[12] Weininger, again one of the half-assimilated Jews of the Viennese monarchy, had committed suicide at the beginning of a promising professional career. Wittgenstein thought well of him and his work.[13] Abrahamsen reports the following synoptic judgment of pre-war Vienna:

A new moral evaluation crept through the thought of the philosophers, Ibsen, Nietzsche, Kierkegaard, and many others, who claimed that the

---

[10]   Pitcher, *The Philosophy of Ludwig Wittgenstein*, 10.
[11]   Malcolm, *Ludwig Wittgenstein*, 100.
[12]   David Abrahamsen, *The Mind and Death of a Genius* (New York: Columbia U. Press, 1946), 36-37.
[13]   Erich Heller, "Symposium: Assessments of the Man and the Philosopher", in Fann (ed.), *Ludwig Wittgenstein*, 65.

action of man should be dependent upon his whole personality with all its emotional and intellectual content and, therefore, that all ideals, even the sacred ones, would have to be abandoned if the personality were to survive. This could mean no less than that the act and the ego would have to be one [Does *Tractatus* 6.422 reflect a refinement of this position which has an almost Aristotelian flavor?] and that the act and the ego would together win or die. . . . Hence the spasmodic despair, the relentless doubt; the twilight mood emerged as men strove to correlate their own existence with reality.[14]

We know that similar thoughts oppressed many of the French symbolists and that it was against this mood of despair that Eliot became a Christian and became the kind of Christian that he did.

World War I came to men and women who were already in grave doubt about everything. Initially it was greeted with a kind of joy on both sides because it substituted an immediate action for the brooding which had preceded it; but it soon became a horror show. Nevertheless, to those who survived it, it provided a breathing period and an alembic in which some also seemed to find themselves. Ludwig Wittgenstein seems to have been one of those who found themselves. Intellectually, the endlessly striving and mindlessly creating Will of Schopenhauer became attenuated to *das Höhere*. *Das Höhere* does not create yet provides the sense of the world (6.41). It may be that Wittgenstein still thought of the Will in connection with *das Höhere;* but, if he did, it is a Will emptied of its viciousness and provided with those positive qualities at which Schopenhauer hints as a possibility in the last section of the first volume of *The World as Will and Idea*. Schopenhauer is definite that these possibilities are open only to the religious man, the saint, and that they can never be achieved by thought; nevertheless, the empirical fact of sainthood is a warrant for believing that such qualities may exist and are attainable to one who has denied himself.

If the Will has become *das Höhere,* which is indifferent to the world (6.432), then there is the necessity for accounting for the world and what goes on in the world. It is obvious that *das Höhere,* if a god, is not a creating god and that it is different from Fate

14 Abrahamsen, *The Mind and Death of a Genius*, 36-37.

(6.372). Could Fate be *empirische Realität,* the womb out of which worlds and men accidentally come to be (6.41)? In that event we are still faced with a radical dualism: *das Höhere* and *Realität* are polar opposites. Logic and the world are of indifference to what is higher (6.432); but *das Höhere* may choose to interfere; or someone from the lower realm, the realm without values, may have caught a glimpse of that which is higher. In that event, the world becomes a place in which tasks are now set; and he who has been called finds: "Die Tatsachen gehören alle nur zur Aufgabe, nicht zur Lösung" (6.4321). If the distinction which has just been made between *das Höhere, empirische Realität,* and the world is a valid one, then the distinction between two kinds of mysticism referred to at 6.45 and 6.522 is equally valid. Drug mysticism undoubtedly belongs to the first; the second is not a feeling at all. It is a point of view (7).

3

Several pages above it was suggested that we may understand Wittgenstein better if we look for parallels in other religious-existential writing. According to his biographers, Kierkegaard was the most admired of Wittgenstein's predecessors.[15] Kierkegaard did not go to war, but he was self-consciously alienated by the commonplace belief of his time that all problems had been solved by science or the Hegelian system of philosophy. Wittgenstein says it thus: "es bei dem neuen System [nineteenth century science] scheinen soll, als sei *alles* erklärt" (6.372). Neither Wittgenstein nor Kierkegaard believed that everything had been explained. As he records in his journal and in *Fear and Trembling,* Kierkegaard, determined that it was his job to make people aware that there was no purely rational solution to the riddle of life.[16] Perhaps the following quotation from Kierkegaard's *Either/Or* will show forth the con-

---

[15] Drury, in Fann (ed.), *Ludwig Wittgenstein,* 70.
[16] *The Journals of Søren Kierkegaard,* trans. and ed. by Alexander Dru (London: Oxford University Press, 1938), 32-35.

clusions to which Wittgenstein came in the midst of the first World
War, and will also explain his deep distress after the war in his
inability to put away his pride,[17] his sense, therefore, that he was
a most loathsome being. The quotation from Kierkegaard reads:

So it is an edifying thought that against God we are always in the
wrong. . . . There is no edification in recognizing that God is always
in the right, and so, too, there is none in any thought which follows
from this by necessity. When you recognize that God is always in the
right you stand aloof from God, and so, too, when you recognize as a
consequence of this that you are always in the wrong, then you are
hidden in God. This is your divine worship, your religious devotion,
your godly fear. . . . Against God we are always in the wrong. This
thought checks doubt and calms its distress, it encourages and in-
spires to action. . . . Do not check your soul's flight, do not grieve the
better promptings within you, do not dull your spirit with half wishes
and half thoughts. Ask yourself, and continue to ask until you find the
answer. For one may have known a thing many times and acknowled-
ged it, one may have willed a thing many times and attempted it; and
yet it is only by the deep inward movements, only by the indescribable
emotions of the heart, that for the first time you are convinced that
what you have known belongs to you, that no power can take from
you; for only the truth which edifies is truth for you.[18]

The sermon from which the quotation is taken is bound up with
the *Or* volume of *Either/Or*. It illustrates, as probably many other
words could not, Wittgenstein's life-long problem: to put away his
pride. He was, in fact, touchy to the very end,[19] and touchiness is
really incompatible with the kind of world-denying life that he gave
himself to in the midst of World War I and which led him to live
austerely and to give away his fortune. Yet, there was a kind of
childlikeness to the older Wittgenstein which has always been the
mark of a saint. His resignation of his professorship and his retreat
to the coast of western Ireland is entirely consonant with a fundamental resolve to deny the world and its glories. Sainthood is never
achieved; it is a gift from *das Höhere*. We cannot then say that

[17]   Engelmann, *Letters*, Letters 12, 22, 23, 26, 28, 31.
[18]   Søren Kierkegaard, *Either/Or*, trans. by Walter Lowrie (2 vols.; Garden
City, New York: Doubleday, 1959), Vol. II, *Ultimatum*.
[19]   Malcolm, *Ludwig Wittgenstein*, 56.

Wittgenstein achieved sainthood before his death; but it is significant that Drury, Malcolm, and others felt that there was a quality of holiness in Wittgenstein's life and that if there is such a quality as saintliness, Wittgenstein possessed it.

It may help us to understand the uniqueness of Wittgenstein and his holiness if we will return to Kierkegaard for a moment. For Kierkegaard, the life dedicated to God is not necessarily different from any other life since it is the inner disposition which counts. The saint is one who lives as a knight of faith despite the absurd; yet there are a few clues which help the knight with his journey. It is from this Kierkegaardian viewpoint that we may well rewrite 6.432 to read: *"How* the world is, is completely indifferent for what is higher. God does not reveal Himself (as such) in the world." The words "as such" have been added. From a basically Christian point of view, the Divine is always *incognito,* and only those who have faith are able to observe the wonderful works of God;[20] others pass the works by, either without seeing them, or seeing them as the merest of commonplaces. Malcolm tells us that Wittgenstein felt sometimes that he himself would be able to live until his own work (*Aufgabe*) was finished.[21] If the above is a fair analysis of Wittgenstein's religious position, it is not very far from that which seems to stand in back of Kant's *Critique of Judgment.* The significant accidental is made significant by our attitudes toward it; and it is a clue that something is going on in the world which is different from those things which are described by the rigid categories of the first two critiques. With Wittgenstein, since the rigid categories had been much more attenuated, there is the possibility of much more of the purely accidental and spontaneous and, therefore, of more significant communication between man and man, and men and God.

4

Wittgenstein apparently talked in very limited ways about himself.

---

[20] Malcolm, *Ludwig Wittgenstein,* 70, 71.
[21] Malcolm, *Ludwig Wittgenstein,* 70, 71.

Even those who knew him as well as Malcolm and Miss Anscombe could disagree on the number of siblings who committed suicide. The correct number seems to be three. Similarly there are conflicting reports about his reading. It is usual to deny that he took a serious interest in earlier philosophers. It is much more likely that he read where he needed in order to help himself with his task, the *Aufgabe*, to which he refers at 6.4321. He did not see his task as one which required him to explain the thoughts of another philosopher. He did see his task as that of trying to find a way to make the realm of values secure from the philistines. To fulfill his purpose, he read, studied, thought about anything which would help him complete his task; and in this sense he was dependent on earlier philosophers and religious thinkers who had thought about the problems with which he was concerned.

In Chapter V an attempt was made to draw parallels with certain aspects of Spinoza's thought. Another concern has been to show that the *Tractatus* cannot be divorced from certain intellectual patterns which developed in France and central Europe in the years before the first World War. The parallels with certain aspects of Schopenhauer's and Nietzsche's thought are obvious, although they seem to have been obscured for those who see Wittgenstein as little more than a logician. Finally, there seems to be very little awareness of the parallels with Kant. It is unlikely that Wittgenstein read Kant, Spinoza, or Schopenhauer after he went to England several years before World War I; and, if he did read Nietzsche during the war, it was likely that he did so only as a diversion. Earlier in this essay it has been suggested that Wittgenstein's primary philosophical reading in the period before he went to England may have been limited to Schopenhauer, with occasional forays into other philosophers who could help him with his problem of finding a *Weltanschauung* with which he could live; but this is a limitation which is quite unrealistic. Even in 1950 a well-reared young man in Vienna would have been expected to have more than a nodding acquaintance with Kant; and it is the intent of this section of the essay to show that Wittgenstein's awareness of the Kantian philosophy is more than he could have derived from a dilletante glancing at the three *Critiques*. The crucial parallels are to be found in Wittgenstein's reassessment of the boundaries of the transcendental unity of apperception and the place of the unique and the accidental. As a philosopher of science, as Ryle called him in his memorial lecture, Wittgenstein was concerned with the topics of the *Critique of Pure Reason;* as a religious man, he was concerned with the validity of ethical, religious, and esthetic experience, concerns of the later *Critiques*.

Kant's critical philosophy came into being, at least for the most part, as the result of his reaction to Hume's devastating dissection of the possibilities of human knowledge. Kant's reaction was to devise a tool, *The Critique of Pure Reason,* to demonstrate that knowledge within certain areas of experience was not only possible, but developes necessarily out of a set of inter-related transcendental rules and modes of intuition as the modes and rules apply to possible experiences. Hume's criticism was shown to apply only if we assume that those things which are sensed are things in themselves. If we do away with that assumption and limit our scientific inquiries, we find, in fact, that the world proceeds in terms of rules; but those rules have their transcendental origin in the very character of rational thought. Kant called the inter-related set of rules and intuitions the transcendental untiy of apperception. As just stated, the transcendental unity of apperception may be seen as identical in both the first and the second edition of the *Critique of Pure Reason*; but we must recognize that Schopenhauer in his criticism of the Kantian philosophy preferred the first edition with its psychologizing qualities to the more abstract character of the later edition. The Kant with which we will be concerned is the Kant of the second edition, but there is an apt quotation from the first edition which illustrates what is meant by the transcendental unity of apperception. It may be that Wittgenstein, himself, preferred the first edition because of Schopenhauer's influence.

Thus the understanding is something more than a power of formulating rules through comparison of appearances [essentially Hume's position]; it is itself the lawgiver of nature. Save through it, nature, that is, synthetic unity of the manifold of appearances according to rules, would not exist at all (for appearances, as such, cannot exist outside us — they exist only in our sensibility); and this nature, as object of knowledge in an experience, with everything which it may contain, is only possible in the unity of apperception. The unity of apperception is thus the transcendental ground of the necessary conformity to law of all experiences in one experience.[22]

The transcendental unity of apperception which Kant introduced into philosophy may be called a philosophical "I" correlated to the world considered in the most general terms, the world revealed by Newtonian science and Euclidean geometry. Without the philosophical "I" there would be no world, at least as we understand it; and all regularity would disappear. The reader is reminded of the constant references to a philosophical "I" in the *Tractatus* (5.557-5.64). There is a constant tendency in most commentaries, such as Black,[23] to consider Wittgenstein's discussion of the philosophical "I" as an attack on a metaphysical subject; but it is, on the whole, more consistent with actual material in the *Tractatus* to see the philosophical "I" as the final attenuation of Kant's transcendental unity of apperception.

At this point a distinction must again be made between accidental and universal or logical generality. The generality which is the result of the a priori nature of the transcendental unity of apperception is universal or logical. Russell's failure to see this distinction in the *Tractatus*, despite the fact that Wittgenstein makes an issue of the matter (6.031, 6.1232), is the greatest weakness of his "Introduction"; but empiricists are, by the nature of their assumptions, driven both to a blurring of distinctions and a fundamental irrationalism. In the *Tractatus* Wittgenstein is describing the general form and limits of all possible objects, the same thing that Kant is attempting to do in the first *Critique;* and, as we shall see later, he, like Kant, is attempting to show that individual worlds may vary within those limits. In no sense of the matter is either Kant or Wittgenstein attempting to make a general description by

[22] *Immanuel Kant's Critique of Pure Reason,* trans. by Norman Kemp Smith (New York: Humanities Press, 1950), 148, A127.
[23] Black, *A Companion,* 308-11.

abstracting that which is common to a large number of objects. Neither Kant nor Wittgenstein is an empiricist, and the attempt to place them within empiricist molds of thought is to falsify them. Nevertheless, each, by his method, is attempting to account for the regularities to be found in human experience; and both are prepared to state without hesitation that without a transcendental unity of apperception there is no world and that any world vanishes with the disappearance of the "soul". The best statement of Kant's earlier position is to be found at A382-383.

But although rational psychology cannot be used to extend knowledge, and when so employed is entirely made up of paralogisms, still we cannot deny it a considerable negative value, if it is taken as nothing more than a critical treatment of our dialectical inferences, those that arise from the common and natural reason of men.

Why do we have resort to a doctrine of the soul founded exclusively on pure principles of reason? Beyond all doubt, chiefly in order to secure our thinking self against the danger of materialism. This is achieved by means of the pure concept *(Vernunftbegriff)* of our thinking self. . . . For by this teaching so completely are we freed from the fear that on the removal of matter all thought, and even the very existence of thinking beings, would be destroyed, that on the contrary it is clearly shown, that if I remove the thinking subject the whole corporeal world must at once vanish: it is nothing save an appearance in the sensibility of our subject and a mode of its representations.

I admit this does not give me any further knowledge of the properties of this thinking self, nor does it enable me to determine its permanence or even that it exists independently of what we may conjecture to be the transcendental substratum of outer appearances; for the latter is just as unknown to me as is the thinking self.[24]

Both Wittgenstein and Kant were concerned to distinguish a philosophical or rational "soul" from a soul or psyche which could be investigated empirically. Wittgenstein's discussion is complicated, however, by the latent dualism of which he himself does not appear to have been conscious (4.128). In the first *Critique* Kant makes every effort to avoid giving an ontological status to anything including the philosophical "I". With Wittgenstein, on the

[24]   *Immanuel Kant*, 353-54.

other hand, there is the assumption that the philosophical "I" is of a different quality from the world correlated to it. The world comes to be out of *empirische Realität* and is of a different substance than the soul which is its boundary (5.631-5.641), but the soul and its world are inter-related and interdependent. The world and the soul live and die together (6.431-1.4312).[25] What causes a world to come to be is left unexplained in the *Tractatus,* but there is an implication that it is through the power of the *Logos,* language and logic, that there is a world at all (5.6-5.62).[26] The explicit doctrine of the *Tractatus* is that any actual world or, for that matter, any actual object is an accident (6.41). Nevertheless, at least in connection with worlds correlated to souls, there is a correlation of logic with what goes on in the world (5.557). Logic seems to have no relation with *empirische Realität* or to be a quality of the worlds correlate to souls; but logic seems to be a quality of the simple "I"s which bound the several worlds and which may be discovered through the expedient of holding up a mirror to those languages. Then logic is revealed as a *Spiegelbild* (6.13) of language and the several worlds.

Since, by definition, if not by empirical investigation, souls cannot be found in a world anymore than Kant's transcendental unity of apperception can be found in a world of appearances, it is evident that most of what we may have to say about the soul must be stated negatively. Nevertheless, to say some things negatively is to say something; and Wittgenstein has left us several hints as to his understanding of the soul as a transcendental, although not as a transcendent, object. The first appears in an argument with Moore and Russell about the truth-functional character of such ordinary language sentences as "A judges p" where "p" is

---

[25] Wittgenstein gives no ontological status to souls nor to anything else, yet his souls function very much like Bradley's finite centers. In many respects, the *Tractatus* is an examination of Bradley's appearances as seen through the alembic of the language of the *Principia Mathematica.* As for Bradley's *Reality,* that is the inexpressible.

[26] Although Neo-Kantianism is not named in the *Tractatus,* it was a widely spread doctrine in Wittgenstein's youth. The position summarized in the text could have been borrowed from it.

itself a proposition. The logical problem is not our concern, at least not at this place. Rather, we are concerned about the implications which Wittgenstein drew, in the midst of the argument, for the simplicity of the soul. The most that needs to be said about the logical or syntactical problem is what Wittgenstein himself says: the problem concerns the relations among *Gegenstände* or locutions within language itself. The important hint that Wittgenstein gives us at this point about the simplicity of the soul reads as follows:

Dies zeigt auch, dass die Seele — das Subjekt, etc. — wie sie in der heutigen oberflächlichen Psychologie aufgefasst wird, ein Unding ist. Eine zusammengesetzte Seele wäre nämlich keine Seele mehr (5.5421).

It is significant, as is true with so many of Wittgenstein's statements, that "wäre" (would be) is in the subjunctive. Wittgenstein wishes to cast doubt on the character of the whole argument. Nor does Wittgenstein tell us the locus of logic. It is not an aspect of *empirische Realität* because, if it were, it would not have to be approached obliquely in order to be observed. Rather, it appears that logic is the constituent of the soul even as the Kantian forms of sensibility and the categories are the constituents of the Kantian transcendental unity of apperception.

Die Logik ist *vor* jeder Erfahrung — dass etwas *so* ist. Sie ist vor dem Wie, nicht vor dem Was (5.552).

Before quoting the next proposition, I must remind the reader of the earlier discussion of Wittgenstein's unique use of Occam's razor. In sum, the discussion affirmed that Wittgenstein's position was that a *Gegenstand* does not become a *Sache* or a *Ding* until there is an interaction between the potentiality of the *Gegenstände* and the creating *Logos*.

Die *Anwendung* der Logik entscheidet darüber, welche Elementarsätze es gibt. Was in der Anwendung liegt, kann die Logik nicht vorausnehmen. Das ist klar: Die Logik darf mit ihrer Anwendung nicht kollidieren. Aber die Logik muss sich mit ihrer Anwendung berühren. Also dürfen die Logik und ihre Anwendung einander nicht übergreifen (5.557).

This statement, together with the understanding of the matrix-like character of *empirische Realität* goes far to explain the cryptic remarks which begin at 2.1 and carry through to 2.223, but it appears likely that this same view of the inter-relatedness of logic, the world, and *empirische Realität* stands in back of the large number of remarks in which logic is called the scaffolding of the world, e.g. 6.124. There are no worlds, at least as we know them, which do not have this logical scaffolding.

Die Logik erfüllt die Welt; die Grenzen der Welt sind auch ihre Grenzen (5.61).

Does this imply that there may be worlds in which the writ of logic does not run, but that we are unable to think of what they might be like (3.031, 3.032, 6.361)? This seems to have been Schopenhauer's position; and it is quite evidently the position of the *Philosophical Investigations*. The singularity of my world is demonstrated by the following quotations.

Dass die Welt *meine* Welt ist, das zeigt sich darin, dass die Grenzen der Sprache . . . die Grenzen *meiner* Welt bedeuten (5.62).

Surely, Wittgenstein is using "bedeuten" in a purely Fregian sense at this place. The boundaries of my language in becoming the boundaries of my world have become almost palpable.

The relations between Wittgenstein's "I"'s and their several worlds are not easily determined. Obviously, the world and the "I" correlated to it are neither of them creatures of the other since "die Welt is unabhängig von meinem Willen" (6.373); but, on the other hand "die Welt und das Leben sind Eins" (5.621), and "beim Tod die Welt sich nicht ändert, sondern aufhört" (6.431). Again, in an old, old phrase he says "Ich bin meine Welt. (Der Mikrokosmos.)" (5.63). If there is a microcosm, there is a macrocosm; and the "I" and the world correlate to it have something in common. The world is not "my" projection; it has its own "whatness" apart from "me". But "I", considered as a transcendental unity of apperception, give *Wirklichkeit* the structure that it has. Perhaps this understanding will go far to explain such difficult statements as 3.13.

Zum Satz gehört alles, was zur Projektion gehört; aber nicht das Projizierte. Also die Möglichkeit des Projizierten, aber nicht dieses selbst. Im Satz ist also sein Sinn noch nicht enthalten, wohl aber die Möglichkeit ihn auszudrücken. ("Der Inhalt des Satzes" heisst der Inhalt des sinnvollen Satzes.) Im Satz ist die Form seines Sinnes enthalten, aber nicht dessen Inhalt (3.13).

Empirische Realität maintains its quasi-existence, its meontic nonbeing, apart from "my" life or any other life. The potentialities within *empirische Realität* are given life, made into facts, by the several philosophical "I"s. Therefore, "die Welt ist alles, was der Fall ist' (1) (in that particular world), and "die Welt ist die Gesamtheit der Tatsachen, nicht der Dinge" (1.1).

In unpacking the many Chinese boxes of the *Tractatus,* one is apt to become very confused and to impose his own thinking on the author's and to make the author say things he obviously did not say. This can be seen even in such a competent scholar as Max Black who interprets Wittgenstein's arguments in such a way as to assert that Wittgenstein was intending to prove that there is no soul.[27] In the sense that a soul is necessarily an immaterial substance, Black is quite right, but if the soul is thought of as an active point of view (Wittgenstein's equivalent of Kant's transcendental unity of apperception), then Black's handling of Wittgenstein's arguments is patently false. Wittgenstein is a rationalist, but he is not an ontologist. His analyses are attempts to probe various suppositions about the nature of the world and to show that any ontology falls from its own self-contradictions.

To say that Wittgenstein was not an ontologist does not say that he was uninterested in ontological problems; for he found himself and all of mankind imprisoned, as far as ultimacy is concerned, within language worlds. There may be gods, there may be elements, there may be souls; but let us avoid going beyond the evidence which is available to us; that evidence is limited to the symbols of our languages. Having recognized the lack of evidence beyond language, let us go on to admit, however, that as we search the *Tractatus* for clues to its meaning we find an implicit radical dual-

27 Black, *A Companion,* 308-11.

ism of which Wittgenstein, himself, may have been unaware.

What in fact seems to be the case is that Wittgenstein modified the Kantian-Schopenhauerian doctrines in his own particular way so as to affirm a soul as the boundary of a particular world and God as the boundary of the totality of all possible worlds. There are parallels to this view in the New Testament, particularly Saint John's Gospel and the Epistles to the Hebrews and to the Colossians (5.552); but, Lord Russell notwithstanding, the doctrine of the *Tractatus* is not Christian. If we did what Wittgenstein himself did not do, we would have to place him within the framework of the speculative systems of the Gnostics: the constituents of his total ontology seem to be *das Höhere,* a most high God, individual psyches each to a degree imprisoned in a world not of its making, and an ultimate reality which is radically different from both God and the psyches. The constituents with which Wittgenstein is dealing are not, in fact, different from those of the early Christians; but the early Christians took the *Logos* up into *das Höhere,* made the psyches mortal, and claimed that all possible worlds were created from nothing rather than something. Nevertheless, as Saint Augustine was careful to admit, the unity which the Christians found in their world was based on faith; and theology was an explication of that faith.

5

Although there are many parallels between Kant's first *Critique* and the *Tractatus,* to pursue them all would necessitate an examination of the critical philosophy which would be far beyond the scope of this essay. In summary, Kant was concerned to provide a framework within which the observed regularities of nature could be understood as something other than chance occurrences. In addition, he wished to find a basis for moral judgments other than the consensus of a particular community; and, finally, he wanted to demonstrate the place of the unique, the beautiful and sublime, and purpose within a world whose main outlines had been sketched in *The Critique of Pure Reason*. The *Tractatus* is a more limited work than the critical philosophy, but its purpose seems to have been similar: to draw careful distinctions between what can be said and what can only be shown; and to say what can be said with clarity (4.116).

In the critical philosophy, the first *Critique* demonstrates that the world shows itself in its regularity through the operation of the schematized categories of the understanding. The categories, like Wittgenstein's logic and mathematics, are transcendental; but they may not, except as heuristic devices, be applied to the purely transcendent. Whether there is, in fact, a transcendent cannot be known; but we can know this at least: that categories of a lower level are not applicable to a higher level. Wittgenstein stated it thus: "Propositions cannot express anything higher" (6.42). Hence there can be no ethical nor esthetic propositions since both ethics and esthetics belong to the realm of *das Höhere*, the transcendent — before which we must be silent (7).

Schopenhauer thought of himself as the true heir of Kant, and there seems little doubt that Wittgenstein was influenced in his understanding of Kant by his earlier understanding of Schopenhauer's system. Schopenhauer reduced Kant's twelve schematized categories to one: causality understood as the principle of sufficient reason. It is not necessary for our purposes to examine the Schopenhauerian analysis of the principle of sufficient reason; but, as with Kant, the category of causality applied only to the world of appearances. Schopenhauer's big leap was to the belief that Kant's *Ding-an-sich* is an ontological Will which ceaselessly seeks to objectify itself. Wittgenstein reassessed the Will; and it is most likely that out of this reassessment we get the implied doctrine of many wills and *das Höhere*. But it is in his handling of the category of causality that we find his biggest break with Schopenhauer; he was at the same time breaking with most of nineteenth century science.

Alles Folgern geschieht a priori (5.133).

Aus einem Elementarsatz lässt sich kein anderer folgern (5.134).

Auf keine Weise kann aus dem Bestehen irgend einer Sachlage auf

das Bestehen einer, von ihr gänzlich verschiedenen Sachlage geschlossen werden (5.135).

Einen Kausalnexus, der einen solchen Schluss rechtfertigte, gibt es
nicht (5.136).
Die Ereignisse der Zukunft können wir nicht aus den gegenwärtigen
erschliessen. Der Glaube an den Kausalnexus ist der *Aberglaube*
(5.1361).

Nevertheless, Wittgenstein's rejection of causality is not complete.
We do not live in Mauthner's nor Hume's random worlds. Rather,
causality is the form of a law (6.32). It is the way our minds, and
therefore our languages, work (6.361).

As we examine the matter of the Kantian categories closely we
find that, although Wittgenstein rejected the categories as the forms
of a transcendental unity of apperception, he did pick up an aside
(B 303n) which Kant himself had considered in the second edition
of the *Critique of Pure Reason*. Kant did not believe that the
aside was worth pursuing because it did not provide enough of a
framework, at least for him, for a reasonably constituted world.
Wittgenstein, on the other hand, found the logical modalities: possibility, certainty and impossibility all that we could rely on; but he
did not understand possibility as Russell did: that sometimes an
event will occur.[28] In Wittgenstein's worlds there is a present king
of France; in Russell's, never. In Russell's understanding of the
modalities, they are ultimately related to the on-going course of
events in this particular world line. In Wittgenstein's understanding, there are many world lines; and the modalities are purely
logical and a priori. The quotation from Kant reads:

In a word, if all sensible intuition, the only kind of intuition which we
possess, is removed, not one of these concepts can in any fashion
verify itself, so as to show its *real* possibility. Only *logical* possibility
then remains, that is, that the concept or thought is possible. That,
however, is not what we are discussing, but whether the concept relates
to an object and so signifies something (B303n).[29]

In this connection, it is probably wise to remember that Kant, in

---

[28]   Russell, *Logic and Knowledge*, 231.
[29]   *Immanuel Kant*, 263.

the first *Critique*, was analyzing the framework for any possible world; but at the same time he held to the belief that there is at least one world. Wittgenstein, on the other hand, was always puzzled by the fact that there is any world at all.[30] Logic is itself prior to any world (5.552), and any world is, in fact, an accident (6.41).

If we accept Wittgenstein's analysis as legitimate, in fact the only permissible analysis, we are left with a much more disordered world than Kant or Schopenhauer left us, although it is by no means as disordered as Hume's. Some things are impossible, e.g. logical contradiction within the world of experience. But Wittgenstein's world or worlds are much more open toward the future than are Kant's or Schopenhauer's. The possible need not occur, but it may. The certain will necessarily occur, but the certain itself can exist only in language (4.46-4.466); we manufacture the tautologies, including the equations of mathematics. In practice, the *Tractatus* leads to the conclusion that the only significant statements are those which describe the accidental or the spontaneous. In fact, it is the accidental which is the real, and of the accidental we can make only one a priori statement — that the event may not contradict itself (6.3751). Mauthner had also said that only the accidental was real; and he had claimed that contradictions exist only in language itself.

In discussing Wittgenstein's handling of the modalities, it is very important to recognize that he did not confuse the possible with the necessary. In terms of the epistemology and metaphysics which has been demonstrated as apparently lying under the *Tractatus* it would seem most likely that that which is possible necessarily comes to pass, if not in this world, then in some other. But Wittgenstein carefully avoids making such an assumption. The world may be infinitely complex (4.2211). If so, we cannot assume that all possibilities are actualized in some *Wirklichkeit*. In other words, Wittgenstein, here as elsewhere, refuses to go beyond the necessities of his analysis to some speculative vantage point. Secondly,

---

such a point of view would have been contrary to his understanding of the nature of language and its core: logic. What is thinkable is also possible (3.02-3.032); but such a statement does not insure the existence of that which is thinkable or of that which is possible. Nevertheless, "das angewandte, gedachte, Satzzeichen ist der Gedanke" (3.5), and "der Gedanke ist der sinnvolle Satz" (4). If we will think again of the matrix out of which all worlds arise, the two different views can be reconciled. All worlds come into being through the inter-reaction of meontic non-being with souls. The worlds are composed of materials in the matrix (3.13), but their form is dependent in each case on the "I" to which it is related. There is a common form described by the general proposition, but the appearance of any particular feature of a world is dependent on the inter-action between the natural matrix, *empirische Realität*, and an "I" of some kind. That "I" could be a man or a god; but the "I" itself would never appear in the world (5.5571-5.641). Furthermore, as the "I" thinks about its world, it thinks about the world in terms of facts, arranged congeries of names, rather than discretely ordered things (1.1, 3.221, 3.26, 3.262). Nevertheless, the significant event, considered as a fact (2.141) can become a means of communication between two or more "I"s and between any number of "I"s and God (3.1, 3.14, 3.2, 3.201, 3.25, 3.262). Language communities exist because "I"s do talk with each other; and faith communities exist because of alleged revelations.

It seems quite common to see Wittgenstein's development of the truth tables as something apart from the rest of the *Tractatus*. This is certainly Miss Anscombe's approach; and, if Miss Anscombe is correct, the truth tables are only interesting toys. But it is most likely that Miss Anscombe is wrong and that the truth tables are an integral part of the whole development of the *Tractatus*. They are an integral part because we can never get outside of our language worlds and must, therefore, find some way within the language world which is ours to discern whether we are being consistent or not. Much as we would like, we cannot check our statements against *empirische Realität*. The truth tables are an artificial matrix whereby we can test any statement for its consistency and identify the linguistic *Gegenstände* which are the elements of the statement and our world.

6

At the level of analysis of Kant's first and second *Critiques*, individual variations from a norm, even if they exist, are at most accidental and therefore irrelevant to the presuppositions of cognitive and moral action. Several statements at the end of the *Tractatus* may be compared with statements in the first *Critique*; but the moral position taken in the *Tractatus* is very different from that taken in the second *Critique*. Essentially, the parallels with the first *Critique* are attempts to trace out the implications of the general proposition for our understanding of the physical world. The physical world may be described in various ways, and how it is described is a matter of decision; but the descriptions which we choose imply that the world may be described with rigor (6.342). *Mechanics*, for instance, is an attempt to describe the world with rigor; and *mechanics* is able to do this because the propositions of *mechanics* are generalizations which concern any objects whatsoever (6.342-6.361). A significant aspect of the development of the *Tractatus* is Wittgenstein's successful attempt to make a secure base for general propositions and to distinguish general propositions from the significant propositions which describe unique states of affairs — the elementary propositions. Both general and elementary propositions exist in our language and refer to the facts which we find in the world; but they exist in our language in quite different ways, ways which the middle portions of the *Tractatus* explore quite carefully. The inter-relation of significant propositions, general propositions and the several worlds of various observers or actors may be seen in the following quotation:

Es verändert ja die Wahr- oder Falscheit *jedes* Satzes etwas am allgemeinen Bau der Welt. Und der Spielraum, welcher ihrem Bau durch die Gesamtheit der Elementarsätze gelassen wird, ist eben derjenige, welchen die ganz allgemeinen Sätze begrenzen (5.5262).

In theory, although not in practice, only the significant or elementary propositions are phenomenologically true or false because only logical modalities and accidental or significant events have existence; and even the latter have existence only as parts of facts (1.1, 3.142, 6.375, 6.41). General propositions exist only within language and have no reference outside of language (4.125-4.12721, 3.311-3.317); nevertheless, as parts of language and, therefore of logic, the general propositions in their application to the world express a creative function (5.471-5.472).

It is we who make a decision as to what constitutes a fact and what does not; and it is we who give a fact an interpretation. In the Fregian sense, we give a fact meaning by postulating bearers within *empirische Realität* for our facts. Neither our rational souls nor God are parts of nature;[31] but if there is any sense to nature, it is we or God, or both who give it sense (6.41). On the other hand it is equally true that the events within nature are meanings (*Bedeutungen*) for God and ourselves; although what exactly the meaning is is a question of hermeneutics or semantics. The *Tractatus* is concerned primarily with syntax, with the most general frame of reference for experience that it was possible to formulate. Nevertheless, if one is going to provide the framework for a complete philosophy, one must provide some way of handling the accidental, the apparently spontaneous. It was Kant's awareness of the intellectual problem of the accidental and the necessity of accounting for our development of empirical laws which led him to write the *Critique of Judgment*. The *Critique of Pure Reason* is a framework for all possible experience; but it tells us nothing about actual experience. The *Critique of Judgment* is concerned with actual experience and it tells us how to cope with the actual event in terms of canons of esthetic and teleological judgment. In no sense may it be asserted that in the third *Critique* Kant is denying anything that he was saying earlier in the first. Rather, he is telling us how to live in the world of our experience where the actual events, as

---

[31] The word "nature" is introduced at this point as a synonym for the actualization of all possible worlds. It is to be distinguished from *empirische Realität* in that it is actual rather than potential.

we reflect upon them, may give us clues to what is beyond our experience and which had to be ruled out in the first *Critique* as dogmatic and illegitimate extensions of the power of reason. A guide to all of Kant's work must be found in the statement: "Concepts without percepts are empty; percepts without concepts are blind."

It will perhaps clarify the distinction between Kant's purposes in the first and third *Critiques* if we turn to an earlier philosopher who obviously had thought much about the difference between certain, or necessary, knowledge and empirical generalizations. In the *Physics,* and the corresponding passages in the *Metaphysics,* Aristotle tells us that science is concerned with that which is always, or for the most part, true;[32] but at the same time he recognizes that in our actual experience we find many events which occur with irregularity, accidentally or with apparent spontaneity.[33] Again, in the sixth book of the *Nichomachean Ethics* he speaks of the practically wise man as one who is able to move from singular to singular proposition without subsuming the two described events under a universal law. In the *Tractatus,* there is the recognition of the accidentality of most events which happen in the world and of the significant propositions which attempt to describe them. If we stay within the limits of our analysis, which on the whole Wittgenstein does, we can say little more; but there is a subtle implication toward the end of the *Tractatus* that the accidental has a kind of a cause which itself is outside of the natural order. That cause is the "inexpressible"; but the cause may very well be *das Höhere* or a rational soul. Neither *das Höhere* nor rational souls are parts of the world, parts of nature; and they themselves can never appear in the world; but there would be no world if rational souls, and God, were not in some way in dialogue with *empirische Realität.* If we are to have converse with our fellows or with God, it must be through the medium of events which occur in the world; and a fact is an event within the world. We know *das Höhere* particularly

---

[32] *The Basic Works of Aristotle,* ed. by Richard McKeon (New York: Random House, 1941), 243-47, 195-198a.
[33] McKeon (ed.), *The Basic Works of Aristotle,* 243-47, 195b-198a.

through and in the moral demands which we find imposed upon us; and we feel that it will be *das Höhere* which will reward or punish us for our failure or success at completing the tasks set before us (6.41-6.422). The *Tractatus* prepares the framework for the possibility of a *Heilsgeschichte,* which to a philistine would be nothing more than the meaningless succession of events. The theory of knowledge presupposed by the *Tractatus* is Hebrew rather than Greek. A similar theory of knowledge underlies the work of another great Jew: Martin Buber. Greek ways of thought and Hebrew ways of thought are quite different in their understanding of objectivity. To the classical Hebrew, reality is that which appears as the result of the dialogue between persons (*psyches*), between souls and the world, and between souls and God. Objectivity, *per se, an und für sich,* is not a part of Hebrew thinking. In fact, if we are to believe Heidegger, it came into the Greek world only with Plato. Ludwig Wittgenstein, functioning within a fundamentally Greek world, attempts in the *Tractatus* to put limits to Greek modes of thought in order to provide a scope for those who would and could think otherwise.

Were we to summarize the importance of the *Tractatus* in a few words, we would see its value primarily in terms of its warning against reifying myths, no matter how compelling they may be. This includes scientific as well as religious myths. But Wittgenstein would also force us to recognize that any over-simplified language such as Fortran's or Rosser's inevitably excludes certain aspects of "reality". Occam's razor cuts two ways: to sheer away redundancy; but equally to cause us to disregard that which in another context might fit a different factual statement. In another context, in another statement, the *Gegenstand* might be terribly important. Surely, this is what the biblical authors had in mind when they stated that the discarded stone had, indeed, become the corner stone.

BIBLIOGRAPHY

Professor K. T. Fann, Florida State University, has prepared a comprehensive Wittgenstein bibliography which contains works by Wittgenstein and books, dissertations, theses, and articles about him and his writings. This bibliography may be found in Dr. Fann's book, *Wittgenstein's Conception of Philosophy*, which is listed below. A supplement to this bibliography, bringing it up to date, was printed by the *Revue Internationale de Philosophie* XXIII (Brussels, 1969), 363-370. The books and articles listed below are those cited in the dissertation. In the case of articles which have been made part of an anthology, only the anthology is listed.

Abrahamsen, David, *The Mind and Death of a Genius* (New York: Columbia University Press, 1946).

Anscombe, G. E. M., *An Introduction to Wittgenstein's 'Tractatus'*, 2d. ed. rev. (New York: Harper & Row, 1965).

Aristotle, *The Basic Works*, ed. by Richard McKeon (New York: Random House, 1941).

Austin, J. L., *Sense and Sensibilia*, ed. by G. J. Warnoch (Oxford: Clarendon Press, 1962).

Beth, Evert W., *The Foundations of Mathematics: A Study in the Philosophy of Science* (New York: Harper & Row, 1966).

Black, Max, *A Companion to Wittgenstein's 'Tractatus'* (Ithaca, New York: Cornell University Press, 1964).

Bradley, Francis H., *Appearance and Reality*, 2d. ed. (London: George Allen and Unwin, 1897).

Cassirer, Ernst, *An Essay on Man: An Introduction to a Philosophy of Human Culture* (Garden City, N.Y.: Doubleday, 1954).

Cassirer, Eva, "Review of Anscombe", *British Journal for the Philosophy of Science* XIV (1964), 359-366.

Copi, Irving M., and Robert W. Beard (eds.), *Essays on Wittgenstein's 'Tractatus'* (New York: Macmillan, 1966).

Copleston, Frederick S. J., *A History of Philosophy*, 8 vols. (Westminster, Md.: The Newman Press, 1955-66).

Engelmann, Paul, *Letters from Ludwig Wittgenstein with a Memoir*, trans. by L. Furtmuller, ed. by B. F. McGuiness (New York: Horizon Press, 1968).

Esslin, Martin, *The Theater of the Absurd* (Garden City, N.Y.: Doubleday, 1961).

Fann, K. T., *Wittgenstein's Conception of Philosophy* (Berkeley: University of California Press, 1969).

Fann, K. T. (ed.), *Ludwig Wittgenstein: The Man and His Philosophy* (New York: Dell, 1967).

Finch, Henry LeRoy, *Wittgenstein – The Early Philosophy: An Exposition of the 'Tractatus'* (New York: Humanities Press, 1971).

Holthusen, Hans Egon, *Rainer Maria Rilke: A Study of His Later Poetry*, trans. by J. P. Stern (New Haven, Connecticut: Yale University Press, 1952).

Immanuel Kant's Critique of Pure Reason, trans. by Norman Kemp Smith (New York: Humanities Press, 1950).

Jones, Genesius, *Approach to the Purpose: A Study of the Poetry of T. S. Eliot* (New York: Barnes and Noble, 1966).

Kenner, Hugh (ed.), *T. S. Eliot: A Collection of Critical Essays* (Englewood Cliffs: Prentice Hall, 1962).

Kierkegaard, Søren, *Either/Or*, trans. by Walter Lowrie, 2 vols. (Garden City, N.Y.: Doubleday, 1959).

——, *The Journals of Søren Kierkegaard*, trans. and ed. by Alexander Dru (London: Oxford University Press, 1938).

Klemke, E. D. (ed.), *Essays on Frege* (Urbana: University of Illinois Press, 1968).

——, *Essays on Wittgenstein* (Urbana: University of Illinois Press, 1971).

Malcolm, Norman, *Ludwig Wittgenstein: A Memoir* (New York: Oxford University Press, 1962).

Maslow, Alexander, *A Study in Wittgenstein's 'Tractatus'* (Berkeley: University of California Press, 1961).

Mauthner, Fritz *Beiträge zu einer Kritik der Sprache*, 3 vols. 3rd ed. (Leipzig: Felix Meiner, 1923. Photocopy: Hildesheim: Georg Olms, 1969).

Merleau-Ponty, M., *Phenomenology of Perception*, trans. by Colin Smith (London: Routledge and Kegan Paul, 1962).

Murdoch, Iris, *Bruno's Dream* (New York: Viking Press, 1969).

Newman, John Henry, *An Essay in Aid of a Grammar of Assent* (Garden City, N.Y.: Doubleday, 1955).

Plato, *Dialogues*, trans. by B. Jowett (New York: Random House, 1937).

Pitcher, George, *The Philosophy of Wittgenstein* (Englewood Cliffs, N.J.: Prentice Hall, 1964).

Plochmann, George K., "Review of Anscombe", *Modern Schoolman* XXXVII (1960), 242-46.

Rhees, Rush, "Miss Anscombe on the Tractatus", *Philosophical Quarterly* X (1960), 21-31.

Russel, Bertrand, *Human Knowledge: Its Scope and Limits* (New York: Simon and Schuster, 1948).

——, "Introduction", *Tractatus Logico-Philosophicus* (London: Routledge and Kegan Paul, 1960).

——, *Logic and Knowledge: Essays 1901-1950*, ed. by Robert Charles Marlh (New York: Macmillan, 1968).

Schopenhauer, Arthur, *The World as Will and Idea,* trans. by R. B. Haldane and J. Kemp, 3 vols. (London: Kegan Paul, Trench, Trübner and Co., 1907).

Spinoza, Benedict De, *The Chief Works,* trans. by R. H. M. Elwes (New York: Dover Publications, 1951).

Stenius, Erik, *Wittgenstein's 'Tractatus', A Critical Exposition of Its Main Lines of Thought (Oxford:* Oxford University Press, 1960).

Toulmin, Stephen Edelston, "Ludwig Wittgenstein", *Encounter* XXII (January 1969), 58-71.

Weiler, Gershon, *Mauthner's Critique of Language* (Cambridge: Cambridge University Press, 1970).

Werkmeister, William H., *Cassirers Verhältnis zur Neukantischen Philosophie, herausgegeben von Paul Arthur Schilpp. Sonderdruck* (Stuttgart: W. Kohlhammer, n.d.).

Whitehead, Alfred North, *Dialogues,* recorded by Lucien Price (New York: Mentor Books, 1954).

——, *Process and Reality: An Essay in Cosmology* (New York: The Humanities Press, 1955).

Wiener, Philip, and Nolard, Aaron (eds.), *Roots of Scientific Thought: A Cultural Perspective* (New York: Basic Books, 1957).

Wittgenstein, Ludwig, *On Certainty,* ed. by G. E. M. Anscombe and G. H. Von Wright and trans. by Denis Paul and G. E. M. Anscombe (New York: J & J Harper, 1969).

——, *Philosophical Investigations,* 2d ed. trans. by G. E. M. Anscombe and ed. by G. E. M. Anscombe and Rush Rhees (New York: Macmillan, 1958).

——, *Tractatus Logico-Philosophicus,* Trans. by C. K. Ogden (London: Routledge & Kegan Paul, 1960).

——, *Tractatus Logico-Philosophicus,* Trans. by D. F. Pears and B. F. McGuiness (London: Routledge & Kegan Paul, 1961).

——, *Prototractatus.* An early version of *Tractatus Logico-Philosophicus,* ed. by B. F. McGuiness, T. Nyberg, G. H. von Wright and trans. by D. F. Pears, B. F. McGuiness (Ithaca, N.Y.: Cornell University Press, 1971).

Wright, Georg Henrik von, *Biographical Sketch.* Bound with Malcolm's *Ludwig Wittgenstein: A Memoir* (London: Oxford University Press, 1962).

INDEX

In preparing this index I have been moved by three considerations: (1) to make it as short as possible because to make it complete would have been practically to duplicate indexes already made for the *Tractatus;* (2) to use either the German word or its translation, but not both; (3) to make a complete list of all citations to the *Tractatus* to which reference is made in the text. Although I have thrown the *Tractatus* against many other pieces of literature, it has been equally my intent to allow the *Tractatus* to speak for itself and to offer itself as a ladder by which one may climb in order to see the world aright.

Aberglaube 136, 179, 197
Abgebildeter 67
Abrahamson 182
absurdity 167
accident 31, 84, 93, 123, 180, 189, 191, 198, 201
accidental generality 94
allegorical 140
anagogic, 88, 140
Anscombe 14n, 42, 52, 71, 78–80, 82–85, 90, 112, 128, 150, 152, 159, 161–163, 181, 187, 199
Anwendung der Logik 139
Aquinas 45, 152
Aristotle 45, 109, 112, 120, 202
artillery 177, 178
atomism 23, 61, 106
Atman 92
Aufmerksamkeit 20, 76
Avenarius 20, 106, 116
aufheben 161
Augustine 143, 160, 195
Austro-Hungarian Empire 182
axiomatic method 96, 98

axiom of infinity 68, 69
axiom of reducibility 70, 99, 130, 134
Ayer 36, 170

Baudelaire 34
Bedeutung 47, 49, 65, 167, 201
Begriff 29, 123
Begriffsbildung 50, 51
Begriffsinhalt 28, 29, 30, 32, 34, 66
Begriffsumfang 28, 29, 30, 32, 34, 66
Begriffswelt 56
meontic non-being 64, 199
Beiträge zu einer Kritik der Sprache 20, 21, 33, 55
Beiträge zur Analyse der Empfindungen (Mach) 116
Bestehen 67, 121
bezeichnen 38
Beziehungen 67
Bible 130
Bild 32
Black's *Companion* 63, 149–154, 156, 170, 194

Bradley 37, 92, 161
Brahman 92
Bruno's Dream 71
Buber 203

Calvin 152
Carnap 18, 77, 95, 144, 174
Carroll 160
Cassirer, Ernst 26, 154, 155
Cassirer, Eva 85, 154, 155
causal 135, 136, 179, 196, 197
chaos 109
Christian 182, 186
coherence 56, 170
Colossians 161
common notions 100
conatus 108, 122, 129
connotation 19, 43, 170
constructionism 97
contradiction 27, 56, 57, 153
cosmos 109

Dante 50, 141
Darwin 33
definition 49
Democritus 106, 168
denotation 19, 43, 45
Descartes 29, 102, 110
Deus Absconditus 130
Deus Revelatus 153
Ding 34 ,36, 120, 180, 192
Ding-an-sich 55
The Drunken Boat 74, 92
dialectic 113
Dilthey 156
dualism 116, 117, 137

Eigenschaften 37
'elements' 106, 109, 131
Elementarsätze 40, 41, 46, 121, 123, 135
Eliot 141, 159–161, 164, 171, 173
Empfindung 118, 121
Engelmann 18n, 24, 82, 141, 142, 146, 147, 162, 163, 174–177
epistemology 115, 198
Erfahrung 107, 124
Erkenntnistheorie 30

Ethics (Spinoza) 96, 100, 102, 107, 108, 112
extension 19, 32, 117, 172, 180
existence 72
existentialism 143
external world 68

facts 40, 41, 65
Fall 27, 36
faith 60, 92, 195
Fann 45, 204
fate 178, 184
Ficker 24, 25, 148
Finnegan's Wake 74
form of any object whatsoever (physique de l'object quelconque) the general proposition (6) 91, 93
Four Quartets 173
Frege 26, 47, 52, 53, 79, 80, 93, 117–119, 137, 141, 151, 155, 159, 165, 201

games 51
Gegenstand 37, 38, 56, 64, 116, 120, 121, 128, 168, 180, 192, 200, 203
general notions 100
general proposition (6) 90
generality 70
genius 133
genre (literary) 44
sui-generis 133
Geschehen 31
Gestalt 156
God 103, 104, 110, 111, 122, 130, 134, 144, 152, 160, 166, 170, 172, 174, 180, 181, 186, 195, 199, 201, 202
Gnostic 137
Gödel 84
Goethe 165
Gounod 164
Grammar of Assent 12
Grammatik 22
Grenzen 36

Haiku 173, 174
Hebrew 203
Hegel 125, 129

Heilsgeschichte 203
Heraclitus 26
hermeneutics 201
Hertz 165
heuristic 32
hinaussteigen 148
das Höhere 41, 124, 131, 133, 138, 142, 166, 169, 170, 182, 184, 185, 195, 196, 202, 203
holiness 78
Human Knowledge; Its Scope and Limit 75
Hume 13, 17, 45, 70, 79, 93, 115, 128, 136, 164, 188, 197, 198

'I' 41, 57, 68, 92, 93, 106, 107, 124, 132, 134, 137, 168, 169, 189–191, 193, 197
idealism 107, 115
Illative Sense 13
incoherence 33, 66, 153, 160, 164
individuation 119, 133
intension 19, 32, 113, 117, 172
intention (*Aufmerksamkeit*) 20, 32, 48, 51, 117

Jewishness 102, 109
Joyce 74

Kant 24, 53, 70, 95, 103, 104, 125, 128, 132, 136, 137, 145, 149, 155, 158, 161, 174, 186–188, 190, 194–198, 201
Kantianism, neo- 115
Kierkegaard 16, 17, 93, 133, 143, 165, 176, 182–186
King of France (the present) 73, 74
Kritik der reinen Erfahrung (Avenarius) 116

language 15, 16, 18, 21, 22, 23, 32, 36, 50, 55, 65, 94, 109, 119, 123, 135, 145, 152, 153, 154, 161, 178, 180, 181, 191, 194, 198–201, 203
Lebensprobleme 138
Leibniz 70
Lenin 65, 116
Locke 30

logic, *Logik* 19, 23, 36, 47, 49, 57, 90, 94, 98, 99, 101, 104, 107, 109, 116–118, 131, 139, 153, 161, 165, 170, 178–180, 189, 192, 193, 197–199, 201
Logos 26, 43, 45, 89, 107–109, 132, 161, 191, 192, 195
Luther 130, 152

Mach 20, 106, 116, 120, 121, 127, 128, 130, 132, 164
Marburg School 116
material implication 90
materialism 115
mathematics 178, 198
matrix 199
Mauthner 20, 28, 30, 31, 33, 48, 50, 51, 54–56, 65, 66, 80, 86, 88, 89, 91, 117–120, 123, 129, 130, 132, 137, 151, 153, 178, 197, 198
mechanics 200
Meister Eckart 31
metaphysics 18, 145, 198
microcosm 193
Mill 13
Milton 141
Mitleid 146
modus ponens 94
modus tollens 94
modality 27, 67, 72, 84, 104, 105, 112, 197, 198, 201
monism 116–118
Murdoch 71
music 19, 161, 175
mystical (*mystisch*) 37, 41, 103–105, 137, 143, 161, 162, 165, 166, 169

natura naturans 102–107, 112, 126, 129, 172, 181
natura naturata 44, 103–105, 107–109, 112, 172
Naturtatsachen 50, 51
natural theology 97
nature 201, 202
Naturgesetze 32
negativa, via 142
Newman 12–14, 17, 176
New Testament 195

Nietzsche 44, 71, 73, 129, 182, 187
nirvana 103, 146, 173
Notebook: 1914–16 177
Null-methode 94
number 91

Occam's razor 46–48, 192, 203
Ogden 14n, 153
On Certainly 13, 14, 23
'The One and the Many' 123
ontology 23, 84, 118, 135, 174, 190,
    194–196

pantheism 102, 104
Pascal 143, 176
penultimate proposition 88
phenomenal 23
phenomenalism 116, 164
phenomenology 201
Philosophical Investigations 19, 23,
    40n, 47, 50, 51, 71, 82, 84, 93,
    97, 119, 120, 130, 134
phronesis 13
Pilgrim's Progress 141
Plato 45, 79, 82, 93, 111, 115, 129,
    131, 149, 203
Plotinus 102, 104, 161, 171, 172
pluralism 118
poetry 18, 19, 140, 142, 160, 161,
    167, 170, 171, 175
Poincaré 95
Popper 78, 79
positivism 164
predicate 91
Principia Mathematica 50, 51, 119,
    120, 160
principle of sufficient reason (Satz
    vom Grunde) 132, 136, 196
Projektionsmethode 67, 132
proper relations 90
propositoin, the general 200, 201
proposition, synthetic apriori 174
propositional function 65, 72, 90
pseudo-concept 90

quality 101, 112

rationalism 50, 101, 194

Realität, empirische Realität 106,
    107, 121, 123, 124, 131, 134, 137,
    138, 142, 150, 168–170, 180, 184,
    191–194, 199
realism 92, 134
reality 32, 41, 161
reference 64, 90
Relationen 37, 90, 112, 117
relativism 33
'le Rêve' 34
riddle 88
Rilke, 25, 34, 35, 76, 77, 138, 141,
    143, 159, 164
Rimbaud 34, 74, 92, 164
Rosser (artificial language) 158, 203
Russell 21, 26, 42, 47, 52, 53, 57,
    65, 66, 70, 72, 75, 77, 80, 90, 93,
    95, 118, 127, 128, 130, 136, 137,
    140, 141, 143, 151, 154, 155, 159,
    164–166, 177, 181, 189, 191, 197
Russell's 'Introduction' 26, 53, 57,
    62, 63, 75, 91
Logic and Knowledge 62, 73, 106

saint 125, 133, 147, 185
samsara 173
Satz-Sinn 132
saying 43, 140, 142, 143, 175
Schopenhauer 14, 17, 53, 57, 61, 71,
    78, 92, 108, 122, 161, 165, 169,
    173, 181, 187, 188, 193, 195, 196,
    198
scaffolding (logic) 139
science 134, 174, 179, 184, 188, 196,
    203
self-evidence 94
semantics 201
sense 90
sensibility 35
set theory 68, 99, 132
showing 16, 43, 140, 142, 143, 175
singular 17
Sinn 31, 47
sinnlos 27, 28, 153
sinnvoll 153
Socrates 35, 176
solipsism 57, 70, 71, 75, 93, 100,
    123, 124, 130, 134, 152, 168

solution (*Lösung*) 138
Sophist (Plato) 120
soteriology 107
soul 190–192, 194, 195, 202, 203
species 17, 133
Spiegel 43, 50, 87, 94, 104 131
Spiegelbild 137, 191
Spinoza 24, 28, 44, 45, 53, 71, 78, 97–99, 110, 113, 122, 129, 161, 172, 176, 181, 187
Stenius 150, 151, 155–157
Stirner 71
Subjekt 192
substance 97
suicide 101
symbolism 28, 34, 183
synonymity 49
syntax 47, 123, 138, 154, 170, 192

Tagore 77
Tao Teh Ching 45, 46
Tatsache 27, 66, 67, 121, 180
Tautologie 27, 56, 57, 153, 198
theology 61, 174, 195
theory of types 47
Tolstoy 143, 176
totality (*Gesamtheit*) 167
Toulmin 144, 145
Tractatus Logico-Philosophicus 14n
as a poem 43
transcendent 87, 103, 131, 149, 196
transcendental 32, 85, 103, 131, 149, 179, 180, 191
transcendental unity of apperception (from Kant) 188, 189, 191, 192, 194, 197
tropology 140
truth tables 46, 135, 154, 199

Übermensch 76
Übersetzung 49
Umgangssprache 22, 49, 117
Unaussprechliche 105, 138, 149, 151
unequivocal 45
unicorns (Russell's argument against their nonexistence) 73, 74

universal 180, 189
unsinnig 27, 28, 33, 45, 130, 148, 153

Valéry 34
variable 90, 91
Vedanta 125
verification principle 171
Verstand 15, 38
Verstehen 156
Vienna Circle 18, 36, 42, 77, 95, 116, 144, 164, 174
Virgil 141
Vorstellung 38, 51, 55

Wagner 72
Wahrheit 22, 55
wahrnembar 67
Waste Land, The 161
weak disjunction 90
Welt 27, 31, 36, 55, 121, 124, 134, 137, 138, 169, 170, 191, 193, 194
Wert 31
Wesen der Sprache 54, 56, 76
Whitehead 52, 58, 178, 179
Will, the 129, 137, 181, 183, 196
Wirklichkeit 21, 50, 55, 56, 67, 107, 121, 123, 124, 134, 150, 168, 169, 193, 198
Wirklichkeiten 167
world lines (in Minkowski's sence) 197
Wortaberglaube (superstition produced by the misuse of language) 30

Yeats 11, 141, 159, 164

Zahl 38
zahllos 117
Zen 173
zero method 94
zero premise 94
zero sum 94
Zukunft 197

LIST OF CITATIONS

1. .... 23, 157	2.1–3.02 180
1.1 ...... 69, 121, 157, 194, 199	2.203–2.225 56
1.11 23	
1.13 27	3.02 130
1.2 157	3.03 .... 28, 130
1.–2.01 56	3.031 .... 28, 56, 130, 193
	3.032 .... 131, 193
2. 121	3.1 .... 67, 131, 199
2.01 .... 69, 120, 121, 180	3.11 .... 67, 131
2.011 23	3.13 .... 132, 193, 194, 199
2.012 180	3.14 .... 67, 132, 199
2.0121 .... 23, 27, 180	3.141 68
2.022 84	3.142 132
2.0231 23	3.2 199
2.02421 23	3.201 199
2.025 23	3.221 199
2.027 23	3.25 199
2.03 .... 106, 120	3.26 199
2.034 121	3.262 199
2.04 .... 106, 120	3.325 94
2.05 121	3.328 158
2.06 .... 121, 129	3.33 .... 47, 94
2.061 121	3.331 47
2.062 121	3.342 .... 48, 94
2.063 121	3.3421 .... 48, 94, 180
2.1 66	3.343 49
2.1201 67	3.344 49
2.141 199	3.42 139
2.16 67	3.5 .... 119, 199
2.202 67	3.–3.0321 84
2.011–2.207 68	3.02–3.032 199
2.027–2.063 84	3.032–3.1432 56
2.1–2.1512 56	3.04–3.26 49
2.1–2.223 193	3.34–3.3421 49

3.342–3.343	50	4.463	56
3.5–4.04	84	4.464	179
		4.52	167
4.	199	4.01–4.0141	180
4.001	119	4.01–4.023	49
4.002	22, 55, 119	4.014–4.032	88
4.003	20, 27	4.1–4.111	95
4.0031	20, 21	4.111–4.113	76
4.01	67	4.121–4.1251	90
4.013	87	4.1211–4.1272	180
4.014	118	4.1211–4.2	19
4.022	49, 67	4.1213–4.2	117
4.023	50, 67, 139	4.122–4.128	90, 114
4.031	67	4.126–4.1272	180
4.0312	88	4.1272–4.128	91
4.0412	116	4.1272–4.2211	120
4.061	67	4.12721–4.24	91
4.1	67, 89	4.2–4.211	84
4.10031	20	4.46–4.66	198
4.11	89	4.46–4.661	84
4.111	83		
4.112	76, 77	5.135	197
4.1121	116	5.136	197
4.115	144	5.1361	197
4.12	90, 91	5.153	179
4.121	43, 90	5.262	167, 199
4.1211	68, 69	5.461	90
4.1212	143	5.471	180
4.1216	77	5.4711	180
4.122	37, 112, 143, 158	5.473	48, 73
4.123	131, 158	5.4731	47
4.124	37, 90	5.47321	47, 158
4.125	37	5.4733	47, 84, 117
4.1252	69	5.511	43, 50
4.126	158	5.512	43
4.127	158	5.514	43
4.1272	90	5.525	84
4.128	69, 117, 137, 166, 190	5.526	70
4.2	67	5.5262	180
4.211	158	5.541	116
4.22	69, 158	5.5421	116
4.2211	131, 198	5.5423	56
4.25	135	5.5432	56
4.27	107	5.552	71, 94, 107, 109, 139, 198
4.3	179	5.5521	71
4.46	27	5.555	97, 123, 135
4.461	27	5.556	106, 121, 135
4.4611	27	5.5561	106, 121, 135, 167, 168, 174

5.5562 134
5.5563 . . . . 49, 56, 117
5.557 . . . . 107, 118, 121, 138
5.6 . . . . 19, 28, 48, 107
5.61 . . . . 19, 193
5.62 . . . . 35, 49, 71, 123, 134, 193
5.621 193
5.63 193
5.634 . . . . 124, 180
5.64 . . 35, 106, 124, 134, 168, 180
5.641 116
5.55-6. 69
5.552-5.556 101
5.555-5.556 113
5.555-5.5661 95
5.5543-5.551 88
5.5563-5.62 110
5.5563-5.63 95
5.5571-5.641 199
5.6-5.62 . . . . 55, 191
5.6-5.63 170
5.6-5.641 . . . . 57, 123
5.631-5.641 191

6. . . . . 91, 180
6.002 97
6.022 91
6.031 . . . . 68, 99
6.111 97
6.113 97
6.12 97
6.121 94
6.1222 139
6.1231 94
6.1232 . . . . 91, 99, 130
6.1233 . . . . 70, 130, 134
6.124 . . . . 94, 139, 193
6.1271 . . . . 94, 99
6.13 43, 46, 50, 103, 131, 139, 191
6.22 179
6.3 134
6.32 . . . . 134, 197
6.34 134
6.342 199
6.343 121
6.36 32
6.361 121, 137, 178, 179, 193, 197
6.362 . . . . 105, 180

6.363 48
6.3631 48
6.37 . . . . 32, 51, 178, 180
6.371 32
6.372 . . . . 178, 184
6.373 . . . . 137, 178
6.375 180
6.3751 . . . . 131, 198
6.41 . . . . . 94, 109, 123, 129, 170
           180, 183, 184, 191, 198
6.42 170
6.422 183
6.423 . . . . 116, 132, 133, 137
6.43 . . . . 103, 107, 132, 138
5.431 . . . . 110, 169, 191, 193
6.4312 . . . . 178, 184
6.432 . . . . 105, 129, 166, 183, 184
6.4321 . . . . 105, 137, 138, 169
             178, 184, 187
6.44 . . . . 71, 103, 105, 109
6.45 . . . . . 103, 105, 106, 173, 183
6.5 124
6.51 14
6.52 . . . . 18, 108
6.521 138
6.522 . . . . 57, 103, 108, 144
             161, 166, 184
6.53 167
6.532 103
6.54 . . . . 20, 167
6.5751 41
6.632 166
6.111-6.12 174
6.1261-6.1264 104
6.3-6.361 95
6.3-6.3751 177
6.32-6.361 174
6.34-6.361 . . . . 46, 178
6.342-6.361 199
6.343-6.372 95
6.3432-6.41 101
6.36-6.361 105
6.362-6.372 109
6.362-6.374 104
6.362-6.375 109
6.362-6.372 174
6.37-6.372 144
6.373-6.374 169

6.375–6.41 104
6.41–6.422 138
6.41–6.44 101
6.43–6.4311 123
6.43–6.4321 177

6.431–6.4312 123
6.4311–6.521 107

7. .... 18, 109, 173, 184